JACK THE RIPPER

Revealed and Revisited

JACK
THE
RIPPER

Revealed and Revisited

JOHN WILDING

EXPRESS NEWSPAPERS

Copyright © John Wilding February 2006

First published in 1993
by Constable and Volcano Books Ltd
This revised edition first published in 2006 by Express Newspapers

Phototypeset directly from author's discs by
Discript Ltd, 24 Bedfordbury, London WC2N 4BN
www.discript.com

Printed and bound in Poland EU by Polska Book

Cover design by Michael Kearton
www.michaelkearton.co.uk

John Wilding is hereby identified as author of this work in accordance with Section 77 of the Copyright, Designs and Patents Act 1988

A CIP record for this book is available from the British Library

ISBN 0–850793–23–8

FOR MY GREAT NEPHEWS, JOSHUA YOUNG, ALEXIS AND
ANDREAS ORSMOND,

WITH LOVE FROM UNCLE JOHN.

Contents

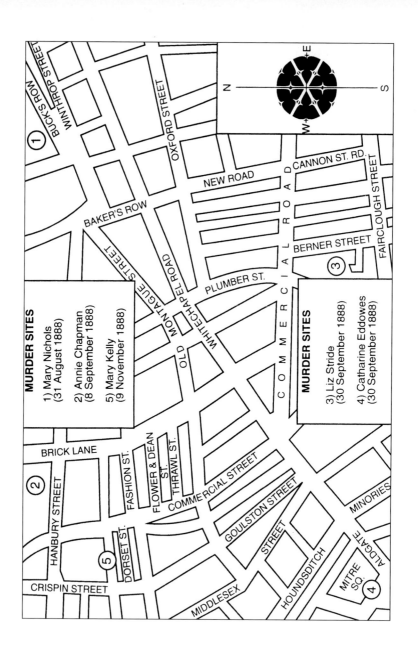

MURDER SITES

1) Mary Nichols
(31 August 1888)

2) Annie Chapman
(8 September 1888)

5) Mary Kelly
(9 November 1888)

MURDER SITES

3) Liz Stride
(30 September 1888)

4) Catharine Eddowes
(30 September 1888)

BUCK'S ROW
WINTHROP STREET
OXFORD STREET
CANNON ST. RD.
NEW ROAD
FAIRCLOUGH STREET
BAKER'S ROW
BERNER STREET
COMMERCIAL ROAD
PLUMBER ST.
MONTAGUE STREET
OLD MONTAGUE ROAD
WHITECHAPEL ROAD
BRICK LANE
HANBURY STREET
FASHION ST.
FLOWER & DEAN ST.
THRAWL ST.
COMMERCIAL STREET
GOULSTON STREET
STREET
MINORIES
DORSET ST.
CRISPIN STREET
MIDDLESEX
HOUNDSDITCH
MITRE SQ.
ALDGATE

Foreword

A new book, a new set of people to thank. I must immediately thank Lynda Finney who wrote to me and provided such extraordinary help. Vicky Reed from the Daily Express has been saintly.

I must thank that excellent, and most talented young actor Adam Rickitt for his endless email encouragement. My much valued friend Ron Moody and Ron's wife Teresa, have also been highly supportive. Ron's brilliant acting performances on DVD still provide great relief when I need a rest from reality. In this category I must not forget the ever-young and delightful actress and writer, Susannah York. Peter Wilson, MBE, producer of such hits as the long-running *Woman In Black* has been his usual kind self, and his secretary, Jill Fox, is ever-helpful. My long-standing friend Blanche Marvin has always been at the end of a telephone, and I am also grateful to Blanche's daughter, Niki Marvin, the brilliant American film producer of such films as *The Shawshank Redemption*, for reading my play script and giving me her expert and welcome opinion, as the did the retired, noted actor, John Fraser, the author of the splendid autobiography *Close Up*. I really couldn't put that book down.

Unexpectedly, my work on *Jack the Ripper* brought me into contact with two of my long-standing heroes – the wondrous soprano, Dame Joan Sutherland and her multi-talented husband, Richard Bonynge. I am delighted to salute these two giants of music.

Dr Trevor Joslin has been unwavering in his support for my Ripper theory, and many thanks are due to my brother, Donald (who provided the line illustrations; these are meant only to serve as an outline for clarification); my nephew David Osmond and his lovely wife Sofia; my niece, Louise Orsmond and her husband Mark. Thanks to Ray Cooney, the brilliant farce writer along with my close friend Driss Laamoumi.

My thanks to John B. Hobbs, who was responsible for so many memorable BBC television series, and to Philip Martin and Frederico de Angelo. Greg Iverson can deal with obtuse computer problems better than anyone I know, and I must also thank my long-standing artist friend, one of Australia's foremost illustrators, Matthew Ottley, along with Edoardo and Luigi Matarazzo and Paul Burrows.

Professor Fred Piper from the Royal Holloway has been patient in the extreme and immensely helpful, as was the professor's secretary,

Pauline Stoner. My excellent agents Kenneth Ewing and Giles Smart from PFD must be given thanks, along with my friends, the translator Osvaldo Lama and the world's best cook, Fabrizio D'Emilio – along with the excellent Richard Bates at Discript Ltd. Batuk Gathani helped, in no small measure, to launch the original book, and the distinguished writer William Pearson, my original editor Roderick Brown, Sally Partington and Robin Butler made valued suggestions for which I was deeply grateful. My friend Stuart Potterton lent me valuable reading material on *Jack the Ripper*, and the distinguished Australian psychiatrist, Dr Anthony Orsmond, advised me most ably. Robert Dyer displayed endless patience, and I am most grateful to him and his charming wife, Yuko. Last, but certainly not least, I would like to thank the three Ripper experts with whom I have been in personal touch, Paul Begg, Keith Skinner and Martin Howells. All three have been kind, charming and helpful. And it is perhaps appropriate to mention my late, and much-missed friend, the distinguished writer Stephen Knight. To finish, I must mention Mark Corrin, Les Eley, Margo and John Cain, Jenny McClaren and Tom Riley and my dear, long-standing friend, Annis James.

Permission to use copyright material has been granted by:

Paul Begg and Robson Books. (*Jack the Ripper The Uncensored Facts*); Paul Begg, Martin Fido, Keith Skinner and Headline Books (*The Jack the Ripper A to Z*); Tom Cullen (*Autumn of Terror*); Martin Fido and Weidenfeld and Nicholson (*The Crimes and Detection of Jack the Ripper*); Martin Howells and Keith Skinner and Sidgwick and Jackson (*The Ripper Legacy – The Life and Death of Jack the Ripper*); Chambers Publishers for Stephen Knight (*Jack the Ripper – The Final Solution*); Donald Rumbelow and Virgin Publishing (*The Complete Jack the Ripper*); David Abrahamsen, Penguin Group (USA) Inc. (*Murder and Madness*).

I am grateful for the generous permission to use short extracts from the above books. W.H. Allen, an imprint of Virgin Books, has generously given permission for use of photographic material from *The Mystery of Jack the Ripper* by Leonard Matters.

Crown copyright material in the Public Record Office is reproduced by permission of the Controller of Her Majesty's Stationery Office. Files HO/144/221/A49301C8a, HO/144/220/A49301C, MEOP/3/140, MEOP/3/141.

My special thanks to Anne Crawford for her help.

Chapter 1

Background

London has always been a violent City, from the earliest recorded times, during the Roman occupation, up to the present day. A Roman historian, Cassius Dio, writing in the third century, relates details of Boudicca's attack on Londinium:

> 'As to the male prisoners, there was nothing of the most dreadful kind which was not inflicted on them. Of the women, they hung up the noblest and the most beautiful naked, cut off their breasts and sewed them to their mouths.'

Imported Roman cruelty involving fights to the death between gladiators and slaves pitted in savage contests against wild animals is well documented. That was the start of London's violent two-thousand-year history, a history full of martyrdoms, murder and painful death. However, the invaders found the native Britons equally barbaric.

Sir William Wallace, who led Scottish resistance to the English king, Edward the First, was betrayed by a friend, Sir John Menteith. Wallace was captured and imprisoned in 1305. After abusive treatment from his gaolers he was dragged from The Tower by horses, hanged and, while still alive, disembowelled before being beheaded and quartered. His head was displayed on a pole on London Bridge. Arbitrary beheading was commonplace throughout the Middle Ages. In 1431 an unnamed weaver from Abingdon who had threatened to 'make priests' heads as plentiful as sheeps' heads', lost his own head, which was displayed on a pike. There were many other kinds of death. 'Smoothfield', then a large open plain to the north of Saint Paul's, which became 'Smithfield', the famous meat market, was once the site of spectacular cruelty. Here, for several centuries throughout the Middle Ages, any person who had been convicted of the charge of poisoning was slowly boiled alive. The leader of the Peasants' Revolt, Wat Tyler, was torn to pieces at Smithfield in 1381 after brandishing a dagger before King Richard II. Protestant martyrs were bound in chains and burned to death on the plane in the sixteenth century. Near present-day Marble Arch is the site of Tyburn, where the rage of King Henry VIII was vented on five monks who refused to acknowledge the King's supremacy over the English Church: they were hanged until they were semi-conscious, the rope was then cut and the bodies were laid on a plank before their stomachs were slit open and the entrails pulled out. Ten other monks who refused to sign the necessary declaration were chained up in Newgate Prison and allowed to starve to death.

Terrible though these events were, such barbaric tortures and cruelties are now largely forgotten, while a series of nineteenth-century murders committed by a man nicknamed Jack the Ripper has become the most famous in the history of crime. *The Star* newspaper summed up public feeling about these murders in a famous article printed in September 1888:

> London lies today under the spell of a great terror. A nameless reprobate – half beast, half man – is at large. The ghoul-like creature who stalks through the streets of London, stalking down his victim like a Pawnee Indian, is simply drunk with blood, and he will have more.

That prediction was to prove correct.

∽

Londoners of the nineteenth century were used to reading and hearing about violence in their city. This violence was aggravated by the use of alcohol, which was plentiful and cheap. That great chronicler of London life, Henry Mayhew, in his famous 1885 publication, *Mayhew's London*, reports that:

> In a 'good time' it is not unusual for a costermonger to spend 12 shillings out of every 20 shillings on beer and pleasure.

Most public houses throughout London were open from before dawn until late at night, and they were well patronised at all times, which means alcohol must have played its part in the violence, thieving, and petty crime that was endemic in the poorest, most deprived and most notorious part of London, the East End. The area was a maze of badly lit, narrow streets, criss-crossed by unlit, foul smelling, litter strewn alleyways that led to dangerous cul-de-sacs. Criminal gangs regularly patrolled the East End streets dodging police patrols. These gangs often contained pimps who controlled local prostitutes, beating them up with impunity on the slightest pretext. The prostitutes themselves frequently solicited in riverside public houses, plying sailors with gin. Once intoxicated the seamen were taken to dark, lonely areas where, instead of rendering a sexual service, the women would hit their clients with a stone, leaving them drunk, unconscious and robbed. Despite repeated warnings sailors continually allowed themselves to be tricked. Fights between rival gangs, neighbours, and, of course, husbands and wives continually disturbed the peace, and murder was reasonably commonplace. The list of East End homicides involving women in 1888 was long. To quote just two examples: a middle-aged prostitute, Emma Smith, was attacked in Whitechapel by a gang of young men. She was robbed, beaten and raped, and a member of the gang then forced a blunt instrument into her vagina, causing serious internal injuries; the unfortunate woman died in agony a few days later. Martha Tabram, a thirty-seven-year-old prostitute was discovered dead on an unlit Whitechapel staircase. She had been savagely and repeatedly stabbed. With incidents such as these occurring on a regular basis, East Enders were not easily shocked. Yet Jack the Ripper's crimes caught the public imagination; local East End shock soon spread to the remainder of the capital, then the whole country, and finally world-wide.

These are the basic facts. In 1888, over a period of approximately ten weeks, between the hours of midnight and dawn, and only towards the end of the week, a savage killer roamed the mean East End streets, where he met and subsequently murdered five prostitutes. Three of the victims were laid out in public, their stomachs ripped open and their vaginas slashed. Policemen regularly patrolled the streets where Jack would kneel over his corpses, cutting into the flesh, then pushing his hands into the hot guts. The East End was busy both day and night but this did not seem to worry Jack: he appeared to carry out his work with impunity. After the fourth murder, *The Times* newspaper remarked:

> The assassin, if not suffering from insanity, appears to be free from any fear of interruption whilst on his dreadful work.

To add to the puzzle, Jack the Ripper's hunting ground was not large: the East End comprised Whitechapel, Spitalfields and several surrounding parishes – an area of only a few square miles. The district had once been fashionable. Nicholas Culpeper, the noted herbalist, had lived in Spitalfields in the seventeenth century, as had Lord Bolingbroke, the writer and MP. The area was then colonised by French Protestants who were forced to flee from their own country in the late seventeenth century for political reasons. An earlier French king, Henri IV, after abandoning his own Protestantism, nevertheless signed a decree known as the Edict of Nantes guaranteeing toleration for his Protestant subjects. This Edict was revoked by Louis XIV, causing great bloodshed. Large numbers of French settlers fled to London where they quickly established a silk trade around Spitalfields. When the French moved in, the East End was still a delightful country district, an oasis cut off from the hurly-burly of London life. John Stow, writing a century before the settlers' arrival, describes the silk-weavers' environment:

> On all sides without the houses of the suburb are the citizens' gardens and orchards, planted with trees. On the north side are pastures and plain meadows, with brooks running through them,

3

turning water mills with a pleasant noise. Not far is a great forest, a well-wooded chase, having a good covert for harts, bucks, boars and wild bulls.

As late as 1799, less than ninety years before the murders, Horwood's map shows a single road starting at Blue Anchor Lane, Bermondsey, and running eastward. This road meandered through deserted country-side until it reached the East End villages.

Rapid industrialisation soon changed this charming landscape. The settlers' silk trade grew into a major industry, and by 1832 50,000 people were employed as weavers. Then mechanisation replaced the hand-worked looms and production was quickly transferred from workers' cottages to vast, soulless factories. These factories attracted large numbers of workers, especially immigrants, into the area – more workers than there were jobs. As a result, by 1888 the East End contained a collection of the poorest people in the world. Thieves, derelicts and prostitutes lived alongside hard-working, honest citizens: citizens who were held back by low wages and unreliable employment, unable to rise above the barest level of subsistence. Houses were dirty and dilapidated and had only the most basic facilities. While some houses had a single cold water pipe in the back yard, other buildings had only a standby cold water pipe in the street.

Sewage was piped raw into the Thames, causing a terrible stench along the entire stretch of the waterway. Even at Westminster the smell from the river was so appalling windows had to be kept shut during debates in the House of Commons. If the open air was so polluted the atmosphere in the sewers must have been atrocious, yet, incredibly, some East Enders, nicknamed 'toshers' made a living from wandering around the sewerage system searching for lost treasure. That mine of information, Henry Mayhew, discusses toshers at some length:

> To enter the sewers and explore them to any considerable distance is considered, even by those acquainted with what is termed 'working the shores', an adventure of no small risk. The brickwork in many parts – especially in the old sewers – has become rotten through the continual action of putrefying matter and moisture, and parts have fallen down and choked up the passage with heaps of rubbish; over these obstructions, nevertheless, the sewer-hunters have to scramble in the best way they can.

Mud-larks, men, women and children of all ages, would wade along the river banks in a slime composed of sewage mixed with mud, searching for small pieces of coal, chips of wood, old iron or copper nails. Mayhew vividly describes mud-larks:

They may be seen of all ages, from mere childhood to positive decreptitude, crawling along the barges at the various wharfs along the river; it cannot be said that they are clad in rags, for they are scarcely half covered by the tattered indescribable things that served them for clothing; their bodies are grimed with the foul soil of the river, and their torn garments stiffened up like boards with dirt of every possible description. Among the mud-larks may be seen many old women, and it is indeed pitiable to behold them, especially during the winter, bent nearly double with age and infirmity, paddling and groping among the wet mud . . .

A glance at Mayhew's list of contents reveals the vast number of East Enders who eked out a living as street sellers – sellers of ham sandwiches, bread, hot peas, sherbet, elder wine, curds and whey, milk, boiled puddings and cough drops, to name but a few.

Some comparatively affluent workers with reasonably steady employment could afford to rent rooms on a semi-permanent basis. Their families often owned animals but there was no safe outside place in which to keep their livestock: the animals would have been stolen even from their own backyards. It was, therefore, not unusual to find whole families living with their goats, pigs and hens indoors. When the time came to eat the animals they would frequently be slaughtered in the street, their blood mixing with an assortment of filth in the gutters.

Many poorer families could not afford to rent decent rooms – they lived in semi-darkness in deep cellars built under houses. The only entrance to and exit from these dungeons was a wooden trap door let into the pavement above, and if objects were placed on these traps the family would be entombed until the obstacle was removed. As late as 1928, when the Thames burst its banks, fourteen people were trapped in basement rooms and drowned. These underground cellars often doubled as both living and working quarters, the most usual employment being an amateur attempt at cobbling. An anonymous writer in 1878 graphically describes the condition of these 'cave dwellers'.

To look down into one of these cellars at night-time and find father, mother, and the elder male and female branches of the family clustered in all their dirt and raggedness in the midst of the unsavoury heap of half-rotten leather, with wisps of wax-end to keep their hair from bobbing into their eyes as they hammer and stitch by the light of the tallow candle or paraffin lamp, is not a spectacle to make a man thrill with pride. They fetch their material from their employers in a great sack, and it consists of a pell-mell collection of 'oddments' in the way of foot coverings, reeking of mould and mildew. In one place I found, besides the parents toiling at the heap of malodorous leather, four small children crouching, half naked and unclean, by the fire hearth, and looking exactly as one might expect children to look, who, all through the long winter, live in semi-darkness, and breathe air that would ultimately undermine the constitution of a horse or donkey, and who see no more of the living and moving world than the muddy boots of pedestrians hurrying to and fro above their ceiling.

Old people with adult diseases bedded down with children suffering from childhood diseases, the bed being often no more than a heap of shavings, straw or filthy rags. Occasionally a dead body would remain in the living quarters for an extended period until arrangements for a burial could be completed. Overcrowding was endemic in the East End. Many people found temporary shelter in houses which provided rooms for up to sixty lodgers. A 'deputy' would sit in a doorway hutch demanding money from clients as they entered. Terms were strictly payment in advance. One landlord complained that 'unscrupulous rival establishments' had reduced rents from the standard four pence for lodgings, to three pence, in order to attract more patrons. Even this cut-price lodging proved too expensive for many East Enders; large numbers of destitutes were forced to creep into graveyards to sleep among the tombstones, while many others slept in the parks. A garden alongside Christchurch, Spitalfields, became so infamous for its congregation of patrons who suffered from ticks, fleas or skin diseases that it became known as 'Itchy Park'. An anonymous 1878 writer records one member of the Victorian judiciary who had his own solution to the homeless problem. A petty East End offender who had been brought before this judge remarked, 'We've all got to live'. The judge offered his own opinion in reply. 'I really don't see why,' the learned gentleman said, 'but if that is the case, then it will be necessary to make persistent vagabondism a capital offence'.

The law itself was kinder – but not much. Policemen regularly harassed people sleeping in the open, and, in order to curb the large number of destitute people who drifted into Trafalgar Square, many East Enders among them (including Mary Nichols – the Ripper's first victim), Sir Charles Warren, the Metropolitan Police Commissioner, demanded and received new powers: he closed Trafalgar Square on various dates, an act that led to riots described in later chapters of this book. Many landlords were quick to grasp the new opportunities afforded them by this new, if limited, restriction, on open-air sleeping. They placed rope across their rooms and charged customers a few pence to lean against the webbing all night. This at least provided indoor shelter. Occasionally an establishment allowed its patrons to lie in rows on the floor, using their arms folded under their heads as a pillow. Sick people were not allowed to remain in any lodging house for more than twenty-four hours. Whatever the illness the sufferer had to be moved away.

A missionary was, on one occasion, summoned to treat a sick child in an East End lodging house. He discovered the six-year-old girl near to death from scarlet fever lying on the floor of a small room amongst fifteen other lodgers: a mixture of old and young, males and females. Included in the standard four-penny rent might be the guarding of one's clothes by the deputy and the use of a communal kitchen. Here, thirty to forty lodgers would share dirty utensils and cook together. A grate would extend five or six feet along a wall, with half a dozen large frying pans on the coals. Lodgers would drop their pieces of raw meat onto a chosen spot in a pan, then pay close attention until the food was cooked. A custodian would stand guard armed with a long iron spit to help settle the many ownership arguments that broke out. Yet these were the luckier ones – the ones who had shelter and food. Many hungry, sick people had to make a choice between sleeping rough or trying to gain admittance to a workhouse, and Victorian workhouses were notorious for their harsh regimes. The writings of a Reverend Milman from the 1880s illustrate Victorian sentiments on this subject:

> The workhouse should be a place of hardship: of coarse fate: of degradation and humility, where we must learn to love our enemies and discover only our duty to God. The workhouse must be administered with the greatest severity and strictness, where you must avoid the sin of anger or malice. The workhouse must be as repulsive as it is consistent with humanity.

Clearly the workhouse administrators agreed wholeheartedly with that dogma. Meals usually consisted of rock-hard bread served with a bowl of watery gruel which often contained dead insects or the occasional drowned mouse. Inmates were told when to go to bed and when to rise – usually before dawn: their every movement was controlled. To pay for this spartan food and shelter the inmates were expected to work – and work hard – at a variety of tasks. Even children as young as eight were made to work, often having to grind corn or bones until the dust settled as a paste on their sweaty faces. Grit or small pieces of bone frequently flew into the paupers' eyes causing serious damage. Inmates were also expected to collect left-over meals from the various infirmaries. Such debris often included food from infectious wards – food that had been sprinkled with disinfectant, but the tainted scraps were still frequently stolen for consumption or for sale. After the day's labours up to twenty inmates were expected to bath in the same water.

It was in these appalling conditions that Jack the Ripper hunted, and it was his crimes which focused the whole of London's attention onto the disgraceful living conditions of many East Enders. George Bernard Shaw, after the Ripper murders had caused such an outcry, wrote:

> Whilst we conventional Social Democrats were wasting our time on education, agitation and organization, some independent genius has taken the matter in hand . . .

Jack, that independent genius, began his work on 31 August 1888, when he found his first victim.

Chapter 2

Mary Nichols

The number of murders attributed to Jack the Ripper varies from four to around eleven, but most authorities on the crimes agree with Sir Melville Macnaghten, who, in private notes wrote: 'The Whitechapel murders had five victims, and five only'. Sir Melville joined Scotland Yard as Assistant Chief Constable in 1889, approximately eight months after the Ripper crimes had finished, but he took an intense interest in the case, which he was able to examine in detail from a privileged position inside the police force.

On that basis Jack's first victim was Mary Nichols, a petite forty-two-year-old prostitute who had a delicate bone structure and grey eyes. Five of her lower front teeth were missing, either lost in a vicious fight with another prostitute – such disputes were commonplace – or lost through poor dental care, another common defect in East End life. Yet despite the dental disfigurements and greying hair, several people who saw Mary after her death remarked that she looked much younger than her age.

Writing biographical material on the Ripper victims is difficult as only minimal information was ever recorded – after all, why would anyone have written about these women *before* their deaths? Even if a contemporary had noted the women's every move there would have been little to record; they led typical lives of unparalleled dreariness – lives ruled daily by two endlessly repeated questions:

1 Where do I get enough money to buy alcohol and food? (In that order). Answer: from trying to sell my body.
2 Where can I sleep? Answer: in a doss-house if there are a few pennies left over at the end of the day.

To any alcoholic, drink is more important than sleep, and it was cheap – a cup of coffee cost more than a nip of gin. A popular sign in public houses read, 'Drunk for a penny, dead-drunk for two-pence. Clean straw free.' Gin ruled the murdered prostitutes' lives – and this was understandable. Enough drink could dull the pain of East End living and no one could blame the women for wanting to do that.

Mary (nickname 'Polly') was the wife of a printer, William Nichols, and the union had produced five children, three boys and two girls. This was not an especially large family in Victorian times, when provision had to be made for the high infant mortality rate: only about one-third of all children born lived to the age of five. Life was, of course, especially hard for poor families with a high survival rate of offspring: children as young as seven often had to start work to help support the unit: half-starved, terrorised young boys forced to climb high, thickly-sooted chimneys, and child matchbox-makers spring instantly to mind. The day-to-day living conditions of the Nichols' family is not known, but a great many poor families lived in one room, the whole unit usually sleeping in two beds. Charles Booth's written account of contemporary life (started in 1889, only one year after the Ripper murders had ended) records that the 'one room' system led to acts of gross indecency and incest. In the 1880s Marchant Williams, Inspector of London Schools, visited an East End lodging house and asked the female tenant, 'How many in the family?' 'Eleven.' 'How many beds?'. 'Two.'

In 1881 the Nichols' marriage failed; William blamed his wife's heavy drinking. There is no doubt that Mary was a typical alcoholic, a lady who would sell her body and soul for a drink. Mary's family claimed that the parting was caused by William's affair with another woman – the midwife who attended the birth of the Nichols' fourth child, which, if true, seems singularly callous. Whatever the truth, William certainly thought that he was the aggrieved party, while Mary appears to have had no compunction about leaving her family behind – the power of mother-love was easily defeated by the might of alcohol. Only the eldest boy left home with his mother; William therefore cared for the other four children. He even provided maintenance of five shillings a week for his wife, but when he discovered that she had turned to prostitution in order to fund her alcoholism the maintenance was stopped. Mary, supported by local parishes, hounded William through the courts to try and regain support, but once William proved to the judiciary's satisfaction that he was caring for the children, Mary lost her case.

After leaving home, Mary and her eldest son moved in with her father, Edward Walker, a blacksmith, who lived in Walworth, South East London. As might have been expected, her drinking habits soon caused friction, and after rows and arguments Mary moved lodgings once more, this time leaving her eldest son to stay with his grandfather. Once she was free from all family restraints Mary embarked upon the itinerant lifestyle that would eventually lead to her death. She moved between various workhouses, and, on occasions, required unspecified medical attention in various infirmaries – perhaps for sexual ailments – a common East End complaint. Children as young as nine would frequently require treatment for venereal diseases.

Occasionally Mary slept rough on the streets, which cannot have been much worse than living in the workhouse. The repeated scandals of these institutions, often reported in the press, caused a variety of undercover agents to worm themselves into various establishments. One reformer, James Greenwood, slept in a Lambeth workhouse, then reported the indescribable sounds of men scratching their itchy skin – itches no doubt caused by either disease or fleas. Greenwood also described the continual sound of coughing. 'The hollow cough; the short cough; the hysterical cough; the bark that comes at regular intervals . . .' and so on. Inmates would be roused at six o'clock and ordered to wash from a single bucket of cold water in the yard. After a bowl of disgusting gruel the men would be forced to work at corn-grinding. An equally redoubtable woman researcher reported that the straw pallets that served for beds in the women's quarters were alive with fleas. The stench in the wards was appalling, as many of the women did not wash.

To be a penniless middle-aged prostitute with faded charms and an incessant craving for drink (and with few means of satisfying that craving) must have been a torment. Mary's life, however, was not without opportunities. Between April and July 1888 she was employed as a maid by a respectable couple, Mr and Mrs Cowdry, who lived south of the Thames at Rosehill Road, Wandsworth. The Cowdrys were an upright, religious, teetotal couple. Surprisingly, they did not recognise that Mary would be an unsuitable addition to their home. Or perhaps they did recognise that fact, and in engaging her they were indulging in good work attempting to save Mary's soul, a fashionable Victorian pastime. If so, they did not succeed. The couple foolishly trusted their new maid to the extent of leaving her in charge of their home from time to time. In a letter to her father dated April 17 1888, Mary wrote:

> . . . you will be glad to know that I am settled in my new place, and going all right up to now. My people went out yesterday, and have not returned, so I am left in charge. It is a grand place inside, with trees and gardens back and front. All has been newly done up. They are teetotallers, and religious, so I ought to get on. They are very nice people and I have not much to do. I hope you are alright and the boy has work. So goodbye for the present – From yours truly, Polly. Answer soon please and let me know how you are.

Edward was never to hear from his daughter again.

One would have imagined that after a hard life in workhouses and on the streets, Mary would have clung tenaciously to her new and easy lifestyle, living in a 'grand place' with food and lodgings provided and not much work to do. Unfortunately she betrayed the Cowdrys' trust and stole clothing valued at £3.10s, a considerable sum in those days. That act of dishonesty led Mary back to the East End, and eventually cost her her life.

After absconding from the Cowdrys' house Mary stayed for a couple of nights at the Gray's Inn Temporary Workhouse, then she moved to Thrawl Street where she shared a room with three other women before she moved once more, this time to Flower and Dean Street. That was her last known address. On 31 August 1888, the final night of her life, Mary was seen wandering around Whitechapel, clattering along on the cobblestones wearing a pair of men's boots. She roamed the grim streets until, in the early hours, she tried to find lodgings back at Thrawl Street, only a block away from Flower and Dean Street, but she could not meet the rigid requirements of the East End doss-houses – pay first or no bed. Mary, later described as 'slightly tipsy', had been turned away from the doss-house because she was penniless, not because she was drunk, but first she uttered the infamous words, 'I'll soon get my doss money. See what a jolly bonnet I've got now.' Such optimism was misplaced, because Mary was soon to meet Jack the Ripper.

From around 1.30 a.m. the pathetic prostitute wandered the streets of Whitechapel, no doubt exhausted, but, apparently, not without trade. The last reported sighting of her was made by a prostitute friend, Ellen Holland. The two women met on the corner of Whitechapel High Street at 2.30 a.m.: the exact time had been set by the striking of a church clock. A melodramatic scene is conjured up by the picture of two penniless prostitutes standing together in a dangerous East End street touting for clients, not knowing that Jack the Ripper was on the prowl, while a church clock solemnly chimed away the hours. They were to be the last hours in Mary Nichol's life.

Ellen Holland described her friend as 'very drunk'. As Mary had been reported penniless and only 'slightly tipsy' a few hours earlier, she must have found several clients but spent the money on gin. In various unlit corners, Mary would have offered herself, standing up, her dress raised high to expose her 'surprisingly clean thighs' (a doctor's comment after he had examined her body in the mortuary). On the night of her murder, Mary confessed to Ellen Holland that she had, 'had her doss-house money three times'. Unfortunately on each occasion the craving for alcohol had proved too strong. Then Mary, another glass of gin on her mind, met her last client: the bargaining with Jack the Ripper completed, the prostitute would have led her killer to a dark place.

Although no one can be certain, strong medical evidence suggests that Jack stood before several of his victims; he would have grabbed Mary's throat – probably as her hands were holding up the voluminous Victorian outfit. Jack then choked his victim into unconsciousness, and, as the body sank down, he slashed viciously at the throat with a sharp knife, before kneeling over the dead woman to complete his work. That scenario has been generally accepted. The facts concerning the finding of Mary's body have been told and retold many times. Buck's Row was a typical, dirty, cobbled East End thoroughfare, running from Brady Street through to Baker's Row and lit by a single gas lamp. Warehouses on one side faced shabby terraced houses. A stableyard gateway was placed between the houses and a school.

On Friday morning, 31 August 1888, around 3.15 a.m. no less than three policemen, each on his own business, passed along Buck's Row within a short space of time. All was peaceful. Half an hour later, Charles Cross was walking along Buck's Row on his way to work. Halfway along the street he saw a bundle lying near the stableyard gates which he thought looked like a tarpaulin. Being a carter he thought a serviceable tarpaulin could be put to good use. Cross moved over to the bundle and, after a quick examination, found not a piece of canvas but a woman collapsed onto the pavement.

Robert Paul, also a carter, was also on his way to work at Smithfield Market. He was presumably startled when a figure rose from the shadows in Buck's Row and asked him to come over and look at a body. After a brief examination the men, unable to see properly in the dark, could not decide whether the woman was hurt, drunk, raped or dead. It was not, of course, uncommon to find alcoholics lying around the streets of London, so 'drunk' would probably have been the men's first assumption. Then Cross decided that as the woman's hands were cold and limp she was dead, but Paul thought he detected a faint heartbeat, which indicated to him that she was alive. As both men were on their way to work and did not want to be late (that could have meant dismissal) they went in search of a policeman.

Shortly after the men had hurried away PC John Neil walked along Buck's Row on his return beat. The bundle also caught his attention – it had not been there on his patrol of the street half an hour earlier. The policeman's lantern now revealed that the woman's throat had been slashed. Mary Nichols, Jack's first victim, had been discovered. PC Neil hailed a colleague who went to find a doctor, and while waiting for medical assistance, Neil made his own examination. Mary's hands may have been cold but other parts of her body were still warm. Her left arm was stretched out, her hand touching the stableyard gate. A Dr Llewellyn arrived quickly but under such difficult conditions, with the corpse lying in darkness sprawled out on the pavement, he could make no more than a cursory examination – sufficient only to pronounce the woman dead. An ambulance was called – this would have been little more than a cart – and the body was taken to a shed (which served as a mortuary) at the rear of the Old Montague Street Workhouse Infirmary.

Police Inspector John Spratling, who went to Buck's Row after the body had been removed, then went on to the mortuary to compile notes for the coroner. It was while making a description of the body that Spratling lifted the skirt and discovered a series of terrible mutilations. The stomach had been stabbed and slashed deeply in several places, allowing the intestines to protrude, and the vagina had also been savagely cut. Dr Llewellyn, who had meanwhile returned home, was quickly called back, but by the time he reached the mortuary, several elderly attendants had undressed and washed the corpse.

Inspector Spratling recorded details of the body's mortuary examination:

> ...her throat had been cut from left to right, two distinct cuts being on the left side. The windpipe, gullet and spinal cord having been cut through, a bruise apparently of a thumb being on the right lower jaw, also one on the left cheek. The abdomen had been cut open from centre of bottom of ribs on right side, under pelvis to left of stomach: there the wound was jagged. The omentum or coating of the stomach was also cut in several places, and two small stabs to private parts appeared done with a strong bladed knife...

An identification of the body was now required. Various people in the neighbourhood wandered into the mortuary to view the corpse – many would have made the visit out of curiosity – but no one could identify the dead woman.

The clothes in which she was dressed were Mary's entire worldly possessions. These were a brown ulster; a brown linsey frock; various underclothes; a black straw bonnet; and a pair of men's boots, cut on the uppers. It was the underwear that revealed the secret of Mary's identity. A 'Lambeth Workhouse' mark led the authorities to William Nichols, who went to the mortuary on 1 September.

The drama of identifying Mary's corpse was compounded by William meeting with his eldest son (Edward John) for the first time since the lad had left home with his mother. Edward Walker, Mary's father, also attended the grim affair, but it was William who formally identified the body. Bitterness towards his dead wife can be recognised in William's comments as he viewed the corpse: 'I forgive you, as you are, for what you have been to me.' Mary's father was less forgiving. On viewing his daughter's body, he is reported to have said, 'I knew she'd come to a bad end.'

Mary's inquest was held almost directly after the body had been formally identified. The affair was presided over by Coroner Wynne Baxter, who appeared brightly dressed in a dashing ensemble more suitable for the races than a murder inquest. He appeared to be enjoying his authority as he threw his weight around and snappishly criticised the police for failing to find the mutilations before the corpse was undressed at the mortuary, conveniently ignoring the difficulties accompanying the finding of the body. Baxter also criticised the police for allowing the body to be washed before Dr Llewellyn could examine it. This caused a row, as one of the elderly paupers who had assisted in washing the corpse, James Hatfield, denied that the police had instructed that the body should not be touched, while the police said the opposite; this contretemps was closed without any satisfactory outcome. The coroner then presided over a rigorous examination of the case.

Residents of the cottages adjoining the murder site were questioned. A Mrs Emma Green, who lived next door to the stableyard, had been sleeping with her daughter in a front room that almost overlooked the murder site. Mrs Green was a light sleeper, but she had heard no suspicious sounds during the night. The manager of Essex Wharf, Walter Purkiss, along with his wife, had spent the night in a bedroom directly opposite the murder site; they had not been disturbed either. Despite a thorough examination by Coroner Baxter no significant clues to the murderer's identity emerged, but Baxter was in no hurry to close the case. The inquest was adjourned several times, and before a final verdict could be recorded ('Wilful murder by person or persons unknown'), Jack had sensationally and successfully stalked a second victim.

Chapter 3

Annie Chapman

Annie Chapman was a short, beefy woman aged forty-five. Rumour (possibly encouraged by Annie herself in an attempt to enhance her miserable social standing) encouraged the community to believe that her husband had been a vet. In fact, John Chapman was a coachman to a farm bailiff in Windsor; very little else is known about him. The couple had wed in 1869. There were several versions as to the cause of the Chapmans' marriage breakdown in 1882. There was a rumour that John had lost a previous job as a gentleman's valet due to his wife's dishonesty. If this was true it could certainly have soured the relationship, but there is no proof to confirm the story. Inspector Frederick George Abberline, while investigating the murder, reported that the husband and wife had separated because of Annie's drinking habits, but John died in 1886 from cirrhosis of the liver, which would infer that he was the heavy drinker. Moreover, friends of Annie insisted that she drank only modestly, although she was 'prone to get drunk on a Saturday'. This is not the behaviour of a chronic alcoholic. Annie's immorality was also blamed as the cause of the marital break-up, but an examination of the facts would seem to refute this rumour. Once alone, Annie tried pathetically hard to earn an upright living by selling crochet work, matches and flowers, presumably without any great success. John Chapman had acted decently and made Annie an allowance of ten shillings a week up to the time of his death, which does not indicate any deep-seated animosity. After that, Annie, a middle-aged widow, would have been in the same position as many other Victorian women with no money and no possessions: soliciting arose from absolute necessity not from choice. With no state benefits, prostitution was often the only way to earn the money needed to provide food or to help raise children left pauperised by the death or desertion of the father.

Annie, a middle-aged, unattractive woman, destitute and ill, had few people from whom she could seek help. There were three children from the marriage, one daughter had died, the second daughter was reputed to be living in France in an unnamed institution, and one son was said to have been placed in a home for cripples. There are records of at least one brother and sister. Shortly before her death, Annie mentioned her intention of trying to borrow boots from her sister so that she could go hop-picking. Clearly this scheme did not materialise. Her brother, Fountain (Fontain?) Smith, attended both the inquest and the funeral. Fountain testified that he had seen Annie shortly before her death and had given her two shillings. Clearly her family could provide only limited and infrequent help.

A week before her death Annie had been involved in a fight with another prostitute, Eliza Cooper, who testified:

> On the previous Saturday, she [Annie Chapman] brought Mr Stanley into the house where I lodged in Dorset Street, and coming into the kitchen, asked the people to give her some soap. They told her to ask 'Liza' – meaning me. She came to me and I opened the locker and gave her some. She gave it to Stanley who went outside and washed himself in the lavatory. When she came back I asked for the soap, but she did not return it. She said 'I will see you by-and-by.' Mr Stanley gave her two shillings and paid for her bed for two nights. I saw no more of her that night. On the following Tuesday I saw her in the kitchen of the lodging house. I said 'Perhaps you will return my soap?' She threw a halfpenny on the table and said, 'Go and get a halfpenny worth of soap.' We got quarrelling over this piece of soap, and we went out to the Ringers public-house and continued the quarrel. She slapped my face and said 'Think yourself lucky I don't do more.' I struck her in the left eye I believe and then in the chest. I afterwards saw that the blow I gave her had marked her face.

Annie had received severe bruising which must have been especially painful for a woman in such a poor state of health. At the time of the fight she was suffering from two potentially fatal illnesses: a chronic disease of the brain and another affecting her lungs. Had she not been murdered, a rapid death from natural causes would have been likely, probably before the end of 1888.

On the night of her murder Annie had been to an infirmary. This, presumably, would have been the outpatients' department at St Bartholomew's Hospital near Newgate Street, East London, which was within walking distance of her usual lodgings. St Bartholomew's was renowned for its free treatment of the poor. This benefit was frequently abused by rich patients. One freeloader was told, 'Madam, this is a charity for the destitute, not for ladies in rich silk dresses. Order your carriage and get out'. There would have been no such trouble for Annie. She was given liniment for her bruises and pills to treat the more serious conditions.

On the eve of her murder Annie had been drinking in a public house. She returned to her usual lodgings in Dorset Street some time after midnight: here the deputy, Timothy Donovan, found Annie in the kitchen eating a baked potato. Her box of pills had broken and she had placed the tablets in a torn envelope which was crested 'Sussex Regiment'. When asked to pay for her bed Annie replied that she did not have the money, adding, 'I am weak and ill and have been in the infirmary'. Donovan callously observed that she could afford food and her breath smelt of drink. He wanted his money, and, in keeping with the inflexible East End rule of payment in advance, Annie was asked to leave. She protested that apart from the potato she had had no food all day. Annie also protested that she felt unwell, which must have been an understatement: a middle-aged woman suffering from severe lung and brain diseases, her body badly bruised and with very little food over an extended period (an inquest report mentioned malnutrition) would have been feeling extremely unwell. Even so, Annie was forced to leave the doss-house at around 2.00 a.m. and search for clients willing to pay eight or nine pence (if she was lucky) for her sexual favours. As we know from Eliza Cooper's inquest evidence, a gentleman friend, Edward Stanley, occasionally gave Annie money. At least this truly sad woman had some warmth and affection in the last few months of her life. Unfortunately her friend was not around on the night of 8 September.

After being turned out of the doss-house Annie accepted her misfortune stoically, and, like Mary Nichols, she seems to have been full of optimism: she asked for her bed to be kept, promising to be back soon. John Evans, a night watchman, saw Annie leaving Dorset Street at approximately 2.00 a.m. as she prepared to tramp the dark, dangerous streets looking for trade to provide at least a cut-price four-pence for her night's lodgings. This would have been no easy task as she was not an alluring woman, with her moon face, bulbous nose and double chins, her dumpy body wrapped in layers of clothing to keep out the cold, and unsteady on her feet due to illness. When Annie took her last walk, did the vicious murder of Mary Nichols only a week earlier prey on her mind? We will never know, but we do know that within four hours of being turned away from the doss-house Annie was destined to meet Jack the Ripper and her death.

Hanbury Street, approximately ten minutes' walk from Buck's Row, was another dirty East End street, lined with neglected, over-populated houses. A door between 27 and 29 Hanbury Street led, by way of a twenty-foot passageway (which contained stairs leading to the rooms), to a swing door and three stone steps. These steps gave access to a small, enclosed back yard (somewhere around twenty-square feet in area) which was in constant use at all hours of the day and night (often for use as an outdoor lavatory) by the sixteen or seventeen tenants (accounts vary) squeezed into 29 Hanbury Street. This fact did not prevent prostitutes from taking their clients there from time to time. And although on

8 September the house was packed with tenants both asleep and awake crammed between the thin wooden partitions, no one was disturbed by unusual sounds during the night.

Amelia Richardson rented two floors at 29 Hanbury Street, where she sub-let part of her premises. At 4.45 a.m. before dawn had broken, Mrs Richardson's son John went into the yard at the rear of the house to check that the cellar entrance was secure and to loosen his boots, which were hurting him. After finding everything in order John sat on the rear steps and trimmed leather from his footwear before leaving the yard. Nothing was amiss; but at some point during the next hour the unfortunate Annie, tired and ill, led Jack the Ripper down the long, dark and no doubt smelly passageway into the yard. Had they conversed, apart from settling terms? What had Jack said to gain Annie's confidence? How and where had they met?

Conflicting reports of Annie's last hours on earth make the facts difficult to assess. At 5.30 a.m. on the Saturday morning, a Mrs Elizabeth Long, one of a large band of labourers setting out before dawn, was walking along Hanbury Street on her way to work. Once again the chiming of a church clock confirmed the time. Mrs Long saw a couple standing together outside 29 Hanbury Street – a man whose face she could not see, and a woman whom she later identified as Annie Chapman. As Mrs Long passed the couple, she heard the man ask, 'Will you?' to which the woman replied, 'Yes'.

However, fifteen-minutes earlier, at 5.15 a.m. a carpenter, Albert Cadosch, went into the yard at 27 Hanbury Street, and heard sounds from the adjoining yard at number 29: a noise which might have been the crash of a body falling against the fence. If that sound was indeed that of Annie's death fall then Mrs Long's testimony was incorrect.

At 6.00 a.m. – after dawn had broken – John Davis, an elderly resident of the over-crowded slum-house, went into the yard and found the butchered remains of Annie Chapman lying in a pool of blood between the stone steps and a bloodstained fence. The usual Ripper myths accompany the finding of the body. One report had Davis hysterically rushing into the street yelling 'Murder', a cry that was heard by Detective Inspector Joseph Chandler, whose involvement is outlined below. A second version had Mr Davis running along to the Commercial Road Police Station to report his find, ignoring the fact that he was an elderly, stooped, pensioner. In fact, Davis was too terrified to examine the body. After a quick glance he ran into the street and summoned help from several passers-by. They examined the remains of Annie Chapman then hurried to Commercial Street Police Station where Inspector Chandler was on duty. Chandler's official statement records the scene:

I at once proceeded to number 29 Hanbury Street, and in the back yard found a woman lying on her back, left arm resting on left breast, legs drawn up, abducted, small intestines and lap of the abdomen lying on right side above right shoulder, attached by a cord with the rest of the intestines inside the body; two flaps of skin from the lower part of the abdomen lying in a large quantity of blood about the left shoulder; throat cut deeply from left and back in a jagged manner right around the throat.

News of the murder quickly circulated and a crowd of curious onlookers gathered. Once this mob had been cleared by the police, entrepreneurial neighbours charged customers a few pence to survey the scene from windows overlooking the murder site.

Dr Bagster Phillips was called to examine the body officially: he arrived on the scene at 6.30 a.m. and quickly declared that Annie had been dead for around two hours, which would have set the murder at 4.30 a.m. thus contradicting the statements of both Mrs Long and Albert Cadosch. After his medical examination Dr Phillips then turned detective. He examined the area around the body, and discovered that Annie's pocket had been slashed open and the contents – a piece of muslin, a comb, and several brightly polished coins – 'placed in order at her feet'. There is conflicting evidence about the coins; Dr Bagster Phillips, who was called to the corpse, did not mention money at the inquest, but several notable writers have mentioned both farthings and pennies. I have been unable to trace the pennies, but Inspector Reid, Head of the local CID, when commenting on a blood-stained farthing being found under a later unrelated killing, mentions, 'similar coins were passed upon the Hanbury Street victim'. There were also reports that several brass rings that Annie had been wearing when she left the doss-house had been wrenched from her fingers and stolen by the killer, but these could have been taken while the body was in the mortuary. One puzzle – why did Jack bother to search the dead woman's clothing to find, cut open and rifle her pocket? Such women were invariably penniless. What was the killer looking for?

From Dr Phillips's report, we discover that Jack had stood in front of his victim and strangled her. Newly-raised bruises, mixed with contusions from the fight, were discernible on Annie's face. Her tongue was swollen and protruding from the teeth and her face was livid – further signs of strangulation. After her death, Jack appeared to have attempted complete decapitation and almost succeeded. Annie's stomach was slashed open, after which her intestines were lifted on to the shoulder, which means Jack must have scooped the guts from Annie's belly with his hands. The vagina was slashed open and the uterus cut out. Jack took this part of the body away with him. Once again the murderer had carried out his crime with people, both awake and asleep, in the surrounding houses – possible witnesses who had heard no cry, no scuffle, no noise, apart from Mr Cadosch and his brief 'sound of falling against the fence'.

There was some excitement when a leather apron was found partly submerged in a dish of water in the yard. After Nichols' murder an Inspector Frederick George Abberline wrote a report about several prostitutes who had revealed their terror of a man known as 'Leather

Apron': he had been demanding money from the women, ill-using them and threatening to rip them open with a knife. The press quickly latched on to this new story and on 5 September the *Star* featured an article on 'Leather Apron'. It was widely assumed that he was the killer and a detailed description of this suspect was soon in circulation. 'Leather Apron' was described as short, thick-necked, with small closely-set glistening eyes and a leering expression, a description straight out of a pantomime. Given this widespread belief of the man's guilt it is not surprising that finding a leather apron in the yard at Hanbury Street seemed to be a major clue, and perhaps the authorities were disappointed when Amelia Richardson revealed that the apron belonged to her son. She had recently washed it, leaving it on the fence to drain.

The second inquest on a Ripper victim was again presided over by Wynne Baxter, who was now firmly into his stride, seeming to delight in his authority. He cross-examined Dr Phillips relentlessly, but the doctor appeared curiously reluctant to state the full facts and made a strange statement, which, as we shall see, would be echoed at a later Ripper murder inquest. 'I feel that in giving these details to the public you are thwarting the ends of justice.' It is difficult to understand what injuries a doctor thought he should conceal, and Phillips was under a legal obligation to disclose all medical information in his possession. The purpose of an inquest is to record and preserve all relevant facts in regard to the death. In his summing up, Baxter launched into grand melodrama:

> ...with Judas-like approaches, the wretch must then have seized the deceased. He pressed her throat, and whilst thus preventing the slightest cry, at the same time produced insensibility and suffocation. There is no evidence of any struggle. The clothes were not torn. Even in these preliminaries, the wretch seems to have known how to carry out efficiently his nefarious work. The deceased was then lowered to the ground and laid on her back; and although in doing so may have fallen against the fence, this movement was probably effected with care. Her throat was then cut in two places with savage determination, and the injuries to the abdomen commenced. All was done with cool impudence and reckless daring; but perhaps nothing is more noticeable than the emptying of her pockets and the arrangement of their contents with business-like precision, in order, near her feet. The murder seems, like the Buck's Row case, to have been carried out without a cry. Sixteen people were in the house. The partitions of the different rooms are of wood. Davies was not asleep after 3.00 a.m. except for three-quarters of an hour or less, between 5.00 and 5.45 a.m.; Mrs Richardson only just after 3.00 a.m. and heard no noise during the

night. Mrs Hardman who occupies the front ground-floor room, did not waken until the noise succeeding the finding of the body had commenced, and none of the occupants of the house by which the yard is surrounded heard anything suspicious...

Baxter made his final summing up of the case (possibly to everyone's relief given his verbosity) on 26 September. Annie had, by this time, already been buried. The verdict was predictable. 'Wilful murder by some person or persons unknown.'

Reconstructed image of Annie Chapman (by the artist Peter Fry)

Chapter 4

Panic and Investigation

The murder of Mary Nichols caused great alarm in the East End and considerable press comment throughout the land. Why, in those violent times, when it was fairly routine for women to be attacked, beaten and all too frequently murdered, did Nichols' death create such an impact? Perhaps the catalyst that propelled her murder into such widespread public prominence was the fact that the body was left sprawled on a London pavement, her dress raised high with the deliberate butchery on intimate parts of her body fully exposed. In prudish Victorian times, when the glimpse of an ankle was considered improper, the intimate exposure of Nichols' body may well have been as shocking as the murder and it might have been this aspect that caught the public's imagination. The murder of Chapman so soon after the killing of Nichols created widespread panic. One mutilated, partly eviscerated body laid out on a London street was bad enough, but a second disembowelled woman lying in the open air caused wide-spread panic. The newspapers thundered their opinions. The *Daily Telegraph*, which was not known to be sympathetic to 'wanton women,' used Chapman's nickname 'Dark Annie' in an editorial. But although it described her as a 'forlorn, despised citizeness of London', the editorial continued on a more humane note:

> Dark Annie's dreadful end has compelled a hundred thousand Londoners to reflect what it must be like to have no home at all except the common kitchen of a low lodging house, to sit there, sick and weak and bruised and wretched, for lack of fourpence with which to pay the right of a 'doss': ... 'Dark Annie' will effect in one way what fifty Secretaries of State could never accomplish.

A September issue of *The Times* thundered:

> ...nothing in fact or fiction equals these outrages at once in their horrible nature and in the effect which they have produced upon the popular imagination.

Punch blamed the murders on the popular Victorian melodramas of the day:

> Is it not within the bounds of probability that to the highly-coloured pictorial advertisements to be seen on almost all the

hoardings in London, vividly representing sensational scenes of murder, exhibited as 'the great attractions' of certain dramas, the public may be to a certain extent indebted for the horrible crimes in Whitechapel?

Possible suspects were arrested and questioned daily. Tens of thousands of leaflets were printed and distributed and countless newspaper editorials were written. Contemporary papers report details of numerous arrests; Edward Stanley, Chapman's friend, was taken in for questioning; no charges were laid against any of the suspects.

This vigorous activity did not prevent criticism from being levelled at the police from all directions – including criticism from Buckingham Palace. (After the fifth Ripper killing, Queen Victoria, who took a keen interest in the crimes, wrote personally to the then Prime Minister, Lord Salisbury, enquiring about the murder investigations.) Things were not proceeding well. Despite the large number of men being arrested and closely questioned there were no results and the police grew more and more desperate – a man was taken into custody for 'grinning' at a lady while walking over Westminster Bridge.

The Ripper remained at large. Due to the continuing popular rumour, arrests of men who wore leather aprons became commonplace. This was quickly followed by arrests of men who carried Gladstone bags, as speculation that the murderer carried a similar kind of case had become intense. Meanwhile the police force had other problems: those in charge of the investigations were not entirely in harmony. Sir Charles Warren, the Metropolitan Police Commissioner, was not on good terms with the acting Commissioner for the City of London Police, Major Henry Smith. In addition, relations were strained between the Assistant Metropolitan Police Commissioner, James Monroe and the Home Secretary, Henry Matthews, and neither of these men was on friendly terms with Sir Charles Warren.

The press praised or criticised all of the above officials in varying degrees, adding to the simmering cauldron of bad humour. *The East London Observer* noted on 22 September 1888:

We have had enough of Mr Home Secretary Matthews, who knows nothing, has heard nothing and does not intend to do anything...

The popular press levelled endless criticism at Sir Charles Warren. *The Star* wrote in September:

We can talk of larger reforms when we do away with the centralised, non-efficient military system which Sir Charles Warren has brought to perfection.

On 22 September the *East London Observer* opined: 'It is clear that the Detective Department at Scotland Yard is in an utterly hopeless and worthless condition.' Yet another newspaper commented, 'If sheer fright grows into crazed fury, we shall hold Mr Matthews and Sir Charles Warren responsible'.

Public feeling was becoming inflamed. More criticism came crashing down on Warren and Matthews because the Government did not offer a reward for the capture of the murderer. The Home Office put forward their point of view on this subject:

> Rewards for the discovery of criminals was discontinued some years ago, because the experience showed that such offers of reward tended to produce more harm than good.

There was clearly a fear that offering a reward in the East End would result in a deluge of false or fabricated evidence. 'The excitement in Spitalfields is now rendering the people almost frantic,' one reporter wrote. He was not exaggerating.

In October 1888, *The Times* published an editorial outlining a previous homicide investigation when bloodhounds had been used to track down a murderer. This suggestion evoked a flood of correspondence on the merits and otherwise of *The Times*'s advice. In desperation, the police force heeded the suggestion; they decided to call dogs into action. On 9 and 10 October, trials were conducted in two London parks. On the second outing Sir Charles Warren sportingly allowed himself to become human bait in order to test the dogs' powers. Although the trials in the parks were successful, it soon became apparent that the animals could not follow a scent in an area so densely populated as the East End, and the dogs' services were not retained. Sir Charles then became the object of ridicule, as rumour spread that the dogs had lost themselves and Warren's men had had to go out searching for them.

A trio of insane medical students were the next serious subjects to be sought. Two were traced and intensive enquiries were made concerning the third, who was reported to have gone abroad. That particular investigation, in line with all previous investigation, was eventually abandoned. Despite exhaustive searching, probing and questioning the police appeared to be no closer to finding the killer than they were at the start of their enquiries.

∽

So who was 'Jack the Ripper'? That is a question which people have been asking for well over a century. *The Jack the Ripper A to Z*, written by three leading Ripper experts, Paul Begg, Martin Fido and Keith Skinner, contains a list of around 150 suspects. I feel confident that that list could be considerably reduced if the class structure to which Jack belonged could be established. Was he from the lower classes, who, in the main, populated the East End? Or did he have an upper-class background?

Firstly, we will examine several popular suspects from the working classes, to see whether eliminations can be made there. The 'leather apron' rumour caused suspicion to fall on a shoemaker, John Pizer, a Polish Jew whose unfortunate appearance (black hair almost covered his face) reinforced public prejudice. The shoemaker was known to have used violence towards several prostitutes, as Inspector Joseph Helson made clear in a police report on 7 September. A search was made for Pizer, but when he was eventually arrested he could prove his whereabouts on the 30/31 August, the night of Nichol's murder. He had questioned a policeman in Seven Sisters Road about a large fire in the London Docks which was visible for many miles around, and he had lodged in a Holloway Road doss-house for the remainder of the night. The deputy of this doss-house and the policeman confirmed these details. Pizer's friends and relatives swore that he had not left the house on the days before or after Chapman's murder. Once these enquiries were completed the police were satisfied that Pizer was innocent, but he could not be immediately released from custody for his own safety. The panic and fury which the first two Ripper killings had unleashed continued to rise daily, fuelled by wild rumours and an endless barrage of sensational press stories, not all of them true. Despite irrefutable evidence of Pizer's innocence, he was still summoned to Annie Chapman's inquest for questioning. This appearance led to his innocence being publicly acknowledged. After this court appearance had led to his exoneration, Pizer successfully sued several newspapers that had stated he was definitely the Whitechapel murderer. The sums awarded to him are not known, but no doubt the money would have supplied him with leather aprons for some years to come.

A second popularly accepted suspect from the working classes was also a Polish Jew, Aaron Kosminski, who worked, when he worked, as a hairdresser. The case for Kosminski as the legendary killer has been thoroughly discussed by Paul Begg in his book *Jack the Ripper, The Uncensored Facts*. An American television programme, chaired by Sir Peter Ustinov and broadcast in 1988, decided that Kosminski was the most likely Ripper candidate, as did an English television programme, *Crime Monthly*, broadcast in the London area in 1990. Kosminski was known to harbour a hatred of women and had homicidal tendencies; it was reported to the police that he had once used a knife to threaten the life of his sister. Kosminski was first named as a suspect by Sir Melville Macnaghten in notes which he wrote in 1894. According to this source, Kosminski lived in 'the very heart of the district where the murders were committed'. He appeared to have had a supportive family, who, it was suspected, would cover up for their brother in regard to blood-stained clothing and any other evidence that might prove incriminating.

Macnaghten's notes state that Kosminski was committed to Mile End Old Town Workhouse Infirmary, and then Colney Hatch Insane Asylum in 1890. Workhouse records confirm that admittance: entries in the workhouse's infirmary register state that Kosminski had been insane for two years. Records of the man's personal habits state that he would only eat food he himself found in the gutters, and that he refused to wash or bathe. 'No one ever saw the murderer', Macnaghten's notes claim, but an equally senior Scotland Yard officer, Sir Robert Anderson, who was in charge of the Ripper murders from October 1888, stated, '. . . the only person [unnamed] who ever had a good view of the murderer, unhesitatingly identified the suspect [Kosminski] the instant he was confronted with him . . .' Clearly one of these two high-ranking officers was wrong.

∽

I now wish to argue against the allegations that Kosminski or Pizer was the Ripper. Take Kosminski: his house was only a few minutes walk from Flower and Dean Street and Thrawl Street, and he was known to roam the area which contained the lodging houses used by the murdered prostitutes, which means he must have been known to the victims. Now although the prostitutes were not fussy over their clientele they would surely have drawn the line at a man who stank, who was known to hate women, who was known to be violent and who, presumably, was penniless. Mary Nichols went into a lonely, dark street with her killer and Annie Chapman went through a long, dark, narrow passageway into a small yard with the same man. Neither of the women would have accepted a local lunatic who was known to them as a client.

It has been pointed out that Kosminski was only taken for mental treatment in July 1890, almost two years after the murders ended: but, as we have seen, the Mile End Workhouse Infirmary declared that Kosminski had been insane for two years, which means he must have been adjudged insane *well before* the Ripper murders started. And, of course, such people usually display signs of impending madness over a period of time, as evidenced by Kosminski's refusal to eat food unless he personally found it in the gutter.

It is just possible that Kosminski might have used a knife to force the women to go with him, but the silence of the murders tends to rule this out. The women would have made some kind of fuss – spoken protests or a scuffle – even if they did not yell out. As we shall see, the last murder, allegedly of Mary Kelly, took place in a room. It would certainly have been possible to refuse to take a lunatic vagrant home. Mary Kelly was an intelligent woman. If threatened she would have led the tramp to a place where she could have received help – possibly from the local policeman on his beat or from a friend – and not into her own lodgings. A similar argument could be made against the violent Pizer being the killer. Indeed, there is circumstantial evidence that suggests Jack was not a local man.

The yard at 29 Hanbury Street in which Annie Chapman met her end was, to reiterate, a busy place, especially around dawn, the time when Annie was most probably murdered. To repeat – the residents of the doss-house used this yard for storage and work purposes; they also used it for relieving themselves and might appear at any time of the night. The fact that anyone entering the yard through the swing door at the end of the passage and down the steps could easily have had their only means of escape cut off was well known to locals. It was an area where a man might risk a quick servicing of his pick-up, the partners pressed together and standing up in the dark – if they had been disturbed no great harm was done – however, to commit murder and mutilation in such an enclosed place would have been decidedly risky. It is highly unlikely that a local man with murder on his mind would have taken Annie into such a busy place from which a hasty exit would prove impossible, his escape cut off by the single door leading to the long passageway. Especially when the mutilations to the body and the search of the clothing must have taken a considerable amount of time. And certainly, as we shall see, the East End graffiti, written by the killer, rules out a member of the lower classes. To strengthen my case, a leading policeman thought that Jack belonged to the upper classes; that will be discussed in a later chapter.

Chapter 5

The Double Killing

Three weeks passed after the discovery of Annie Chapman's body in Hanbury Street, with no further murders in the area to arouse excitement. Three weeks in the East End environment, where every hour was a struggle to survive, sharpened the mind in favour of the present and blunted the power of the past. If Jack's killings had finished in Hanbury Street, his deeds would probably have quickly faded into the mists of time – two unpleasant murders in a violent area, made unremarkable by the passing decades. But on 30 September 1888 a double murder took place within the space of around forty-five minutes, the sites being approximately half a mile from each other. This unique savagery immortalised Jack, creating a legend and giving rise to a puzzle that has tantalised millions of people for more than a century: who was Jack the Ripper?

The situation of Liz Stride, who, at the time of her death, was a forty-two-year-old East End prostitute, appears to differ from that of the Ripper's first two victims. On the eve of her murder Liz had worked as a cleaning woman in Flower and Dean Street, earning sixpence for her work. She was not so tragic a figure as Nichols or Chapman: she was better looking and probably in better general health, although she had received treatment for bronchitis and there had been problems with venereal disease in the past. But on the night of her death, in contrast to the earlier victims, she was not turned away from lodgings in the small hours, forcing her to tout for clients in order to earn money for a night's lodgings. Liz appears to have been a genuine free spirit, restless at being in one place for too long and unwilling, or unable, to sustain a steady relationship over an extended period. Accurate details of Liz's former life and upbringing were difficult to distil into a clear picture, as she was in the habit of embroidering her past with fantasies and lies.

Nonetheless, we know that Jack's third murder victim was born in Torslanda, Sweden, the daughter of a farmer. She had one sister and two brothers. Liz left home in 1860 aged sixteen, presumably some time after she left school – her restless spirit clearly dates from early in life. After settling in Gothenburg she worked as a domestic servant, but by 1865 the Swedish police had registered her – now in her early twenties – as a prostitute. Liz had been 'on the game' for almost half of her life.

Although a foreigner she apparently spoke perfect English and she was reputed to speak fluent Yiddish, accomplishments which would indicate intelligence.

It is not known why Stride decided to leave Sweden and move to Britain, which she did in 1866. Perhaps the death of her parents and the fact that she had given birth to a still-born baby drove her away from home. Or maybe her wanderlust had already started to work? Once in London the Swede reputedly settled into a mansion in Hyde Park, a highly respectable area, where she became a 'gentleman's domestic servant'.

In 1869 she married a carpenter, John Stride (Annie Chapman had been married in the same year) but, following the depressing pattern of the Ripper's other victims, at some point in time this union broke down; by 1877 Liz's fortunes had reached a low ebb and she was living in an East End workhouse. Acquaintances spoke well of Liz (nicknamed 'Long Liz'), describing her as 'good hearted'; 'pleasant'; 'clean' and so on. Having arrived in the East End she always declared that she had been widowed and had lost her children in a shipping accident. In 1878, the steamer *Princess Alice* had struck the *Bywell Castle* in the Thames near Woolwich; the *Alice* had sunk with great loss of life. A News Agency report on 8 October 1888 printed a story that an Elizabeth Stride had indeed identified her husband and two children amongst the dead lying in Woolwich Dockyard, but the *Princess Alice* passenger and crew lists did not register the name of Stride.

Liz's story about the loss of her family, and about her own escape climbing onto the funnel of the stricken ship, appears to have been romantic fiction. The prosaic truth was that her husband, John Stride, died of heart failure in 1884 in an East London workhouse. Indeed, Liz's downfall appears to stem from character defects. If her husband did not abandon her, and so far as one can speculate, John Stride appears to have been a decent man, then Liz must have abandoned him, presumably leaving her children (variously numbered from two to nine) and a reasonably secure domestic life for the uncertainties of the street. No doubt the widely-spread East End disease of alcoholism played its part in this choice of action. Liz was frequently arrested for being drunk and disorderly. Once in the dock she was reputed to have given dramatic performances blaming her symptoms on illness. Stride's second nickname was 'Epileptic Liz' but, as I can find no trace of that illness in her medical history, I must assume that the soubriquet referred to her famous performances in the court room. This heavy drinking free-spirit begins to emerge as a distinct individual.

At some point Liz settled down with another partner, Michael Kidney, but even in this relationship the urge to roam made her disappear from time to time. Kidney, an apparently brutal, heavy drinking dockyard labourer whom Liz accused of assault, made an inquest statement that helps to illuminate Stride's lifestyle:

> ...she was subject to going away whenever she thought she would. During the three years I've known her, she has been away from me altogether about five months. I've cautioned her the same as I would a wife. It was drink that made her go. But she always came back again. I don't believe she left me on Tuesday to take up with any other man. I think she liked me better than any other man...

This last statement may well have been more than supposition. Although Liz charged Kidney with assault, she failed to appear in court for the prosecution and the charges were dropped.

∽

On the eve of her murder, 30 September, Liz left Flower and Dean Street mid-evening, presumably in order to enjoy herself drinking in pubs and searching for clients to refill her coffers and provide more gin. She was seen soliciting in the Whitechapel area by a number of witnesses, but, as usual, there is conflicting evidence about these sightings. *The Evening News*, 1 October 1888, recorded an interview with a Mr Best and a Mr Gardner. These gentlemen claimed that when they had entered an East End public house, *The Bricklayers Arms*, at 11.00 p.m on the night of the murder, Liz and a respectably dressed man had been leaving. They were hugging and kissing. The man was 5ft 5ins in height, clean-shaven, apart from a black moustache, wearing a black billycock hat and dressed in a morning suit and coat; forty-five minutes later a William Marshall claimed to have seen Stride with a man in Berner Street: both were travelling in the direction of Dutfield's Yard, a premises situated off Berner Street.

The Evening News tracked down an elderly greengrocer, Matthew Packer, whose shop was situated at 4 Berner Street. On 4 October the newspaper published Packer's statement. He claimed that he had sold grapes to a man and a woman (whom he subsequently identified as Stride) on the night of the murder. Packer also claimed that no detective or policeman had visited him to find out whether he had seen anything suspicious on the night in question. There are many conflicting reports around Packer's testimony, and he appeared to change the time of his transaction according to his audience, which tends to make his evidence unreliable. The main interest in the man lies in the fact that Sir Charles Warren interviewed him personally, a fact established by Stephen Knight, who found Warren's hand-written notes in police files: why should such a highly-placed police officer interview such a minor witness? Warren, in his spidery handwriting, questions the timing that Packer had made in previous police statements (that he believed Stride had bought grapes from him at midnight), against the timing that the man had personally made to him; at 11 p.m . . . But even the former timing was a full hour before Liz Stride was killed. Plenty of time for her to have found another client. So why was there such interest in Packer's evidence, as he could well have been describing an innocent man? Stephen Knight in his widely-read book, *Jack the Ripper, The Final Solution*, makes a strong case for Charles Warren having hired special investigators answerable only to him. If Packer was considered such an important witness, why was he not called to give evidence at Stride's inquest? Clearly something very odd was going on behind the police scenes.

On the night of Liz Stride's murder, Mrs Fanny Mortimer, who lived at 36 Berner Street, only a few doors away from *The International Workingmen's Educational Club* (a locally unpopular establishment which served as a meeting place for anarchists and intellectuals) told reporters that she had been standing outside her door to listen to the community singing from the men's club. Again, there are various differences in the reported timings of Mrs Mortimer's nocturnal vigil, ranging from 12.30 a.m. to 1.00 a.m. *The Evening News*, 1 October 1888, reported that Mrs Mortimer '. . . heard the measured heavy tread of a policeman passing the house on his beat.' Paul Begg records that only a single policeman, PC William Smith, is known to have passed along Berner Street within that time limit. Smith plodded his beat at 12.30 a.m. Mrs Mortimer said that while she was standing at her door, she had seen only one man in Berner Street. He was traced and found to be Leon Goldstein, an innocent pedestrian who had passed Mrs Mortimer around 12.50/55 a.m., but as we shall see, if the lady had indeed been outside her door from 12.30 a.m. she could not have failed to notice two other men, Morris Eagle and Joseph Lave.

A Charles Letchford, who lived at 39 Berner Street, told the *Manchester Guardian* that his sister had been outside her door for about ten minutes, from 12.50 a.m.; it is a reasonable assumption that Mrs Mortimer was the sister referred to. This later timing would fit in with the following evidence, which places Mrs Mortimer outside her door from around 12.45 a.m. to 12.55 a.m. Letchford's timing might well have been incorrect by a few minutes. The lady is said to have returned inside her house about five-minutes before the man who discovered the body, Louis Diemschutz, passed by in his horse and cart. Diemschutz passed by at almost exactly 1.00 a.m.

The most illuminating evidence of Stride's last night on earth was given to Chief Inspector Donald Swanson by an Hungarian immigrant,

Israel Schwartz. Schwartz claimed that at 12.45 a.m. he had turned into Berner Street from the Commercial Road, and, Swanson recorded:

> ... having got as far as the gateway where the murder was committed, he saw a man stop and speak to a woman who was standing in the gateway. The man tried to pull the woman into the street, but he turned her round and threw her down on the footway and the woman screamed three times, but not very loudly. On crossing to the opposite side of the street, he saw a second man standing lighting his pipe. The man who threw the woman down called out, apparently to the man on the opposite side of the road, 'Lipski' and then Schwartz walked away, but finding that he was followed by the second man, he ran so far as the railway arch, but the man did not follow so far ...

Given that Schwartz only watched the struggle for a minute or so, he described an event that took place roughly fifteen-minutes before Liz's death, so he almost certainly saw her being attacked prior to the murder. The police refused to give out Schwartz's name and address, but he was tracked down by the *Star*, which printed a long interview:

> Information which may be important was given to the Leman Street police yesterday by an Hungarian concerning this murder. This foreigner was well-dressed, and had the appearance of being in the theatrical line. He could not speak a word of English, but came to the police station accompanied by a friend, who acted as an interpreter ... As he turned the corner from Commerical Road he noticed some distance in front of him a man walking as if partially intoxicated. He walked on behind him, and presently he noticed a woman standing in the entrance to the alleyway where the body

DUTFIELD'S YARD

⊗ Gates

⊗ Liz Stride's Body

was found. The half-tipsy man halted and spoke to her. The Hungarian saw him put a hand on her shoulder and push her back into the passage, but feeling rather timid of getting mixed up in quarrels, he crossed to the other side of the street. Before he had gone many yards, however, he heard the sound of a quarrel, and turned back to learn what was the matter, but just as he stepped from the kerb a second man came out of the doorway of the public house a few doors off, and shouting out some sort of warning to the man who was with the woman, rushed forward as if to attack the intruder. The Hungarian states positively that he saw a knife in the second man's hand, but he waited to see no more. He fled incontinently to his new lodgings . . .

This newspaper story clearly differs in several respects from the one which Schwartz had given to the police a few days earlier, and which, over one hundred years later, we can now compare. There are several possibilities for these changes. The interpreter might have been adding his own embellishments, but this is unlikely. The detail about a man rushing from a local public house brandishing a knife was also unlikely given the current climate of distrust – a Jew named only as Jacobs became a suspect merely because he wore a leather apron. He was continually attacked in the street and frequently had to run for his life. In September 1888 the *Daily News* reported that doctors were kept busy on cases of serious assault which arose directly and indirectly out of the mere discussion of the Ripper murders. In these circumstances only a lunatic would dare to openly carry a knife. Furthermore, what reason would a man have for attacking a fellow found arguing with a prostitute? Given the suppression of Schwartz's statement and the extraordinary fact that *he was not called to give evidence at Stride's inquest,* could the immigrant have been bullied into changing his story before being hustled away by Charles Warren? It is certainly mysterious that, after his newspaper article, the man, a vital witness in such a widely-reported and infamous case, disappeared, never again to be recorded by any newspaper or any official documents.

The discovery of Liz's body was made by Louis Diemschutz, an entrepreneurial Victorian who managed *The International Workingmen's Educational Club* situated near to Mrs Mortimer's house. The club appears to have been run mainly by Louis's wife while he peddled cheap jewellery from a market stall.

Between 40 and 42 Berner Street, a gateway approximately twelve-feet wide, led into a small yard, Dutfield's Yard, reached along two blind walls which formed a long alleyway between the Berner Street houses and the club.

It was 1.00 a.m. when Louis turned his horse into the twenty-foot long, unlit passageway off Berner Street that led into Dutfield's Yard. The horse, as it was nosed through the gates, suddenly shied and refused to go any further. Singing could still be heard in the club as Louis urged his horse on without success. He then poked with his whip to the right of the pony's head and discovered a bundle lying on the ground. A quick examination in the darkness showed that the bundle was an inert woman lying near to the wall. Unable to see very much in the darkness Louis hurried into the club and collected a lamp and several companions. They all rushed back to the gates. Light revealed a woman lying on her back, head towards the wall, feet towards the street. Her left arm was extended and her hand still clutched a packet of cachous. These scented sweets would have been used to hide the smell of alcohol on her breath. Liz had clearly aimed to present a pleasant package to her clients, a package that included a corsage of fresh flowers pinned to her coat. Her right hand was folded over the stomach; her throat was deeply cut. When Louis and his colleagues examined the body the throat was still oozing blood, indicating that the entry of the horse might have disturbed the Ripper.

A large crowd quickly collected at the murder scene, forcing the police to close off the yard which was then thoroughly searched, without result. The club members were all detained and questioned, again without result. In the mean time, every available policeman in the area was being drafted towards Berner Street, a fact that did not seem to bother Jack. He progressed through the East End in search of a new victim, past alerted policemen, and no one saw him apart from a prostitute, Catharine Eddowes, and she would not be giving evidence. The Ripper was her last encounter.

Liz Stride's inquest opened on 1 October, the day after her murder, and the coroner was once again the indefatigable Wynne Baxter. Identification of the dead woman provided an immediate stumbling block, taking up a great deal of police time, and soon farce entered the proceedings. The police testified that the body was that of an habitual drunk who gave the name of Annie Fitzgerald each time she was arrested. Then a Mrs Mary Malcolm came forward and testified under oath that the body was that of her sister, Elizabeth Watts. Mrs Malcolm bore a strong facial resemblance to the dead woman so her testimony was given serious consideration. The lady then launched into a tirade of abuse against her 'dead' sister, accusing her of gross immorality. It was difficult to disprove Mrs Malcolm's assertions until the 'dead' sister arrived at the inquest and refuted the calumnies which had caused her great distress. Mrs Malcolm was not available for further comment.

The inquest was finally wound up on 24 October, when PC Walter

Stride identified the dead woman as the wife of his deceased uncle, John Stride. At least Liz had been truthful about her name.

∽

We now arrive at yet another fascinating Ripper puzzle, one which has been surprisingly ignored by other writers on the crimes.

Let us examine the comings and goings around Dutfield's Yard half an hour before Liz Stride's murder. With the activity from the men's club it was clearly a busy place – not a spot any sensible man would select for murder. These statements are taken from witnesses at Stride's inquest:

12.30 approx. William West, a printer, was in Dutfield's Yard and noticed that the gates at the end of the passageway were open. He saw nothing unusual.

12.35 approx. Morris Eagle went along the passageway from Berner Street into Dutfield's Yard. He saw nothing unusual.

12.45 approx. Joseph Lave went along the passage. As it was so dark, he had to grope along the right hand wall and would have fallen over Stride's body had it been there.

12.45 approx. The most likely time at which Mrs Mortimer stood outside her front door, staying there until approximately 12.55 a.m.

There is a general consensus that Israel Schwartz did indeed see Liz Stride being attacked at around 12.45 a.m. prior to her murder. We must assume that Mrs Mortimer and Joseph Lave narrowly missed being present at the attack. But this timing provides a further mystery. If Stride was attacked at 12.45 a.m., why did her murder take place almost fifteen minutes later? Her throat was still pouring blood when Diemschutz and his companions examined the body, which means Stride was killed only minutes before she was found; Diemschutz was certain of the time, as he had checked with a clock shortly before arriving at Dutfield's Yard. What happened to Stride in the fifteen- minutes between her attack and her murder? Mrs Mortimer, standing a few yards away saw nothing suspicious happening in the street. Where was Stride after the struggle with her attacker at 12. 45 a.m. up to her death at 1 a.m.?

∽

Catharine Eddowes was a forty-six-year-old prostitute when she was murdered. She had been born 14 April 1842 in Wolverhampton, the daughter of a metal worker. There are confusing reports about her early upbringing and education and it is impossible to sort out fact from fiction. In 1864 Catharine, a young woman, started living with Thomas Conway, an older man; newspapers reported that he was a pensioner. The couple moved to London and it is impossible to say whether they ever married, but Conway was the father of her three children, a daughter and two sons. By 1880 the relationship had broken down. Their daughter Annie blamed the split on her mother's excessive drinking, but

Eddowes's sister claimed that Conway's violence made Catharine leave. If Conway had been a pensioner in 1864 (assuming that he had not been invalided out of the armed forces early), then he must have been an old man sixteen years later. Catharine, a much younger person with a fiery temper, would surely have been able to defend herself, so I tend to believe the daughter's version of the marriage breakdown.

Catharine had met John Kelly, who became her common-law husband, one year after she parted from her first husband, if that was indeed a legal union. Since then Catharine and John had lived together in apparent harmony and happiness for seven years. Although Catharine is usually described as a prostitute, John Kelly and a lodging house keeper both stated that she did not 'walk the streets'. However, her ever-present difficulty was to find money for drink, and alcoholics, when desperate, will perform any service. She had a reputation as a scrounger and even her own daughter is reputed to have moved to an undisclosed address to avoid her mother's cadging ways. Thomas Conway went to the lengths of having his army pension paid to him under the name of Thomas Quinn, to prevent Catharine from making a claim on it.

During September 1888 John Kelly and Eddowes travelled to Maidstone in Kent to earn money hop picking – a traditional combined working holiday much favoured by East Enders. Their hop-picking efforts did not appear to meet with success and the couple returned to London penniless. There are persistent reports that Catharine returned to the capital in order to claim the reward money that had been offered to anyone able to name Jack the Ripper. 'I think I know who it is,' Catharine is reputed to have said to the superintendent of the Shoe Lane Workhouse where she was well-known, and where she went for a bed for the night after returning from the hop fields. When she was warned not to say such things in case she should become the Ripper's next victim, Catharine replied, 'Oh no fear of that'. She was wrong.

On the 29 September the impecunious couple pawned John Kelly's boots; he is said to have stood barefoot on the pavement while Catharine arranged the transaction. The half-a-crown obtained in the morning from the pawnbroker, a not inconsiderable sum in late Victorian times, lasted only until early afternoon. Penniless again, Catharine left her partner in Houndsditch, a road built over the site of the Roman moat which used to surround London in ancient times. The name is said to have originated from the number of dead dogs that were thrown into the water by the Romans. Houndsditch ran between Bishopsgate and Aldgate High Street, places that are associated with Catharine's last night on earth. She left John Kelly at 2.00 p.m. saying she would go to Bermondsey to try and borrow money from her daughter Annie and would be back no later than 4.00 p.m. This statement is puzzling as the daughter had moved away from Bermondsey leaving no forwarding address, presumably to try and dodge her mother's unwelcome cadging, and Catharine must have known this fact; so why did she lie to John?

Ignoring her promise to return within two hours she went on a massive drinking spree, we do not know where, and this creates yet another puzzle. Given the fact that Catharine was penniless (and sober according to John Kelly at the inquest) in the early afternoon and that she did not manage to borrow money from her daughter – she could not even find her daughter – it is difficult to know where Catharine obtained money to spend on drink, if not from clients in return for sexual favours. But where did she find these clients? She was not seen soliciting. The other prostitutes had all been seen with men even in the middle of the night; Catharine's work would have taken place in the middle of the day in an area where she was well known. As it was still light she could not take clients to dark corners in remote alleyways – she would have needed a place to use for her sexual encounters, but at this point in time Catharine did not even have a regular doss-house to go to; and, even if she had, these places were so crowded someone would have seen her with her pick-ups. Given the publicity surrounding the case, these sightings would have been reported. So where did Catharine go from early afternoon to mid-evening to earn the money to supply enough drink to hopelessly intoxicate her?

At 8.30 p.m. she was found in Aldgate High Street profoundly drunk. Although it is not a hard and fast rule, most heavy drinkers need large amounts of alcohol to intoxicate them completely – and as so many people wanted to get in on the act after the murder, someone would surely have mentioned that Catharine got tipsy quickly. No one did. Catharine had clearly imbibed – and spent – heavily. There is no satisfactory answer as to where she got the money to buy alcohol and where she went in the unaccounted hours on the day before her death. More about that in a later chapter. As Catharine was obviously intoxicated and disorderly (she was unable to stand upright) two constables took her into custody and she was locked in a cell at Bishopsgate Police Station. Around 1.00 a.m. – precisely the time Liz Stride was being attacked a quarter of a mile away – a constable looked into Catharine's cell and decided that she had sobered up sufficiently to be discharged, which creates another mystery. The police station in which she had been detained was in the heart of the Ripper territory. The police had issued many warnings that women should not go out alone at night. Why, therefore, in the small hours of the morning, did they discharge the penniless, and presumably still groggy Eddowes? Clearly, with hindsight, this was the most stupid of actions as Catharine did indeed become another Ripper victim. Before being released, Catharine's name had been registered as

'Mary Ann Kelly', a soubriquet she used from time to time. Many of the prostitutes used false names when they were arrested, in order to give the police a difficult time. Intriguingly, the alleged fifth and final victim of Jack the Ripper was also named Mary Kelly.

∽

Mitre Square was one of the more respectable areas of London. At 1.30 a.m., PC Watkins trudged his usual beat through the square – all was quiet. At 1.35 a.m. three men, Joseph Lawende, Joseph Levy and Harry Harris, testified that they had passed Church Passage, which leads into Mitre Square. (See map below.) Here, at the Duke Street end of the passage, they saw a man and a woman talking. They could not see the woman's face, however, Lawende later identified the woman as Eddowes by the clothes she had been wearing ('I noticed she had a black jacket and black bonnet. I have seen the articles at the Police Station, and I recognise them as the sort of dress worn by that woman'). Recognising black clothing worn in a dark place on a dark night does not seem to me to be particularly convincing identification.

About 1.38 a.m. PC James Harvey went along Church Passage as far as the entrance to Mitre Square. Harvey testified that he had been at the end of Church Passage around that time but he saw no one and heard no cry or noise. At 1.45 a.m. when Constable Watkin's beat returned him to Mitre Square (that is about six or seven minutes after PC Harvey stood looking into the area), he discovered the body of Catharine Eddowes in deep shadow, lying on the pavement outside an empty house. She had been appallingly mutilated, with slashes cut into her cheeks, part of her nose sliced off and cuts made across her eyelids. By her side lay an old mustard tin box, containing pawn tickets.

To repeat the police timetable:

1.30 a.m.   Watkins passes the murder site in Mitre Square. No body was seen.

1.38/9 a.m.   Harvey stands at the Church Passage entrance to Mitre Square. All was quiet.

1.45 a.m.   Watkins returns to Mitre Square. Discovers Eddowe's body.

This gave the Ripper six or seven minutes to murder and carry out complicated mutilations on his victim, which is clearly impossible.

Watkins ran to Kearley and Tonge's warehouse in Mitre Square and roused the watchman, George Morris, a former policeman. Morris later testified that although the warehouse door was ajar he had heard no suspicious sounds. A doctor, Dr George Sequeira, was called to the body. He merely declared Catharine dead, which was obvious, and the City Police Surgeon, Dr Frederick Brown was sent for. Dr Brown's examination revealed the full extent of Catharine's injuries. Besides the facial mutilations, her throat had been slashed almost from ear to ear – her right ear lobe fell off when the body was undressed in the mortuary. Catharine's stomach had been exposed and cut open and the intestines pulled out and slung over the right shoulder. A small piece of intestine had been cut away and dropped underneath the left arm. One kidney and the uterus had been removed and were missing. Jack had also cut through the anal artery releasing feculent matter which had possibly smeared him. This clumsiness was a main consideration in convincing the experts, including Dr Sequira and eventually Dr Brown, that the killer had no surgical skill.

Jack's unprecedented night of terror, during which he had succeeded in ripping himself into everlasting fame by committing two terrible murders within forty-five minutes of each other, was over. But worse violence was to follow.

Chapter 6

Prelude to the Fifth Murder

Despite a massive police investigation the murders were baffling, the stealth and cunning of the invisible killer terrifying. Myths began to be born: Jack the Ripper was a vampire; he was an agent of the devil; he was a trained wild animal. Major puzzles arose, puzzles that were hard to solve.

The Ripper murdered Stride in Berner Street at 1 o'clock in the morning then set off in the direction of Bishopsgate and Mitre Square. Going directly to the Square on foot would have taken about ten to fifteen minutes, but somewhere along the route Jack met the recently-released Catharine Eddowes whom he must have engaged in conversation. How did they arrive together in Mitre Square? Dr Frederick Brown's post-mortem report on Eddowes's mutilated body describes her right kidney as '. . . pale, bloodless, with slight congestion of the base.' This signifies Bright's Disease; so Catharine was a sick woman. Typical symptoms of Bright's Disease include hypertension and loss of energy; 29/30 September was a cold night, Catharine was middle-aged and she had just slept off a massive drinking spree in an uncomfortable police cell. Given the above factors she cannot have been feeling too sprightly, so any journey on foot would be slow, yet we know that her murder was committed within forty-five minutes or so of her release from custody.

In between PC Watkin's regular fifteen-minute Mitre Square patrols, Jack, with meticulous timing, murdered his victim, slashed her face, nicked her lower eyelids as though creating the face of a clown, and then carried out time-consuming mutilations on his victim. He cut away a large piece of the intestine and placed it alongside the body, while other parts of the gut were drawn out and placed over her right shoulder. The uterus and a kidney were removed, but the kidney is buried deep in the body and is not easy to find, yet Jack completed his work in seven to eight-minutes at the most. Having finished this butchery, the killer, no doubt bloodstained and with human organs in his pocket or in a bag, escaped through an area where the police had already been alerted by the earlier killing. He must have walked past late-night revellers, yet no one, police or public, caught a glimpse of him.

Other puzzles began to emerge. Catharine's last recorded words to the policeman on duty were, 'I'll get a good hiding when I get home'.

She clearly remembered that she had promised to meet John Kelly eleven hours earlier, which predisposes rational thinking. A Frederick Wilkinson testified at the inquest that Eddowes and John Kelly were always on good terms although they quarrelled occasionally, so the remark to the policeman was most likely made in jest.

Women had been warned to stay off the East End streets after sunset – and following the horrific murders not many warnings were needed. This set of circumstances (along with her hangover and illness) should have sent Catharine scurrying towards the safe company of her partner, yet once she had been released from Bishopsgate Police Station she headed away from John Kelly's lodgings. Why? Better a possible quarrel with her lover than a meeting with Jack.

∽

Londoners, their blood already chilled by the murders, now had to endure a series of frightening letters – and a message chalked on a wall at Goulston Street. The Goulston Street beat was trodden by Police Constable Alfred Long. At approximately 2.15 a.m. on the night of the double murder, the constable passed Wentworth Model Dwellings, tenement buildings in Goulston Street; nothing out of the ordinary caught his attention. Retreading his beat at approximately 3.00 a.m. PC Long noticed a piece of bloodstained apron near the base of common stairs leading to apartments 108/119 of the Model Dwellings. Later tests proved the fragment had been cut from Catharine Eddowes's apron. Jack had passed along Goulston Street and thrown away his memento. Written in chalk on the wall above the apron, were the words:

> *The Juwes are the men that will not be blamed for nothing.*

Was Jack anti-Semitic, trying to put the blame for his terrible deeds onto the Jewish race in order to start riots? That, apparently, was the belief of Sir Charles Warren. On hearing of the graffiti Sir Charles immediately headed to the East End and, according to Sir Henry Smith, the Acting Commissioner City of London Police, personally washed the message from the wall. If Smith was mistaken and Warren did not personally erase this potentially vital clue, he certainly gave the order to do so. The Commissioner's action was backed by Superintendent Thomas Arnold, who wrote in his Home Office report:

> Knowing in consequence of suspicion having fallen upon a Jew named John Pizer, alias 'Leather Apron', having committed a murder in Hanbury Street a short time previously, a strong feeling existed against Jews generally, and as the building upon which the writing was found was situated in the midst of a locality inhabited principally by that sect, I was apprehensive that if the writing were left it would be the means of causing a riot and therefore considered

it desirable that it should be removed. ... had only a portion of the writing been removed the context would have remained.

So removing part of the message (presumably the word Juwes) had obviously been discussed. However, 'if only a portion of the writing had been removed the context would have remained,' is clearly arrant nonsense. What context could the words, '... are the men that will not be blamed for nothing' have held? And why should these words cause riots? Besides, no one, outside the police authorities, knew that the graffiti was linked to Jack the Ripper. Anyone with a little thought, or a grain of sense, would have recognised this truth and left the graffiti until it could have been photographed. I find that the words and writings of some of the top London policemen of the time undoubtedly dubious. A relevant personal letter from Sir Charles Warren proves my point.

> ... The most pressing question at that moment was some writing on the wall in Goulston Street evidently written with the intention of inflaming the public mind against the Jews, and which Mr Arnold with a view to prevent serious disorder proposed to obliterate, and had sent down an Inspector with a sponge for that purpose, telling him to await his arrival. I considered it desirable that I should decide this matter myself, as it was one involving so great a responsibility whether any action was taken or not.
>
> I accordingly went down to Goulston Street at once before going to the scene of the murder: it was just getting light, the public would be in the streets in a few minutes, in a neighbourhood very much crowded on Sunday mornings by Jewish vendors and Christian purchasers from all parts of London. There were several Police around the spot when I arrived, both Metropolitan and City.
>
> The writing was on the jamb of the open archway or doorway visible to anyone in the street, and could not be covered up without the danger of the covering being torn off at once. A discussion took place whether the writing could be left covered up or otherwise or whether any portion of it could be left for an hour until it could be photographed: but after taking into consideration the excited state of the population in London generally at the time, the strong feelings which existed against the Jews, and the fact that in a short time there would be a large concourse of the people in the streets, and having before me the Report that if it was left there the house was likely to be wrecked (in which from my observation I entirely concurred), I considered it desirable to obliterate the writing at once, having taken a copy of which I enclose a duplicate ...

Surely with a police guard any covering would *not* have been torn down until photographers arrived? The police held far more power in dealing with the public than they do today. And what was the 'report'? With such a pressing matter in hand had Arnold sat down and written out the pros and cons? I find that odd. I must also express doubts about the positioning of the graffiti. Sir Charles writes it was, '. . . on the jamb of the open archway or doorway visible to anyone in the street.' Many researchers have accepted this statement.

On a number of occasions I have met and conversed with Paul Begg, Martin Fido and Keith Skinner, three of the most impressive and reliable of all the Ripperologists. Besides finding all these men intelligent and charming, their combined scholarship and their invaluable solo work are the books that I usually consult. Only in one matter do I take issue with this most distinguished trio. Their excellent collaboration, *The A to Z*, states that the graffiti was chalked on the brick fascia edging the doorway. (I have taken 'fascia' to mean jamb.) Other writers repeat this information. I assume that all parties are accepting the words written by Sir Charles Warren to the Home Office. ('The writing was on the jamb of the open archway or doorway visible to anyone in the street . . .') Yet Chief Inspector Donald Swanson, who was in charge of the Ripper investigation up to early October 1888, noted that the graffiti was on the wall of 'a common stairs leading to a number of tenements.' In other words, Jack had entered the entrance to the dwellings, partly out of sight of the street. Furthermore, I have copies of many of the original newspaper reports. The policeman who found the rag stated at a hearing, 'it [the portion of apron] was lying in the passageway leading to the staircase . . . above it on the wall was written, The Jews (sic) are the men who will not be blamed for nothing.' 'In the passageway,' seems quite clear, and, to my way of thinking, is quite different to 'lying in the doorway.' Detective Constable Daniel Halse, who visited Goulston Street before the graffiti was destroyed, wrote that the words were, '. . . written on the fascia . . . the fascia was about the height of a man'. In the *Oxford Dictionary for Writers and Editors* ' fascia' is described as 'a long flat surface between mouldings.' That does describe nine inches of brickwork.

Keith Skinner, in his excellent co-written book *Letters From Hell*, records that the positioning of the graffiti was written on a map by the City surveyor. '. . . on the right hand side of the doorway . . . *found inside entrance* [my italics] to Model Dwellings.' '. . . found inside entrance' seems quite clear. Indeed, the only person to definitely pin-point the positioning on the, 'jamb of the open doorway' was Warren, and he did so in a letter to the Home Office that would go unseen, straight onto file. I also contend that the writing did not fit on the brick framework. We can now view the careful copy made of the graffiti. I have experimented writing a message that might just fit on about nine inches of brickwork. Instinctively, the opening letters are cramped until it is clear there will be enough space to complete the thoughts, then the writing opens up. In the copy the writing is evenly spread out – with no sign of spatial limitations. So, as far as I am concerned, the reports of PC Long, Chief Inspector Swanson, DC Daniel Halse, Thomas Arnold and the City surveyor, along with the spacing, set the graffiti inside the hallway. I am only being pedantic about the positioning as, if I am correct, it would mean that Warren was either mistaken or lying. My contention is that, in the continuing purposes of an official cover-up, Warren was lying. His explanation for the destruction of the graffiti, like that of Arnold, does not hold water; the combined case of these two top-ranking policemen adds up to this:

> members of the general public who happened to be out and about as dawn was breaking might see the words, '...are the men that will not be blamed for nothing,' chalked on a wall, written, as far as they were concerned, by Joe Soap. This message would have led to a violent insurrection, houses would have been wrecked and lives lost.

That certainly doesn't convince me. To continue – *what* was so confidential about a potentially vital Ripper clue that ensured it was kept secret for almost a century? The vague gist of the message was soon printed in all the newspapers, with some quarters printing 'Juwes' as 'Jews', which was more damaging. Why were questions asked in court about the actual wording of the message when a verbatim version was lying on police files? Why did the policeman who found the message not have it written correctly in his notebook? Until the discovery of the graffiti in the Private Letter Book of the Metropolitan Police by my late friend Stephen Knight, no one had any idea about the layout or the exact wording, which, given the world-wide publicity on the case, is strange in the extreme.

Some writers have indicated that the message was an ordinary piece of graffiti which could have been written anywhere in the East End. But it wasn't written anywhere – it was chalked directly above a piece of a victim's blood-stained apron; and if a mischief maker had been trying to stir up trouble, why not just write, 'The Jews Are to blame' or some such straightforward message? Why a convoluted, strangely laid-out sentence with double negatives – a message hard to understand, so defeating its supposed purpose? Furthermore, this is not just an ordinary, run-of-the mill piece of graffiti. We will find out why later in this text.

A flood of obscene letters now began to arrive at newspaper offices, police stations and the Central News Agency. Amongst these letters was one which instantly wiped away the killer's nickname of 'Leather Apron' and replaced it with one of the world's most famous soubriquets.

The letter, written in red ink, and dated 25 September 1888, stated:

Dear Boss,

I keep on hearing the police have caught me but they wont fix me just yet. I have laughed when they look so clever and talk about being on the right track. That joke about Leather Apron gave me real fits. I am down on whores and I shant quit ripping them till I do get buckled. Grand work the last one was.

I gave the lady no time to squeal. How can they catch me now. I love my work and want to start again. You will soon hear of me with my funny little games. I saved some of the proper red stuff in a ginger beer bottle over the last job to write with, but it went thick like glue, and I cant use it. Red ink is fit enough I hope ha. ha. The next job I do I shall clip the ladys ears off and send to the police officers just for jolly wouldnt you. Keep this letter back till I do a bit more work, then give it out straight. My knife's so nice and sharp I want to get to work right away if I get a chance. Good luck.

Yours truly,

Jack the Ripper

A postscript read: 'Don't mind me giving my trade name.' Then at right angles underneath the main text was written: 'wasnt good enough to post this before I got all the red ink off my hands curse it. No luck yet. They say I'm a doctor now ha ha.'

After the double murder a postcard, postmarked 1 October, was received with the same 'trade name':

I was not codding dear old boss when I gave you the tip, you'll hear about saucy Jackys work tomorrow double event this time number one squealed a bit couldnt finish straight off. had not time to get ears for police thanks for keeping last letter back till I got to work again,

Jack the Ripper

A flood of imitative material (around 1,000 letters weekly), much of it from cranks, poured into police stations and newspaper offices. These missives, combined with the general ambience of butchery and blood which surrounded the unsolved crimes and the publicity of the Jack the Ripper letters, sent a tidal wave of terror across the whole of London. Music halls emptied overnight, locksmiths sold out of their wares, and one old lady died of terror, the evening paper which recorded Jack's latest deeds clutched in her hands.

One of the few interesting letters from the flood of material sent to the newspapers was recorded by J. Hall Richardson in his book *From The City To Fleet Street*.

Liverpool, 29th inst. Beware, I shall be at work on 1st and 2nd Inst. in Minories at twelve midnight, and I give the authorities a good chance but there is never a policeman near when I am at work.

Yours

Jack the Ripper

This letter was posted in Liverpool and is now unfortunately missing. Many writers, myself included, have deemed that 29th inst refers to 29 September 1888. However, the 'Dear Boss' letter, with the newly-coined soubriquet 'Jack the Ripper' was not published in the papers until 1 October 1888, so how did the writer of the 'Minories' letter know about the name on 29 September? And, as the authors of the *A to Z* so rightly ask, what did the writer mean by stating in a letter probably dated 29 September that he would be at work on 1st and 2nd inst. [meaning 'of the same month']. It does not make sense to send a letter stating that you will be committing an outrage four weeks after a given date has passed. Is there an explanation for this strange conundrum? I went to considerable lengths to trace any relatives of J. Hall Richardson to try and find the letters in question, but this proved impossible. Once again I must delay a full discussion of this puzzle until later in the text, when a number of relevant points will be gathered together and addressed.

As the weeks rolled by, the popular press continued to fan the fires of hysteria. *The East London Advertiser* opined:

> It is so impossible to account, on any ordinary hypothesis, for these revolting acts of blood that the mind turns as it were instinctively to some theory of occult force, and the myths of the Dark Ages arise before the imagination.

In early September, a Vigilance Committee had been formed, under the presidency of a George Lusk. He was a prominent local business-man. Lusk and other members of his committee were no doubt concerned by the murders, but they must also have been concerned about the dramatic drop in trade brought about by Jack's activities.

On 16 October 1888 Mr Lusk received through the post a small card-board box wrapped in brown paper. The box contained part of a kidney initially assumed to be that of an animal, but on examination the organ was discovered to be part of a human body. Dr Frederick Brown, the doctor who had carried out the autopsy on Catharine Eddowes, had declared that her remaining kidney had shown signs of Bright's Disease. (To repeat: 'Pale, bloodless, with a slight congestion at the base of the pyramid.') The kidney, which had been sent through the post, did indeed show signs of Bright's Disease. And the organ Lusk received was attached to one inch of renal tissue, which would have left two inches of gut remaining in Catharine's body; two inches of renal tissue did remain in Catharine's body. There is a strong assembly of informed opinion who believe that the kidney was indeed from Catharine – a genuine gift from Jack the Ripper, along with a letter from the murderer. This letter read:

> From hell. Mr Lusk.
>
> Sor,
>
> I send you half the kidne I took from one woman prasarved it for you tother piece I fried and ate it was very nise I may send you the bloody knif that took it out if you only wate a while longer
>
> signed
>
> Catch me when
>
> you can
>
> Mishter Lusk.

I suggest that this was another hideous prank, but it is little wonder that, with this kind of material along with the terrible crimes, London's panic continued to grow. Suggestions on how to catch the murderer began to pour into Scotland Yard. One bright spark opined that the next woman approached by Jack should surreptitiously stick a piece of paper on the fiend's back, thus marking him out for the police. No brave lady volunteered to stroll along the dark alleys, sticky paper in her hands, waiting to be approached.

Further discrepancies arose. When Major Henry Smith was told about the Goulston Street graffiti he rushed to the area, although Goulston Street was outside the City boundaries, and therefore within the jurisdiction of his rival, the Metropolitan Commissioner, Sir Charles Warren.

The writing had been erased by the time Smith arrived on the scene. The Major, undaunted, went sleuthing around the East End. In a public sink in Dorset Street he found blood-tinged water still running down the drain. The Major always believed that he was within minutes of catching Jack the Ripper, ignoring the fact that the bloody piece of apron had been dropped at least an hour earlier. Jack was hardly likely to have been wandering around the area hands dripping with blood, dodging the increasing police activity. But who had been washing blood from their hands in a public sink in the early hours of the morning?

Despite a massive police presence in the East End and the arrest and questioning of hundreds of men, the Ripper remained at large. The public waited in abject terror, and on the night 9 November 1888 Jack murdered again. It was to be his most savage and revolting attack.

Chapter 7

Mary Kelly

Commercial Street in 1888 was exactly what its name implies, a crowded, busy street choked with market stalls, shops, pavement vendors and horse-drawn traffic. The Britannia public house, whose main frontage was on Commercial Street, curved into Dorset Street, in all a notoriously dangerous area, its dozens of cheap lodging houses frequented by a wide variety of social mixes, including violent criminals. Any policeman foolish enough to follow a suspect into Dorset Street was likely to be set upon and his life might be in danger.

There was an arched passageway between 26 and 27 Dorset Street which led to Miller's Court, a cul-de-sac of six houses, three on either side. A rear room at 26 Dorset Street had been partitioned off and an entrance (designated number 13, the unlucky number) had been constructed in Miller's Court, the door to this separation being immediately behind the arched passageway. Number 13 Miller's Court was rented by Mary Kelly, a young, attractive, blue-eyed prostitute. The reported colour of her hair has varied, but a woman who knew her described Mary as 'fair as a lily,' which would point towards a blonde. Mary, who paid her rent weekly and thus had no need to search out a doss-house each night, was born in Ireland into a large family. The Kellys were apparently affluent and middle-class. They moved to Wales when Mary was a youngster and she is said to have spoken fluent Welsh.

In a Press Association report a Mrs Carthy, a former landlady of Mary's, described her as academically bright and artistically talented, from a family of good standing. Joe Barnett, Mary's final lover, confirmed that account. Maybe this is all true – very few solid facts are available about Mary's early life, but she certainly appears to have had the positive forces of confidence and enterprise which a comfortable upbringing tends to imbue.

When Kelly was sixteen she married a man named Davies – we do not know his first name; he was killed in a mine explosion several years later. After this tragedy his young widow moved to Cardiff, where she began to work as a prostitute. Such an early fall from grace would point towards a typical, youthful rebellion against family life; an extravagant use, and need of money; or simply a powerful sexual drive that required constant fulfilment. Such an early marriage might point towards the latter.

50

In 1884 Mary moved from Cardiff to London, a move which is easy to understand. London, with its opportunities, its reputation of glamour and streets paved with gold, would have been an understandable magnet for an attractive, ambitious girl with loose morals. It is, therefore, a major mystery as to how a moderately well-bred young lady ended up living and working in the East End of London. Whitechapel (and its surrounding districts) was an area where, in the main, drab, sad, middle-aged women tended to ply their trade. But an attractive and fully-fledged prostitute – and Mary had been that for some years – could have made a substantial living and lead a more comfortable lifestyle in the salubrious surroundings of the West End of London, an area in which Mary is said initially to have worked. According to Joe Barnett, her last lover, once in London Mary was introduced to a rich man who took her on trips to France. This life of luxury had reputedly been arranged by a West End madame. So why, after only approximately eighteen months of high living, did an engaging young woman end up amongst the unfortunate dregs of society? Did alcohol addiction aid Mary's rapid descent from West to East? She certainly had problems in this area. Or was it dishonesty that forced her to flee from the salubrious West End to find anonymous sanctuary in a slum area? We can only surmise.

After reaching the nadir of the East End Mary lived with several men. First there was an unnamed builder, then a man known only as Morganstone (possibly Morgan Stone), and then a tradesman, Joseph Fleming. In 1887 Kelly met Joe Barnett and there was obviously an instant mutual attraction since, within days of one more meeting, they had formed an alliance and started living together, a state of affairs that continued for eighteen months. They initially lodged together at various addresses including Brick Lane, one of the toughest parts of East London, before moving to the now infamous, ill-fated lodgings in Miller's Court, the address at which the fifth Ripper murder was destined to take place.

Barnett, who was aged around thirty years old, was, so far as one can glean, a decent, hard working fellow, but that has not stopped him from becoming a 'Ripper' suspect on the grounds that, by murdering prostitutes and causing a panic, he would keep his lover off the streets. If this had been Barnett's strategy it clearly failed. Mary was reported as being on the streets up to a few hours before the Ripper visited her room. And had the violent murders continued they would have been more likely to drive Mary back into a bordello, which, for obvious reasons, was safer.

Alternatively, any continuing violence might have made her leave London. It was reported in the newspapers that Mary spoke of leaving the capital city several times during the Ripper murders. Part of the case against Barnett is that he was jealous of Mary's associations with other men. A Miller's Court neighbour, Julia Venturney, said that Barnett did not care for Kelly being on the streets. This has been turned into something sinister by certain theorists, but might not his objections have been due to concern for his lover's safety once the Ripper murders had started? He had met Mary while she was soliciting so he knew what she was up to; and he was the person who told the inquest about his girl-friend's string of former lovers. Barnett alleged that one of these men continued to call on Mary, so he does not appear to have been remotely jealous, which should remove the basis of Barnett's indictment. And, of course, had Barnett been the murderer there would have been no cover-up by the authorities. (Again – more of that later.)

The couple lived together in apparent harmony, although at Mary's inquest Barnett admitted that they did have rows which 'were soon over'. The couple had had a violent argument in which a window pane got broken; from Mary's perceived character it is not unreasonable to suspect that it was her quick temper combined with alcohol that led to that violent incident.

Joe was variously a dockside labourer and a market porter but he became unemployed in the mid-1880s, which was not uncommon for Victorian workers without the protection of strong unions or the enforcement of employment laws. This must have been a difficult time for the unemployed Barnett. Life with Mary had grown tempestuous, and at some point, following the usual pattern of the Ripper victims, the relationship broke up. Two theories account for this parting. One story asserts that Mary, due to the loss of Barnett's wages, had returned to soliciting, and that the return to her old ways caused the rift. There is, however, no firm evidence that Mary ever broke away from her chosen profession in the first place. A more interesting view of Joe's departure asserts that he left Mary because she insisted on having another prosti-tute live with them. This act led to charges against Mary of lesbianism, a not uncommon leaning in street women. Joe refused to share the single bed with a second female, and so the couple split up. This episode I find distinctly strange. There is no evidence of strong emotional ties between Mary and women until a few weeks before the end of the Ripper mur-ders. After eighteen months of close association with her lover, Mary must have known that Barnett would not tolerate other women living with them. So quite clearly she knew that her actions would drive him away. Mary appears to have been trying to get Joe to leave their lodg-ings. Why? Another question that will need answering.

On the Wednesday, two days before her death, Mary bought a candle from her landlord's shop in Dorset Street. This was found half burnt in her room after the murder. Later, on that same day, she was sighted by Thomas Bowyer (an employee of her landlord) in the company of a man in his late twenties; this man had a 'dark moustache and very peculiar eyes' and 'was very smartly dressed' said Mr Bowyer. The man was never identified.

Paul Begg, a previously mentioned Ripper expert, remarked to me, with reference to this sighting: 'There is no reason why Mary should not have consorted with upper-class men, but to find one of them visiting her in such an area as Miller's Court is very strange indeed.' Precisely. Well dressed people visited the East End but they would have kept to certain areas. Few would have been foolish enough to visit such a violent area as Dorset Street, even during daylight hours, so who was this man? And was he conducting only a sexual arrangement with Mary?

On Friday, the eve of Kelly's alleged death, Joe Barnett visited Miller's Court where he found Mary entertaining a female whom he did not know. Later investigations proved the woman to have been Lizzie Albrook, and, as she was apparently unknown to Barnett, only a recent neighbour of Mary's. Shortly after 8.00 p.m. Barnett left Kelly and returned to his new lodgings, where he played cards until after midnight before going to bed.

One testimony of Mary's movements on the night of her murder is important, but full of inconsistencies: George Hutchinson, a typical, unemployed, impecunious East Ender who claimed to know Mary well, stated that he met her in Commercial Street at 2.00 a.m. on the night of her death. She asked to borrow sixpence but he did not have any money. Mary moved off towards Thrawl Street which Hutchinson had just passed on his way to lodgings in Commercial Street. George presumably turned around and watched Mary, although why, after a short conversation with a prostitute in the early hours, he should turn and watch the lady walk away, when the night was cold and wet and he was hurrying home, is puzzling. But there are many puzzles in Mr Hutchinson's testimony. As Mary reached Thrawl Street a man coming in the opposite direction stopped and spoke to her. After a short conversation the couple moved towards him then passed by, and Hutchinson 'stooped down' in order to see the man closely. He described Mary's companion in minute detail:

...age about 34 or 35, height 5 foot 6 inches, complexion pale. Dark eyes and dark lashes. Slight moustache curled up each end and hair dark. Very surly looking. Dress, long dark coat, collar and cuffs trimmed with astrakhan and a dark jacket under, light waistcoat, dark trousers, dark felt hat turned down in the middle, button boots and gaiters with white buttons, wore a very thick gold chain, white linen collar, black tie with horseshoe pin, respectable appearance, walked very sharp, Jewish appearance. Can be identified.

For a one-second glance under the brim of a hat, in a badly lit street, on a rainy night, this is a miraculously detailed description. How, in such poor conditions, with the man's head bent, could Hutchinson notice 'dark lashes'?

The couple went into Dorset Street and Hutchinson, in the early hours of the morning, presumably tired, in cold, wet weather, turned away from his own lodgings and followed the couple. This seems further irrational behaviour. If he had hoped for Mary's favours for himself he would, presumably, have fallen into step and moved off with her after their earlier conversation. But it was not until she had been taken up by another man that he turned and followed her.

Hutchinson then watched the couple standing outside Miller's Court for about three minutes, after which they both went into the Court. Hutchinson subsequently stood in bad weather for three quarters of an hour watching for the man's reappearance. Around 3.00 a.m., his patience apparently exhausted, the spy gave up and returned home. If he had been concerned about Mary taking up with a stranger in the wake of the Ripper murders, Hutchinson now took no steps towards her safety. No police were called but then why should they be? There was nothing suspicious about a prostitute entertaining a client all night, so Hutchinson's watch was purposeless if concern for Kelly was to be a motive.

Hutchinson's statement was not made to the police until 6.00 p.m. on 12 November. This was the most perverse timing, as Mary's inquest was held on that exact date and the proceedings had been concluded by 6.00 p.m. This meant that Hutchinson's evidence could not be closely questioned or examined further in court. Why did he (seemingly deliberately) wait until the inquest was over before coming forward? Could the extraordinary story be a fabrication which Hutchinson was encouraged to relate? And if so, who encouraged him? Why should anyone wish to spread such lies?

∽

Apart from Hutchinson, several other people provided information about the period between 2.30 and 4.00 a.m., the hour in which Mary was thought to have been murdered, although there is no certainty about this estimate.

Mary Ann Cox, a resident of Miller's Court, returned home around midnight and passed Mary Kelly (who was bareheaded and drunk) in the company of a shabbily-dressed man of about thirty-five. As she passed the couple Mrs Cox heard Kelly say, 'I am going to sing.' (Why?) She then began to do so. Mrs Cox, a prostitute, quickly returned to soliciting and Kelly was still singing as Cox left the court. After half an hour, another neighbour, Catherine Picket, became irritated by the noise, but her husband prevented her from going to protest. Kelly was still singing when Mrs Cox once more returned home, around 1.00 a.m. Further conflicting evidence in this bizarre case then arose. Mrs Cox tried her luck on the streets once more and finally returned home at 3.00 a.m., later declaring that there was now no noise or sound from Mary's room: the remainder of the night was quiet. However, Mrs Elizabeth Prater, who lodged in a room directly above Kelly's, heard a cry of, 'Oh murder' around 4.00 a.m. This cry was confirmed by another neighbour, Sarah Lewis, but as such cries were commonplace both women ignored the call. They were wrong to do so: on this occasion, a murder was indeed being committed.

John McCarthy, from whose shop Mary had bought a candle two days before her death, was also her landlord. And Mary, amazingly, given the strict, totally inflexible 'no credit' policy of the East End, had been allowed to run up arrears of thirty-five shillings on the rent of Miller's Court; well over £120 in today's money, when less-favoured tenants had been turned out of doss-houses in the middle of the night because they could not produce a few pence. Indeed, Kelly and Barnett had been turned out of other lodgings because they could not pay the rent.

An immediate surmise of payment by sexual favours from Mary to her landlord might solve the problem, but it was Mrs McCarthy who usually dealt with the rents – presumably while her husband ran the shop: and Mrs McCarthy was a stickler for prompt payment, which makes Mary's arrears all the more puzzling. Mid-morning on 9 November, McCarthy sent his employee, Thomas Bowyer, around to Miller's Court to ask Kelly for her rent. Just where the man thought Mary might have been able to obtain such a large sum of money as thirty-five shillings overnight (after all, he had seen her two days previously at the most) is not known. And why he should choose the very morning of Mary's death to try and collect his rent which was three months overdue is a further mystery.

Bowyer went to 13 Miller's Court but his knock went unanswered. After trying without success to peer through the keyhole, and after finding the door locked, he reached through the broken window pane, pulled back a flimsy curtain, and peered into the room. A mass of raw flesh lay on the bed surrounded by pools of blood on the floor. The corpse's stomach had been gutted, her intestines ripped out: her liver, breasts and various cuts of flesh lay near to, or under the body. Bowyer, terrified, ran back and returned with Mr McCarthy, whose comments were recorded in *The Times*:

The sight we saw ... looked more like the work of a devil than a man. I had heard a great deal about the Whitechapel murders, but I do declare to God I never expected to see such a sight as this. The whole scene is more than I can describe.

After the discovery of the body chaotic scenes occurred around Miller's Court and it is difficult to sort out fact from fiction and truth from rumour. Inspector Walter Beck was the first officer to be summoned to the scene, as he was the senior officer on duty at the Commerical Road Station. Several other policemen claimed that they were the first to be called. Reporters and crowds began to gather around Miller's Court, so Beck cordoned off the area and refused to answer any questions or to allow anyone to enter the murder site. This included the police surgeon, Dr Bagster Phillips, who once again was called to a Ripper murder. He had to peer at the cadaver through the broken window before he declared all life was extinct, a statement which, as the corpse was literally hacked to pieces, any man, doctor or not, would have been able to make. Then, according to the reliable Paul Begg, Dr Phillips advised that no one should be allowed to enter the murder site until bloodhounds had been called.

The fact that a medical man was allowed to pontificate on police matters would indicate considerable indecisiveness on the part of Inspector Beck. Policemen were posted outside the door of the murder room where they waited until 1.30 p.m. while a decision on calling in the dogs was sought from Sir Charles Warren. Even official photographers had to poke their cameras through the broken window and do their best under these unsatisfactory working conditions. Finally, having wasted the entire morning, with any possible clues that the murderer might have left growing colder by the minute, it was announced, with the most extraordinary timing, that Sir Charles Warren had resigned: as for the question of the bloodhounds – no dogs were available even if they had been needed, and if they had been available, and had been needed, they would not have been useful. No dog could have detected a single particular scent from the blood-drenched murder site. Farce had taken over the proceedings.

The authorities finally ordered McCarthy to break down the door of his premises. Why this action was thought necessary must be added to the lengthening list of mysteries in this case. The key to the door had been missing for some time and Joe and Mary, to gain access, used to reach through the broken window pane and pull back a spring lock. Why were the police not able to follow the same routine? Smashing down the door might well have destroyed valuable clues. It has been claimed that the murderer, during his work on Kelly's body, had placed a heavy object behind the door, but I can find no trace of this in any official report of the affair. If the door was blocked, it would mean that Jack, after his butchery, must have opened and crawled through the broken window. Why didn't he just remove the heavy object?

As the above details show, the initial investigation into Mary Kelly's murder involved a series of appalling errors on the part of the police. Dr Phillips presumably returned home after his brief adjudication, as a full on-site report on Kelly's body was produced by Dr Thomas Bond, once the authorities had given their belated permission for entry to the murder site. Dr Bond's report was highly detailed. His strange use of capital letters is reproduced in the extract below: was this a sign of mental strain showing in his handwriting? Dr Bond later committed suicide. His report from Miller's Court and his post-mortem examination, stated:

The body was lying naked in the middle of the bed, the shoulders flat, but the axis of the body inclined to the left side of the bed. The head was turned on the left cheek. The left arm was close to the body with the forearm flexed at right angles and lying across the abdomen. The right arm was slightly abducted from the body and rested on the mattress, the elbow bent and the forearm supine with the fingers clenched. The legs were wide apart, the left thigh at right angles to the trunk and the right forming an obtuse angle with the pubes.

The whole of the surface of the abdomen and thighs was removed and the abdominal cavity emptied of its viscera. The breasts were cut off, the arms mutilated by several jagged wounds, and the face hacked beyond recognition of the features. The tissues of the neck were severed all round down to the bone.

The viscera were found in various parts viz: the uterus and Kidneys with one breast under the head, the other breast by the Rt. foot, the Liver between the feet, the intestines by the right side and the spleen by the left side of the body. The flaps removed from the abdomen and thighs were on a table.

The bed clothing at the right corner was saturated with blood, and on the floor beneath was a pool of blood covering about two feet square. The wall by the right side of the bed and in a line with the neck was marked by blood which had struck it in a number of separate splashes. Post-mortem examination:

The face was gashed in all directions the nose, cheeks, eyebrows and ears being partly removed. The lips were blanched and cut by several incisions running obliquely down to the chin. There were also numerous cuts extending irregularly across all the features.

The neck was cut through the skin and other tissues right down to the vertebrae the 5th and 6th being deeply notched. The skin cuts in the front of the neck showed distinct ecchymosis. The air passage was cut at the lower part of the larynx through the cricoid cartilage.

Both breasts were removed by more or less circular incisions, the muscles down to the ribs being attached to the breasts. The intercostal between the 4th 5th and 6th ribs were cut through, and the contents of the thorax visible through the openings.

The skin and tissues of the abdomen from the costal arch to the pubes were removed in three large flaps. The right thigh was denuded in front to the bone, the flap of skin, including the external organs of generation and part of the right buttock. The left thigh was stripped of skin, fascia and muscles as far as the knee.

The left calf showed a long gash through skin and tissues to the deep muscles and reaching from the knee to 5 ins above the ankle.

Both arms and forearms had extensive and jagged wounds. The right thumb showed a small superficial incision about 1 ins long, with extravasation of blood in the skin and there were several abrasions on the back of the hand moreover, showing the same condition.

On opening the thorax it was found that the right lung was minimally adherent by old firm adhesions. The lower part of the lung was broken and torn away.

The left lung was intact: it was adherent at the apex and there were a few adhesions over the side. In the substances of the lung were several nodules of consolidation.

The Pericardium was open below and the Heart absent. In the abdominal cavity was some partly digested food of fish and potatoes, and similar food was found in the remains of the stomach attached to the intestines.

The inflicting of such mutilations must have taken some considerable time but again, no one heard or saw anything suspicious. Once more the Ripper appeared to have melted into thin air. In the grate there were signs that a fierce fire had been blazing, hot enough to melt the spout-solder of a kettle. Burnt clothing, including the brim of a woman's bonnet, was found in the grate. A passer-by would have only had to see the reflection of the flames on the curtain and reach through the broken window to witness the Ripper at work. No one did so. The murderer's extraordinary run of luck had continued.

As would be expected, the dramatic events in Miller's Court produced a flood of anecdotal evidence about Kelly. People who knew her rushed to the press with quotes. Tom Cullen relates in his book *Autumn of Terror* that Kelly's nickname was 'Black Mary', and if this did not perversely allude to her conspicuously fair colouring then it must have referred to her character. John McCarthy, her landlord, said that she was very noisy when she had taken drink but otherwise she was a quiet woman. This statement was confirmed by Elizabeth Phoenix who knew Mary from a past lodging house. She declared that Kelly was quarrelsome and abusive when drunk but very pleasant when sober. Mary's quick temper can be further confirmed by reiterating the violent argument with Joe Barnett – violent enough to break a window in their lodgings.

Tom Cullen, while writing his aforementioned *Autumn of Terror*, talked to a retired market porter, Dennis Barrett, who claimed that as a young man he had known Mary Kelly. Mr Barrett's description of the lady would without doubt have earned her the nickname Black Mary. He stated that if any woman tried to intrude on Kelly's territory then the woman would be violently attacked and stood the risk of having her hair pulled out in handfuls. Mr Cullen was writing some forty years ago and he was enterprising enough to track down people who had been alive at the time of the Ripper murders. This research has provided some fascinating information. According to Mr Cullen:

> Black Mary was no stranger to the Britannia. Many was the time she had rushed into this pub after rolling some drunken sailor, to swop shawls with one of the whores there. Thus disguised, she would take to the streets again, knowing that the police would be looking for her under a different disguise.

Exactly as I had surmised. The writer of *Tornado Down*, William Pearson, assures me that it was common practise for prostitutes to change both clothing and names to outwit the police. Presumably Mary, if she were not just dodging the police but dodging danger, would have been devious enough to make this changeover of clothing appear to be a favour. ('Try on my shawl, it really goes with that dress,' or some such excuse.) She would not have disclosed the real reason for her generosity.

At Kelly's inquest, Joe Barnett revealed that Mary had once lived and worked in the notorious Ratcliffe Highway area near to the East End Docks. Ratcliffe had once been renowned for its collection of shops which housed wild beasts; sailors would visit the place to barter their pets and animals which they had brought from faraway places. It was in the Ratcliffe area that sailors were most likely to be lured into a dark place and robbed, so Mary, while she was living around there, might well have joined in the local sport by violently accosting her clients, as Mr Cullen has alleged. Reading between the lines of various reports on the lady, Mary appears to have been somewhat of a Jekyll-and-Hyde character.

The usual pattern of searching, arresting, questioning and releasing followed by more of the same was carried out by the police after Kelly's supposed murder. At one point Joe Barnett was arrested. He was questioned closely and his clothing was carefully examined but Barnett had an alibi. He had been with company, playing cards all evening at his new lodgings. The police checked this out and were eventually convinced that Barnett was not guilty of his lover's murder.

It quickly became clear that once again Jack had evaded capture.

Mortuary photograph of Catharine Eddowes

Mary Kelly as found in Miller's Court

Chapter 8

Cover-Up?

We must now pose the question, 'Was Jack the Ripper a man from the upper classes of Victorian society?' There is a long-standing belief, which has reached the status of a minor myth, that certain highly placed members of the Victorian Police Force had undisclosed information regarding the Ripper killings and the murderer's identity. Is it conceivable that members of Scotland Yard's hierarchy might have joined forces to organise a cover-up, and if so, why?

The obvious answer to that question is that the Victorian Establishment, for reasons of its own, wished to protect a member of the upper classes. Obviously this would have to be a man of great importance. I believe this general assumption to be correct, and I am not alone in such a belief; it is a suspicion that stretches back to the beginning of the affair. In November 1888 *The Star* wrote :

> We have heard the wildest stories ... it is believed by people who pass among their neighbours as sensible folk that the Government do not want the murderer to be convicted, that they are interested in concealing his identity ...

Paul Begg, in his splendid book *Jack the Ripper. The Uncensored Facts* wrote: 'Beyond question, there was something very strange going on after the murders of Elizabeth Stride and Catharine Eddowes.' On 1 October *The Evening News* reported: 'The police are extraordinarily reticent with reference to the Mitre Square tragedy.' *The Yorkshire Post* on the same date reported: 'The police apparently have strict orders to close all channels of information to the press.' Even *The New York Times* on 1 October was moved to complain of the police that, 'they devote their entire energies to preventing the press from getting at the facts. They deny reporters a sight of the scene or bodies, and give them no information whatever.' After this barrage of criticism there was a complete reversal of this stance by the police. *The Manchester Guardian* reported on 2 October:

> The barrier of reticence which has been set up on all occasions when the representatives of the newspaper press have been brought into contact with the police authorities for the purpose of obtaining information for the use of the public has been suddenly withdrawn, and instead of the customary stereotyped negatives and disclaimers

of the officials, there has ensued a marked disposition to afford all necessary facilities for the publication of details and increased courtesy towards the members of the press concerned.

I will repeat, for emphasis, the extraordinary words of *The Star*: '. . . the Government do not want the murderer to be convicted – they are interested in concealing his identity'. And I will repeat Mr Begg's words: 'Beyond question there was something very strange going on after the murders of Elizabeth Stride and Catharine Eddowes.' My only query about this statement would be to question whether a cover-up started earlier than the third and fourth murder?

My late friend Stephen Knight also firmly believed in a cover-up. In his celebrated book *Jack the Ripper: The Final Solution*, published in 1976, Knight cites the authorities' conduct as being suspicious as early as the Chapman inquest. There is no doubt that the conduct of the police surgeon Dr Bagster Philips, when called to give evidence, was evasive. He clearly did not wish to reveal pertinent facts about Chapman's injuries. The coroner Wynne Baxter was moved to say:

> Dr Phillips, whatever may be your opinion and objections, it appears to me necessary that all the evidence that you ascertained from the post-mortem examination should be on the records of the court for various reasons which I need not enumerate. However painful it may be, it is necessary in the interests of justice.

Yet by the time of the third Ripper victim's inquest (Liz Stride) on 3 October, Baxter, who was again presiding, appears to have been much more lax. As we have seen, on 30 November 1888 Chief Inspector Swanson took evidence from the immigrant, Israel Schwartz. Let us repeat this man's evidence, as it is so important. Schwartz claimed that at 12.45 a.m. he had turned into Berner Street from the Commercial Road, and, Swanson recorded:

> . . . having got as far as the gateway where the murder was committed, he saw a man stop and speak to a woman who was standing in the gateway. The man tried to pull the woman into the street, but he turned her round and threw her down on the footway and the woman screamed three times, but not very loudly. On crossing to the opposite side of the street, he saw a second man lighting his pipe. The man who threw the woman down called out, apparently to the man on the opposite side of the road, 'Lipski', and then Schwartz walked away, but finding that he was followed by the second man, he ran so far as the railway arch, but the man did not follow so far . . .

This statement was in the hands of the police during the extended inquest on Liz Stride but at no time was Schwartz called to give evidence, although he was the only person in the land who saw the Ripper about to begin work: he was the only person who could possibly identify the infamous murderer, a murderer who was being desperately hunted by every policeman in London. This makes the man's evidence absolutely vital, yet, astoundingly, *Schwartz was not called to give evidence, nor was his statement produced in court.* His vital and dramatic account, describing two men, remained, along with other vital documents, on closed Home Office files. There could be no clearer sign of a cover-up by the authorities. And this limiting of justice occurred at an inquest presided over by Wynne Baxter. It is difficult to believe that Mr Baxter was not at least informed about Israel Schwartz, so why did this normally inquisitive man, a stickler for correct procedures, not insist that such an important witness be summoned to appear?

Matthew Packer, who claimed to have sold grapes to a man in the company of Stride some time before her murder, was not called upon to give evidence in court either, yet the police considered him important enough to be interviewed personally by Sir Charles Warren. Mrs Mortimer's evidence, even if evaluated negatively (that she did not see anything out of the ordinary), might have been useful, but she too was not called upon to give evidence. We will never know whether or not Baxter was involved in a plot, but given the above facts, there can surely be no doubt that a cover-up of some sort, by unknown persons, for unknown reasons, was in place during the Ripper murder investigations. Other writers have voiced that concern. Martin Howells and Keith Skinner in their excellent book *The Ripper Legacy* published in 1987, wrote:

> Edwin Thomas Woodhall, writing in the mid-1930s, admits when talking of his own particular search for Jack the Ripper that his main difficulty had been the minimal assistance from those concerned with the crimes.

Woodhall was not writing without considerable experience. He was, at various times, a member of the CID, the Special Branch and the Secret Service. These appointments should have given him unique access to restricted information. Stephen Knight further cites the Coroner's conduct during the inquest into Mary Kelly's death as evidence of something highly suspicious. It certainly was. Indeed, Roderick MacDonald's conduct at this fifth inquiry was so peculiar several newspapers of the day made their own comments. Immediately after the abrupt termination of proceedings, the *Daily Telegraph* wrote:

> Much surprise is expressed that the inquest should have been closed before an opportunity was given to the relatives of the deceased to identify the body. As they are believed to reside in Ireland, there was some delay to be expected in finding them. It is

in the power of the Attorney-General to apply to the High Court of Justice to hold a new inquest, if he is satisfied that there has been rejection of evidence, irregularity of proceedings, or insufficiency of inquiry . . .

The inquest into Kelly's death is so essential in piecing together the truth about the Ripper murders that we need to examine it in great detail. This controversial affair was conducted by Coroner Roderick MacDonald, a distinguished former police surgeon. As such, he had given evidence at many proceedings similar to the Kelly inquest and must therefore have known the court procedure better than most other members of the judiciary. Yet the Coroner did not enquire whether any parts of the body were missing, there was no attempt to discover the extent of the body's injuries, and no attempt to discover any details of the weapon that was used to kill Mary.

King Edward I, who reigned from 1272 to 1307, was a renowned law-maker, although he did not care to be personally held in check by his kingdom's legal system. It was Edward who first established the office of Justice of the Peace and, as Tom Cullen rightly points out, it was during Edward's reign that laws were enacted which made it mandatory to note, in cases of death, all injuries to the body, the depth and extent of all wounds and the weapon which caused the injuries. MacDonald failed in all these requirements, and by neglecting to uncover such basic and important details he broke the law of the land. Mary Kelly's inquest opened with the now famous argument between MacDonald and an unnamed, independently-minded juror who voiced a strong opinion:

JUROR. I do not see why we should have the inquest thrown on our shoulders, when the murder did not happen in our district, but in Whitechapel.

HAMMOND (Coroner's officer). It did not happen in Whitechapel.

MACDONALD. Do you think that we do not know what we are doing here? The jury are summoned in the ordinary way, and they have no business to object. If they persist in their objection I shall know how to deal with them. Does any Juror persist in objecting?

JUROR. We are summoned for the Shoreditch District. This affair happened in Spitalfields.

CORONER. It happened within my district.

SECOND JUROR. This is not my district. I come from Whitechapel and Mr Baxter is my coroner.

MACDONALD. I am not going to discuss the subject with the jurymen at all. If any juryman says he distinctly objects, let him say so. I may tell the jurymen that jurisdiction lies where the body lies, not where it was found.

There is conflicting evidence over MacDonald's assertion that he had every right to preside over the inquest. The affair appears to have been an administrative nightmare, difficult to understand even today. Stephen Knight asserted that the authorities were wrong – he saw this contretemps as an attempt by the authorities to take the case away from that meticulous searcher after the truth Coroner Wynne Baxter, but, as we have already seen, Mr Baxter appears to have slackened his enquiries by the time of the third inquest. In *The Jack the Ripper A to Z*, Paul, Martin and Keith appear to have cleared up the puzzle in their usual efficient manner. The *A to Z* claims that the affair may have been an administrative anomaly. The juror was correct in thinking that the murder site in Spitalfields was normally under the jurisdiction of Whitechapel, but apparently this jurisdiction did not include coroners' inquests, which came under the jurisdiction of Northeastern Middlesex: this would mean that MacDonald was rightfully holding the inquest, unless the Shoreditch authorities had refused to pay the mortuary expenses for Mary Kelly, who died outside their jurisdiction. Such legalities are difficult to understand, even when read over several times, so these complex arguments would have been even more difficult for Victorian working men to understand. Why, therefore, did MacDonald not try to explain to the jurors, as simply as possible, the legal arguments, instead of snapping at them?

The affair obviously rattled the coroner, because once the spat was over he returned to the subject, castigating the newspapers for making such a fuss over the inquest's change of venue and adding that Kelly's body was, without doubt, within his jurisdiction, and there the matter would end. Quite a storm in a teacup. Whatever the legality of MacDonald's appointment, his language in court was arrogant. 'The jury are summoned in the ordinary way, and they *have no business to object*.' Why not? MacDonald then threatens: 'If they persist in their objection, I shall know how to deal with them.' How? 'I am not going to discuss the subject with the jurymen at all.' Why not?

If we continue to examine this strange and significant inquest in more detail other puzzling aspects emerge. Inspector Abberline led the jury to the mortuary where Mary's mutilated body lay. Apart from her slashed, unrecognisable face, she was covered by a dirty sheet which was not removed for the jury to see her wounds. That restricted viewing could only have proved that there was a faceless corpse lying in the mortuary and nothing else. The jury were next shown the murder site, which might have been of some importance in their deliberations, although due to the police bungling after the discovery of the body some clues may well have been destroyed. After this tour the jury returned to the town hall to hear evidence.

Joe Barnett, as we have seen, discussed his relationship with Mary. One particularly pertinent question was put to him. The Coroner asked whether there was anyone of whom Mary had been especially afraid? Barnett replied, 'Yes'. He had read her everything about the Ripper murders, although he added there was no particular individual whom Mary feared. Words that appear to be contradictory. If we think this statement through logically it testifies that Mary Kelly was terrified of meeting Jack, as were, presumably, all the other prostitutes in the area. Yet on the night of her death Kelly fearlessly walked the streets in the early hours, picking up men with impunity before taking them back to her lonely room. Why was she not afraid any more?

The inquest next heard an electrifying piece of evidence, which, in itself, should have heralded a lengthy, more probing investigation. A Mrs Caroline Maxwell, who lived in Dorset Street stated, under oath, that she had seen Kelly standing at the entrance to Miller's Court *at eight o'clock on the morning following Mary's supposed murder*. Medical evidence proved Kelly must have been dead for at least four hours prior to this supposed sighting.

CORONER. Did you speak to her?

MAXWELL. Yes. It was unusual to see her up at that hour. I spoke across the street. 'What, Mary, brings you up so early?' She said, 'Oh Carrie, I do feel so bad.'

CORONER. And yet you say you had only spoken to her twice previously? You knew her name and she knew yours?

MAXWELL. Oh yes, by being about in the lodging-house.

CORONER. What did she say?

MAXWELL. She said, 'I've had a glass of beer, and I've brought it up again.' I imagine she had been in the Britannia beer shop on the corner. I left her saying that I could pity her feelings.

CORONER. Then what did you do?

MAXWELL. I went to Bishopsgate to get my husband's breakfast.

CORONER. Did you see Kelly again?

MAXWELL. Yes. When I returned I saw her outside the Britannia public house talking to a man.

CORONER. This would be about what time?

MAXWELL. It was about a quarter to nine.

Mrs Maxwell maintained that she had been going to a shop in Bishopsgate which she did not use a great deal and that made her certain of the time and date of her conversation. The shop later confirmed Mrs Maxwell's visit. In November *The Times* reported that a tailor, Maurice Lewis, a resident of Dorset Street, had also claimed to have seen Kelly briefly leave her room around eight o'clock on the morning after her supposed death. Mr Lewis maintained that later on that same day, at around 10 o'clock in the morning, he saw Kelly drinking in a local public house. *The Times* also reported that a young unnamed lady claimed to the police that she had seen Mary Kelly alive and well around 8.00 and 8.30 a.m. after her 'murder'. Although MacDonald probably did not know of the other two supposed sightings, he peremptorily dismissed Mrs Maxwell's assertions and, after a day's hearing, to everyone's astonishment, closed the case, commenting:

> There is other evidence which I do not propose to call, for if we at once make public every fact brought forward in connection with this terrible murder the ends of justice might be retarded.

As Tom Cullen asks in his book *Autumn of Terror*, 'What did he mean by this extraordinary statement? ... what were the police trying to hide?' What indeed? MacDonald, after brazenly breaking the law by not establishing the full facts concerning Kelly's injuries and the weapon used to inflict them, closed the inquest with indecent haste and with, to repeat the *Daily Telegraph*'s words, 'undoubted insufficiency of evidence'. As a final insult MacDonald failed (as *The Jack the Ripper A to Z* records) to complete or sign the certificate of findings to which the jurors' signatures had been appended. Did MacDonald at the last moment draw back from adding something so concrete and important as a signature to a document which recorded his bizarre and unlawful handling of the case? There is an inherent reluctance in human beings to sign a false declaration – men have faced death rather than do so in the past. Did MacDonald have that same instinctive misgiving? Certainly the omission of a signature on so valuable a document recording a case of such wide interest is highly unusual.

It was in this air of rushed incompetence and illegality that Mary Kelly's inquest was closed. The mutilated corpse was buried with considerable ceremony at St Patrick's Catholic Cemetery in Leytonstone, the funeral attended by many of the residents of Miller's Court; Joe Barnett was there, no doubt replete with memories.

One question that I find puzzling, a question that seems to have been largely ignored by other Ripper writers, concerns Mary Kelly's relatives.

In a November 1888 interview with a newspaper, Kelly's landlord, John McCarthy, revealed that Mary received correspondence from Ireland, letters which he understood were from Mary's mother. Joe Barnett told Inspector Abberline that Mary had a brother, Henry, who served in the Scots Guards; he added that Henry had visited Mary. Now Kelly and Barnett had only been living together for eighteen months, which means that Mary and at least one or two members of her family were in touch, possibly to the end of her life. Considering that Mary was part of a large clan and considering the worldwide publicity given to the case, it is strange in the extreme that not one of her relatives came forward, either after her death or after her funeral. No member of the family could be contacted despite a search. What had happened to the relatives? Why did they disappear without trace? Mary was reputed to have six or seven brothers and a sister. Surely one of them should have turned up to mourn their close relative?

The authorities complacently accepted the rushed, one-day inquest into Kelly's complicated last night on earth, although, as the *Daily Telegraph* had pointed out, it was possible to recall witnesses and hold a new inquest. Mrs Maxwell's extraordinary testimony, now backed by two independent witnesses (that Mary Kelly was seen alive after she had been declared dead) should by itself have merited a new hearing. And clearly George Hutchinson's evidence should have added further argument for a reopening of the case. If this had been done Hutchinson's disclosures could have been examined under oath and under cross-examination. He could have been asked why he had waited until the inquest was closed before revealing what could have been crucial information about the murderer and so on. There is a list of perplexing issues upon which Mr Hutchinson could, and should, have been asked to shed light. Let us examine some of them.

Everyone in the East End knew that a reward had been offered for the arrest of Jack. George alleged that he had taken a close look at a likely suspect, so why did the impecunious Mr Hutchinson not rush forward with his detailed evidence in the hope that this would result in the man's capture, thus winning himself a fortune of £1,200 (in today's money over £86,000) plus a pension for life? Hutchinson inexplicably kept the possibly vital information to himself until the inquest was closed, ignoring the fact that every day's delay made the arrest of his suspect more and more difficult and so his reward more and more unlikely. In his evidence George described a very rational conversation between himself and Kelly on the night of her death, when they met at 2.00 a.m. in Commercial Street. Mary is said to have asked for the loan of money. This statement might also be open to question. A witness, Mary Ann Cox, testified that she had seen Kelly in Dorset Street at about a quarter to midnight with a man:

> ...as they were going into her room, I said goodnight Mary Jane. She was very drunk and could scarcely answer me, but said goodnight. The man was carrying a quart of beer. I shortly afterwards heard her singing. I went out shortly after twelve and returned about one o'clock, and she was still singing in her room. I went out again shortly after one...

So we have testimony that Mary was 'very drunk' at midnight – barely capable of speech. She was with a man carrying a quart of beer which, presumably, they drank until at least 1.00 a.m. by which time Mary must have been paralytic. Yet an hour later she was reported by Hutchinson as apparently sober, holding a rational conversation, asking for money. If Kelly was merely pretending to be drunk, what was the purpose of such an act? Several other questions arise from this episode. If Mary had had a client less than an hour earlier, what had she done with the payment for services from this man, although the non-stop singing presumably ruled out sex? And if, as seems apparent, Mary had had her fill of alcohol for the night, why did she risk her life roaming the dangerous streets in the early hours of the morning? East End prostitutes generally solicited to find money for either drink or lodgings. Mary had no need of either on the night in question, so once again, why did she risk her life, given her particular fear of the serial killer, as outlined by Joe Barnett? *The Jack the Ripper A to Z* states:

> Conspiracy theorists have alleged that Hutchinson was deliberately excluded from Dr MacDonald's very abrupt inquest. It has been speculated that Hutchinson's very detailed description is too elaborate to be accurate.

I heartily concur with this solid conspiracy reasoning. The facts, on examination, do not add up. There is a strange air of 'staginess' around Mary's last supposed night on earth. It was as though a charade was being played out for public consumption. To summarise, was it reasonable for a prostitute to take a man home at midnight, then proceed to sing to him loudly for around an hour? A chap who had sex on his mind might sit and listen to a few stray bars, but it is difficult to imagine him sitting patiently through 60 minutes of solid serenade. Mary was drunk before midnight and continued to drink for at least an hour. Yet around sixty minutes later she was out and about, seemingly quite sober. Having had her fill of alcohol why did she go out on to the dangerous streets once more? What did she do with the money which she presumably received from her last client? Why did she ask George Hutchinson for sixpence in the middle of the night? The whole scenario is extremely odd.

Let us return to our original query – to what social class did Jack the Ripper belong? As we have seen, there is considerable evidence pointing towards a cover-up of the crimes by the authorities and clearly such an action would only be conducted for someone of very great importance; this would indicate that Jack did indeed belong to the highest class in the land. The question we must now ask is – who could that person be?

Chapter 9

Royal Involvement?

For several decades at least there has been a popular and well-discussed theory which maintains that a member of the British Royal Family was directly involved in the Ripper murders. I firmly believe that the Ripper affair did indeed have a royal link, although direct involvement is absurd. Perverting the course of justice was common practice in Victorian times. Certainly in the 1880s the law sometimes turned a blind eye, within limits, if prosecution would damage members of the aristocracy. Clear evidence of the Victorian police force perverting the course of justice can be found during the early 1890s. The police raided a homosexual club in Cleveland Street and discovered Queen Victoria's grandson, Prince Albert Victor (nicknamed Eddy), on the premises. Although several members of the aristocracy were arrested on this occasion there was no mention of the Prince's involvement in official reports.

Could the blatant suppression of facts and the equally blatant perversion of justice during the Ripper investigations mean that the highest in the land were again being protected? Certainly Eddy, in line to the throne, had that rank. Eddy has been mentioned as a Ripper suspect in the past and this allegation has been taken up by several distinguished writers. Yet Eddy does not fit a psychological portrait of the murderer. Jack's crimes displayed a towering confidence and, it must be said, courage and fearlessness in his total defiance of the London Police Force and the many watchful East End citizens. In their execution and positioning the murders undeniably showed great daring; by all accounts Eddy was a shy and diffident young man who suffered from an inherited partial deafness. It is highly unlikely that a man with hearing difficulties would crouch over dead bodies on a public pavement committing outrages with a knife, when his sole defence against detection would be the ability to perceive the sound of approaching danger. Even if Eddy had been accompanied by conspirators, shouted warnings would be essential, and the murders were famously carried out in total silence. Further, as a future heir to the throne, Eddy's activities and whereabouts would always be monitored and published in the court lists.

To untangle the complicated threads of the Ripper crimes it will be necessary to understand fully the forces that moulded the character of Eddy's father, the Prince of Wales (Queen Victoria's eldest son, nicknamed 'Bertie'). The officials surrounding Bertie knew his every move until he was married, with a home, staff and children of his own: not until then did Bertie enjoy any real freedom. While in his late teens studying at Cambridge University, Bertie found this unremitting surveillance too much to bear and one evening he sneaked out of his lodgings and took a train to London. When he arrived, officials were waiting for him at the station. Presumably Eddy's movements while he remained unmarried and dependent on his parents would have been just as tightly controlled. Also, there is no known link between Eddy and London's low life or between Eddy and female prostitutes. From the information available Eddy was a gentle, charming boy, needing affection, who did not display signs of the violent temper that characterised his father's youth.

However, the words 'female', 'low life', and 'prostitute', immediately bring Bertie to mind. His outrageous exploits, both as Prince of Wales and later as King, are now legendary. It is recorded that Bertie was hailed by low Paris showgirls as he entered their club; the dancers would insolently call out, 'hello Wales'. Bertie was known, when in Marienbad, to follow a set routine by entertaining casual mistresses at his hotel: he would often visit such clubs as *Mott's* and the *Cremorne* – where the waitresses were known as 'soiled doves'. And there is the infamous chair, designed so that the old and obese King Edward VII could be serviced by prostitutes – to name but a few of the sexual exploits in the King's life.

Seeds for the Ripper murders were sown decades before the murders occurred. Surprisingly, it was the behaviour of Bertie, the future King Edward VII, that reached out and destroyed the lives of at least five penniless East End prostitutes. In order for the Prince of Wales's actions to be fully understood – and this is vitally important to the Ripper story – we must consider in detail the formative influences that moulded the future King's character. We must understand why he turned into an irredeemable Victorian rake.

Queen Victoria's first son was born on 9 November 1841 at Buckingham Palace. Her first child had been a girl. 'Don't worry,' Victoria had confidently told the doctor, 'the next one will be a boy'. She was right. There was, naturally, great rejoicing at the birth. Country-wide church bells pealed the entire day and so many military salutes were fired that a wag said, 'My, how they do powder that child'. The baby was christened Albert Edward, and on his birth inherited the title Duke of Cornwall. Less than a month later the titles of Prince of Wales and Earl of Chester were also bestowed on the infant. At other times throughout his life the prince became the Duke of Rothesay, Duke of Saxe-Coburg-Gotha, Prince of Saxony, Earl of Dublin, Earl of Carrick and Baron Renfrew. But to his family, the much-titled prince became known as 'Bertie'.

Victoria and her Consort, Prince Albert, were not ideal parents. Victoria was totally absorbed into the life of her adored husband. In a letter to her uncle after the boy's birth the Queen wrote:

> Our little boy is wonderfully large and strong. I *hope* and *pray* he may be like his dearest Papa. You will understand how fervent my prayers to see him resemble his angelic father in *every*, *every* respect, both in body and mind.

Then Bertie was quickly forgotten as the Queen returned to her favourite subject.

> I delight in the fact that I possess such a perfect husband. I cannot say what a comfort and support my beloved Angel is to me.

Already at birth the wish for the son to become the father had been formed without regard to the child's temperament and tastes, an age-old recipe for disaster. But the Queen's wishes to create a second Albert were warmly welcomed by other members of the court. This transformation was to be achieved by careful training. Planning for the boy's education was placed in the hands of Albert and a German aristocrat, Baron Stockmar, a man Victoria had grown to rely on and to implicitly trust.

Stockmar had been born in 1787 in Coburg, where he received his early education. He served as an army doctor in the Napoleonic wars (which perhaps hardened his character) before he drifted into political matters. The Baron had been sent by the queen's foster-father, King Leopold to direct Victoria's political education. It was Stockmar who was chosen to vet Albert before his betrothal to Queen Victoria. The Baron was delighted to report that Albert appeared quite uninterested in women, and liked to spend his evenings discussing issues with older and wiser philosophers. Stockmar quickly became a trusted adviser on many aspects of court life where he became a law unto himself, often being thought of as 'the power behind the throne.' Certainly the advice of the pedantic Baron was invariably accepted by both Victoria and Albert.

Prince Albert had, as a boy, demonstrated an unusual passion for academic study. He delighted in the discussion of law and metaphysics with his elders. One year he refused a Christmas holiday as this would have interrupted his studies. An hour-long debate on religious and theological subjects at his confirmation apparently gave the young Albert more pleasure than a Christmas break. This was the academic young man who was to become Bertie's father. This was the man they now intended to recreate through the son. While the rigid, humourless and authoritarian Albert clearly made Victoria a good husband, there would be few little boys who would regard him as an ideal father.

Bertie's early years were reasonably untraumatic, although he was denied the company of other children apart from his own brothers and sisters. Albert considered that other boys might pass on bad habits, so the gregarious, friendly Bertie was kept alone in his classroom, studying religion and Latin and similar subjects, or playing four-handed chess with his parents and tutor for relaxation. From the ages of 7 to 9 Bertie's education was placed in the hands of a distinguished scholar from Cambridge University, Henry Birch. Bertie formed a warm attachment to his tutor, and it is not known whether it was the young lad's pleasure at being with Birch or the considered laxity of lessons that displeased Albert and Stockmar.

Whatever the reasons, Henry Birch was dismissed, and a new tutor sought. The young boy was dismayed at the loss of one of his few friends; he wrote affectionate notes and left small gifts under Birch's pillow. The young lad's opinion was not even briefly considered. A recommendation from Sir James Stephen, who was Under-Secretary at the Colonial Office, brought Frederick Weymouth Gibbs to Stockmar's attention as a replacement for Birch. It was Sir James's nephew, J.K. Stephen, who would be chosen decades later as the tutor for Bertie's eldest son Eddy, a choice that would add to the tangled Ripper threads.

Gibbs was considered suitable and he was engaged to conduct the next stage of Bertie's education. The new tutor quickly assessed the mental capabilities of his royal charge: he questioned the advisability of an intense learning schedule for so unacademic a boy, but Stockmar and Albert were unbending: they wanted a recreation of the father; perfection was the goal. Along with traditional studies – reading, writing, arithmetic, geography, history, biology, there was theology, classics and political economy. For relaxation, Albert took the boy on long walks where he had to guess the Latin name for plants along the route. If facts had been food, Bertie would have choked.

Enlightened minds saw the damage that was being inflicted on the young boy's mind. Lord Redesdale wrote of Bertie, 'I can see his poor, bored face even now. It was pitiful'.

The young Prince began to display signs of violent temper.

After various opinions on the Prince's educational progress were collated, it was adjudged that Bertie, in all spheres of education, was far less capable than his elder sister. 'My son is so stupid,' Queen Victoria is reported to have said. This bombardment of criticism lasted for many years and came from several directions. The tutor Gibbs quickly became a first-class sneak, relating his charge's every conceivable fault to the royal parents and keeping his own record of the young Bertie's misdeeds.

The complaints are so petty it is difficult to believe that anyone would take note but Albert considered each misdemeanour carefully. The Prince Consort decided to release some of the fifteen-year-old Bertie's pent-up energy on a four-month tour abroad. He was surrounded by model all-male company on his overseas journey.

When he was sixteen it was decided that the Prince should now have the weighty task of selecting his own clothes, but even here the heavy hand of Queen Victoria fell. She sent warning notes to her son cautioning him against extravagant or immodest attire.

When, while still a teenager, the Prince was given his own home at White Lodge in Richmond Park, a squad of tutors and minders were lodged with him. For their guidance the Queen and her Consort issued a list of instructions. To use the words of the Archbishop of Canterbury's son, E.F. Benson:

> An exhaustive memorandum was prepared in many sections, concerning his dress, deportment, relations with others and conversation. Any tendency towards lounging, loud clothes, frivolity, discourtesy, idleness, vanity, unpunctuality and mimicry must be instantly checked.

The unfortunate (mentally imprisoned) Prince was still not allowed the company of youths of his own age and practical jokes were forbidden. On Bertie's eighteenth birthday he reached his majority as legal heir to the Crown and it seemed that relief might at last be on hand: it was announced that Frederick Gibbs would be retiring. Any joy was short-lived. His new 'aide' was to be Colonel Bruce – a dour, humourless man in the familiar mould. In regard to this new appointment, Victoria and Albert sent their son a directive:

> Your equerries will receive orders from Colonel Bruce. You will never leave the house without reporting yourself to him, and he will settle who is to accompany you, and will give general instructions as to the disposition of the day.

It is reported that Bertie wept when he read this communiqué. Discipline became even more rigid although Bertie was now a young adult. Part of Colonel Bruce's timetable for the Prince's studies is recorded:

> Before breakfast, Italian studies. 11 to 12, read with Mr Tarver. Early afternoon study ancient monuments and works of art. Translate French from 5 to 6. One hour in the evening for private reading and music.

Baron Stockmar's maxim, 'Never relax', was being faithfully maintained.

After reaching the age of majority Bertie was almost immediately enrolled for a short course of study at Edinburgh University. A familiar rigorous schedule of study was drawn up. Such unremitting application would tax the most studious of minds: for the unbookish Bertie, with a strong personality and even stronger sexual urges, the course must have been nightmarish. Every arrangement for the Prince's stay in Scotland appeared to have been designed to frustrate the young man's personality. He was not allowed to live with the other students for fear that their personalities and habits might contaminate his royal mind. Bertie was installed at Holyrood Palace with his governor and tutors.

After the term of study at Edinburgh the Prince was moved to Oxford University and a similar living and working schedule was prepared: however, at Oxford, even working alongside other students was forbidden. Private tutors were engaged for lectures. Meanwhile, Prince Albert made frequent unannounced visits to his son's university, in order to check that the educational standards that had been set for Bertie were being observed. No advisor appeared to find it ludicrous that an eighteen-year-old prince should be treated like a ten-year-old boy. It was at Oxford University that Bertie was introduced to tobacco, but to enjoy his first smoke he was obliged to crouch behind a hedge with a few conspirators, like a schoolboy behind the bicycle sheds.

In a rash moment Queen Victoria had promised that when Canada furnished an infantry regiment for service in the Crimean War she would send her son on a tour of the Dominions. No doubt Stockmar and Albert decided that the lamentably long university vacation would be the ideal moment to fulfil this promise. There was considerable parental surprise when Bertie's tour proved highly successful. On his return, the prince went back to Oxford for a final term, then, for good measure, he was enrolled for a further year of study at Cambridge University. The pressure of such long and rigid discipline was beginning to place a severe – and evident – strain on the young prince and his temper became more explosive.

After careful consideration it was decided that marriage might help stabilise Bertie. Maybe his strong sexual urges had been recognised, although this is unlikely. The shining example of Albert and Victoria's highly successful early union was more likely to have been the marriage catalyst. *The Times* discussed Bertie's marital affairs on 5 July 1858.

> To all present appearances, our future monarch's choice of wife is positively limited to exactly seven ladies of Royal blood . . .

Number five on that list was 'Princess Alexandra (daughter of Prince Christian) of Denmark'. Meanwhile, during Bertie's final university vacation, when most students would travel to their homes to relax and enjoy themselves, Colonel Bruce advised that a spell of military training was the perfect way to fill Bertie's long break. This decision was to lead to the first great scandal involving the Prince of Wales.

The Curragh Camp in Ireland was chosen for the prince's initial military service. The Camp was a remote outpost where, Colonel Bruce doubtless thought, no youthful, lustful adventures could occur. Colonel Bruce could not have been more mistaken.

Albert and Victoria visited their son in Ireland. Bertie had hoped that for his parents' visit, after a short but concentrated period of training, he might be placed in charge of a battalion of soldiers, but Colonel Percy, Bertie's commanding officer, considered that the Prince's drill and his commands to the men were not to the required standard. Bertie was made to march past his parents in a lowly subaltern's position.

Queen Victoria noted her son's humiliation without any great sympathy. She wrote to her Uncle Leopold in Belgium, 'Bertie acquitted himself as well as could be expected in the circumstances'.

Fellow officers cannot have failed to notice the Prince's harsh treatment so they decided to give Bertie a treat. A dark-haired beauty, Nellie Clifton, an actress, was in Curragh in the company of an officer. Nellie was young, healthy and available. The soldiers commandeered her services, smuggled her past Colonel Bruce and tucked her up in Bertie's bed. Bertie knew exactly what to do and clearly enjoyed the experience. Unfortunately for him Nellie could not resist boasting of her royal conquest, the gossip spread, and news of Bertie's debauchery quickly and inevitably reached Buckingham Palace. Queen Victoria appeared to know when her family scratched themselves. Albert went into a state of shock. He ordered an immediate inquiry into the affair and when confirmation of Bertie's actions arrived, the Prince Consort wrote to his son:

> You have caused me the greatest pain I have yet felt in this life. You must not, you dare not be lost. The consequences for this country and for the world would be too dreadful.

Bertie was rushed back to Cambridge where his father hurried to meet – and to castigate – his son. Returning from that meeting it was reported that 'The Consort travelled through cold and stormy weather, and, as a result, caught a feverish cold'. What Albert had really caught was typhoid fever. Bertie was summoned to Windsor Castle, but by the time he arrived his father was unconscious. Albert died on the night of 4 December 1861.

The effect on Queen Victoria was predictable. For twenty-one years Albert had been her constant and singular joy. 'England, my unhappy country, has lost all in losing him,' she wrote to her uncle. The devastated Queen wrapped herself in a mantle of grief and stayed coc-ooned in misery for decades, in what could only be termed 'exhibitive mourning'. Widowhood would have been the perfect time for Victoria to share the increased burdens of state (which now fell onto her should-ers) with her eldest son and heir, and Bertie could have gained valuable experience for his role as future king, but Victoria tenaciously held on to power. Was that because of a strong dislike which she seemed to have for her son? On one occasion she wrote, 'I shall never look at him with-out a shudder'. The Queen apparently believed that the shock over Bertie's sexual escapade with Nellie had seriously weakened Albert's constitution, allowing the fatal fever to gain hold. Whatever the reason, the Queen refused to allow Bertie any participation in State affairs: she even refused to allow her son access to cabinet papers that were available to her private secretaries.

Bertie, now of age, was relieved from the smothering burden of edu-cation, and at the same time he was cut off from any semblance of responsibility. The result was predictable. Freed from all constraints, with power and money and no responsibilities, Bertie launched himself into a life of unrestrained pleasure to make up for the years of unre-strained childhood misery. He could hardly be blamed. Years of educa-tional torment had been wasted. Bertie began to make up for lost time.

Despite Victoria's bereavement, it was decided to continue with plans for Bertie's marriage. A betrothal of his son and heir had been Albert's last wish so it would be carried out. *The Times's* 'number five' choice of bride, Alexandra of Denmark, had been carefully assessed by the Palace authorities. Despite the fact that a Dane marrying into the British Royal Family would cause great offence to the Prussians (the two countries had been engaged in a bitter territorial argument for years), Victoria decided that as no other suitable candidate was available the union should go ahead. Bertie and the Danish Princess had met, and they had liked each other. Victoria had also met Alexandra and they too had warmed to each other. The young princess had been warned not to smile during this meeting; the queen disliked any show of happiness as it reminded her of the lost and happy times she had shared with Albert. An engagement was announced and the anticipated storm of protest from Prussia was brushed aside. Victoria was, after all, Queen of England, so she could do anything she liked.

Bertie and Alexandra were married in St. George's Chapel at Windsor Castle on 10 March 1863 at midday. Although a year and three months had passed since her beloved Consort's death, Victoria arrived at the wedding dressed in deepest mourning, wearing an entirely black outfit, even down to the gloves, relieved only by the blue ribbon of the

Order of the Garter. This assembly was rounded off by a widow's cap. Alexandra, glittering with spectacular jewellery, wore a white satin dress trimmed with garlands of orange blossom covered by Honiton lace; she was surrounded by heralds and trumpeters in brilliant cloth-of-gold tunics, yet after the wedding Victoria wrote: 'What a dismal affair it was', forgetting that she personally had not added much cheer. She insisted on sitting in seclusion, dressed in black, occasionally bursting into tears as she looked at the spot on which Albert's coffin had so recently stood, a spot now occupied by their son about to be wed. There is a wonderfully absurd wedding photograph in which Alexandra in bridal dress looks sternly towards the camera while Bertie glowers at his bride: even on this happy occasion no outward show of pleasure was permitted. Victoria is seated in front of the gloomy couple wearing voluminous mourning robes, staring up miserably at a marble bust of her dead Consort. Just because he had passed away did not mean that Albert should be left out of the wedding celebrations. The portrait is a splendid display of unconscious humour.

Bertie and his wife moved into their own premises at Marlborough House in central London, and finally the prince was master of his own destiny. Fun was to be the order of the day. Bertie's love of food was served by endless official dinners. Balls crowded in on each other. Foreign travel, much to Bertie's taste, was undertaken on a grand scale. In Constantinople they were served meals from solid gold, diamond-encrusted plates. Now that Bertie was free a set of high-bred rakes became part of his inner circle. Henry Chaplin, Sir Frederick Johnstone and other like-minded hell-raisers, all of whom enjoyed gambling, drinking and seducing women, influenced the prince, and after the earlier, dreary company of academics and theologians, Bertie's enjoyment in stepping beyond the bounds of propriety with rakes is fully understandable.

In the days before newspapers had learned the technique of reproducing photographs, Bertie's face was recognised by few of the general public. One day the Prince of Wales and the Bishop of Thetford were driving along a country lane when an old woman, carrying a huge basket of cockles, approached the dog-cart and asked the prince if he would carry the cockles for her. Charmingly, Bertie said that he was unable to do that, but instead, he would give her a picture of his mother. He then handed the old woman half a sovereign. Amazingly, Victoria also frequently went unrecognised by the general public, especially when she was in the wilds of Scotland. This anonymity meant that Bertie was able to dismiss his royal coaches and travel around London in public cabs, visiting clubs with his circle of friends and drinking in bars where no royal personage would be expected to imbibe. There is little doubt that these activities would have been reported to Victoria – she had her spies everywhere – but now that Bertie was married with his own home there was little she could do, apart from sending warning notes and giving motherly advice, most of which Bertie ignored. The days of sending transport to bring the prince back home had long since passed.

Bertie was fascinated by fire and never missed attending a major blaze if he could help it. (See above illustration, Bertie on the right.) Occasionally Bertie and some of his cronies would go every night for a week to Watling Street Fire Station where they would play at being firemen. The prince certainly made up for his lack of fun during childhood. One of the firemen who worked at the blaze which destroyed the King and Queen Granaries in London reported:

> Through the height of the fire, His Royal Highness shared the smoke and water with us all, and gave a hand here and there just like one of ourselves. The walls of the place were very high, and as the water soaked the grain, it bulged the walls out till they fell with a terrific crash. Through it all the Prince, who seemed to bear a charmed life, worked with a zeal and knowledge that would have done credit to any trained fireman, unrecognised by the onlookers, and unnoticed by the rank and file of the Brigade.

The head of the London Fire Brigade had orders to report any fierce conflagration to Marlborough House. Bertie and his circle would then rush out to view. Clearly the prince led the most extraordinary lifestyle for a member of the Victorian Royal Family – or any other royal family for that matter.

By the late 1860s Bertie's reputation as a roué and a seducer of women was well established. His close association with the Marquis of Hastings in particular could well have helped corrupt the prince. The Marquis was young, extremely rich, and intimately associated with brothels and working-class clubs. He had a passion for cruel sports such as cock fighting and liked to associate with criminals and low prostitutes. Bertie much enjoyed the company of the Marquis and allowed himself to be led into the nobleman's sordid world. The two friends often travelled abroad together and it was reported that during a party in Paris, a naked courtesan was served up to Bertie on a silver plate. The Prince of Wales, now much lampooned by sketches and satirical articles, had become the greatest rake of his time. This cruel, mocking cartoon, emphasising not only the women but the champagne and the cigars, is typical of the flood of scurrilous material printed in newspapers and magazines.

THE PRINCE OF WALES PROVIDING COMFORT FOR THE WIVES AND WIDOWS OF THE MEN FIGHTING THE BOER WAR.

The foolish educational programme of Prince Albert and Baron Stockmar had backfired, and, totally unwittingly, they had laid the groundwork for the Ripper murders.

J.K. Stephen

Montague John Druitt

The Prince and Princess of Wales with Prince Albert Victor

The Duke of Clarence

29 Hanbury Street

Sir Charles Warren

Reconstructed image of Liz Stride
(by the artist Peter Fry)

Miller's Court, demolished in 1928.

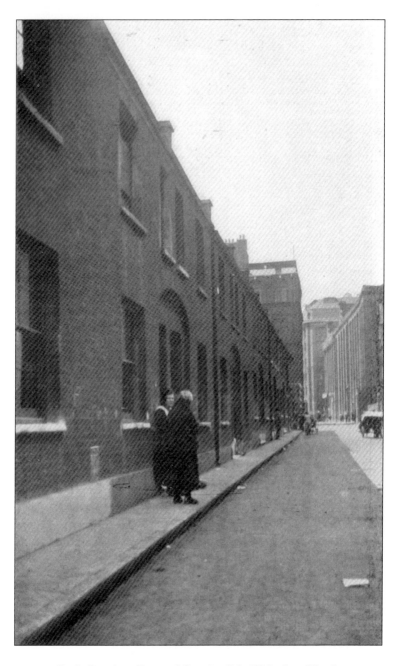

Bucks Row (now Durward Street), off the Whitechapel Road.
The body of Mary Ann Nicholls was found lying across the gutter.

Chapter 10

Eddy

If the Prince of Wales was a first tenuous link in the Ripper murders, then his eldest son, nicknamed Eddy, was a second link. Both of these men take us one step nearer to the solution. For a complete understanding of the puzzle it is essential that Eddy's background is also fully understood. Eddy was born in the wrong place at the wrong time, unexpectedly and without preparation; all rare for a royal child.

On 8 January 1864 Bertie and Alix were staying at Frogmore, a royal house in Windsor Park. The weather was bitterly cold, and a hockey match in which Bertie was booked to play had been organised on a frozen lake in Virginia Water. The royal couple left for the match and Alexandra, whose accouchement was not due for two months, spent a happy time in the company of her husband being pulled around the lake on a sledge. She left Virginia Water at 4 p.m. in good health and spirits, but when Bertie followed his wife home to Windsor several hours later he found her in labour, with the royal doctor many miles away. Complete preparations for the accouchement had been made at Marlborough House, but with the birth so unexpected no preparations had been made at Frogmore. A local medic was summoned and he, with the aid of Alix's lady-in-waiting, delivered Eddy into the world. The baby then had to be wrapped in makeshift clothing.

There was great rejoicing at the birth of a male child, an heir apparent to the throne. Victoria hastened to Windsor to view her grandson; he was frail and small, weighing only three and a half pounds. Victoria found him, ' a poor little bit of a thing'. That did not stop her, however, from deciding that the boy would be named after her dead Consort. No doubt her mind had been made up from the moment she had heard of the pregnancy. Male equalled Albert. 'Albert Victor Christian Edward' the Queen announced, much to the dismay of his parents, who thought they should at least be consulted in the choice of names for their firstborn. Victoria brushed the protestations aside, declaring that from henceforth every king who sat on the throne of England must be called 'Albert'. Her obsession did not lessen with time.

The boy was christened as Victoria wished, the ceremony taking place in St George's Chapel, Windsor, the scene both of Albert's funeral and Bertie's marriage. Once again the Queen was dressed in deepest mourning. Although Victoria won initially over the naming of the boy,

Alix was not without her triumph. From the start she called her son 'Eddy' and that was the name by which he was known to his family and friends throughout his life.

Seventeen months after Eddy's birth a second son was born. He was christened George. Being so near each other in age the boys were educationally compatible. Naturally Victoria tried to interfere in the education of her grandchildren, but Bertie, remembering his own nightmarish tutoring, insisted on a more relaxed programme of study. He firmly believed that little could be learned from books and Alix agreed with him, so the princes were allowed to roam free during their formative years with little enforced education. The result of such freedom was predictable. Victoria called her grandsons, '...ill-bred and ill-trained. I can't fancy them at all', yet despite that statement she was clearly fond of the boys. Eddy was served, from his earliest months, by a personal footman who was also attached to George once he was born, but clearly discipline was not part of the footman's duties.

Once the boys reached the ages of six and seven respectively it was decided that a firm educational stand must be undertaken. After a short search for a suitable tutor, the Reverend John Neale Dalton, a thirty-two-year-old clergyman, was engaged to educate the princes privately. Dalton was a brilliant scholar who had graduated from Cambridge University with first-class honours in Theology, but his high spiritual attainments did not prevent him from emulating the sneaky actions of Bertie's tutor: detailed diaries were kept which noted the boys' behaviour and a steady stream of letters, assessments and notes outlined his young charges' development. Eddy was considered educationally subnormal. It was reported that he could not concentrate for more than a few minutes at a time – he even lost concentration in mid-sentence, when his words would trail away. He was listless, vacant and prone to prolonged daydreaming. Eddy had, according to Dalton, a weakness of the brain, a feebleness and a lack of mental power to grasp even the simplest concepts that were put before him. Although Prince George was more responsive to teaching than his elder brother, his attainments also left much to be desired and he progressed only slowly.

Alexandra, whose own education had been minimal without any ill-effects in later life, wrote back to say how shocked she had been by the tutor's reports, but clearly she remained unperturbed by the teacher's depressingly negative outbursts. I cannot help wondering whether Dalton's reports were unconsciously supposed to defend his own position – the case of a bad workman blaming his tools – but whatever his motives, Dalton remained at his post for fourteen years.

Eddy's education was, in many respects, a recreation of his father's schoolboy difficulties, reincarnated in an even more relentlessly negative form. However, Bertie, during his educational struggles, must have been aware of his engaging and powerful personality. By contrast, Eddy had no such reserves of assurance on which to rely. He was a languidly beautiful boy inclined towards melancholia, and one must feel sympathy for his predicament: a prince unsuited by temperament and ability for his destiny, he was relentlessly squeezed and moulded by royal forces into a shape thought fit for the highest in the land.

Although Alix suffered from an inherited deafness, only Sir Henry Ponsonby, Victoria's private secretary, thought to wonder whether hearing difficulties might be at the root of Eddy's educational problems. Eddy suffered from otosclerosis, a fusing together of small bones in the inner ear. Being cut off from the tutor's voice and from normal conversation would be enough to make any boy appear educationally weak. In later years Eddy proved to be a fine player of whist, a game that requires concentration and mental skill. It is interesting to note that whist requires only sight and a knowledge of the cards held in the hand, and it is best played in total silence. If Eddy's mental powers could concentrate over long rubbers in a card game requiring powers of memory and mental arithmetic, then it was presumably the teaching methods during his schooling (which did not recognise Eddy's disability) that had been at fault and not the quality of the prince's brain. A strong bond of friendship and affection existed between the young brothers. In 1877, when the boys were aged twelve and thirteen, it was decided that travel might broaden their minds and at the same time stimulate their desire for education.

Bertie was, at this juncture, deep into his entanglement with the beautiful socialite Mrs Lillie Langtry, an affair of passionate depth. The educational responsibility for two young boys must have interfered with Bertie's insatiable demands for pleasure, no matter how affectionate his feelings were towards his sons (and there is some evidence that this affection was ambivalent). Was there a touch of cynicism when Bertie decided that the boys should tour the world for two years? The princes were to be accompanied by their tutor. It was suggested that the boys should be placed on separate ships, but the strong bond of friendship between the brothers made it inadvisable to part them at the start of their teenage years. A further consideration was the fact that George appeared to be the only person who could occasionally rouse his brother from a state of semi-permanent torpor. So the princes sailed away together as cadets on the naval training ship *HMS Britannia*. While George, as usual, coped well with his training, Eddy displayed no greater appetite for nautical matters than he had shown for other forms of education.

When he reached the age of sixteen Eddy's mental capabilities appeared as restricted as ever; moreover he had grown into an archetypal 'mother's boy'. Books written in Eddy's short lifetime contain sentimental Victorian statements such as: '... he liked to go for long walks at Sandringham, arm around his mother's waist.' Eddy is reported to have said, 'Mama is so nice, she is fond of everything I like. There is nobody like Mama'.

With such an attitude and with such a low educational standard, Eddy began to draw criticism from his father. Sir Henry Ponsonby had written that while accompanying the boys to their training ship before the world tour, the Prince of Wales 'snubbed Prince Eddy uncommonly'. And this cold behaviour was before a two-year parting. It was Bertie who, recognising his son's liking for immaculate dress, unkindly nicknamed his son 'collar and cuffs', an appellation that became widely used. Despite such difficulties however, it is clear from documented reports of Eddy's activities and friendships, that by mid-teens a split between personality and educational ability had occurred. Eddy had grown into a charming, much-liked young man. It is possible for any person who can listen (or appear to listen) attentively to conversation to be assigned a degree of intelligence by the speaker: such is human nature – intelligence by association. Perhaps this occurred in Eddy's case? There is no doubt that despite his low educational achievements he was a popular fellow amongst those who knew him and much loved by his family and friends.

Alix, after bearing her two sons, gave birth to three daughters. The girls' education was sadly neglected, but their mother did insist on the instillation of good manners and humility in all her offspring. 'They must not assume attitudes of superiority,' Alix continually ordered the retinues of nannies and tutors. This must have been a difficult lesson for such high-born youngsters to stomach but Alix's wishes were obeyed: Eddy in particular proved an apt pupil. Any person coming into contact with the young prince, perhaps expecting a haughty, regal personality, found instead a self-effacing, gentle and friendly young man. By his mid-teens Eddy had the ability to instil in his friends a deep sense of loyalty and love: this quality is a far more important talent to any member of royalty than brain power. Eddy's natural qualities were invaluable and impossible to teach.

After a second lengthy educational tour on board the ship *Baccante*, George, who had developed a passion for life at sea, decided on a naval career. Eddy had to continue his education on land, and so, for the first time in their lives the boys were parted – a wrench for both the brothers but more especially for Eddy. Life must have seemed bleak for the ninteen-year-old prince as he considered the course that had been set for him: study at Cambridge University, competing with the country's finest brains, without the support of his brother, while he was being moulded for a future role to which he was quite unsuited. And these trials and tribulations were being undertaken with impaired hearing which would cut him off from a full integration into university life.

To assist Eddy during his ordeal at one of the world's finest educational institutions, it was decided that he must have a special tutor who could live with him before his enrolment and help to cram his mind with knowledge. The hunt for a suitable tutor did not take long. The Reverend John Neale Dalton recommended a young man from an excellent family, James Kenneth Stephen. Stephen was interviewed and quickly accepted the post.

It is at this point that the plot thickens. With James Stephen by his side, Eddy unexpectedly found himself supported by an extremely handsome, highly intelligent and confident young man; he had found friendship in a hostile world; he had found a replacement for his lost brother. This must have seemed miraculous to the diffident young prince.

Neither men could have known at their first meeting that the relationship would eventually prove disastrous for both of them, or that the pairing would mean death for five women.

Chapter 11

J. K. Stephen

The next link in the Ripper murders moves us very close to the crimes. Once again a complete understanding of our subject is essential. The Stephen family were descended from farming stock, but within several generations literary talent was in evidence, and a series of books and articles had been written by various family members. *Memoirs*, *Imprisonment For Debt*, *A Treatise On Pleading* and *New Commentaries* comprised some of the family's literary output. The study and practice of law also became a recurring occupation of successive generations of the Stephen family.

James Kenneth Stephen was born in 1859, the second son of Sir James Fitzjames Stephen, and he inherited the family's twin talents, writing and the law. J.K. (as he was often known) was initially educated at church schools in Tunbridge Wells and Banbury before being accepted into Eton in 1871, where he remained until Easter 1878. At Eton, one of James's tutors was the notorious Oscar Browning, who was dismissed from the College for 'over-familiarity' with the boys. Browning, a man in his mid-thirties when James entered Eton, preferred the company of younger lads. Did J.K., a handsome, chunky young man, experience some form of sexual harassment from the tutor? A possible answer to this question might lie in one of J.K.'s poems (supposedly written from a woman's point of view) in which a 'Mr B.' is mentioned.

> When I had firmly answered 'No,'
> And he allowed that that was so,
> I really thought I should be free
> For good and all from Mr. B.,
> And that he would soberly acquiesce:
> I said that I would be discreet
> That for a while we should not meet;
> I promised I would always feel
> A kindly interest in his weal;
> I thanked him for his amorous zeal,
> In short, I said all I could but 'yes'.

I suspect that this poem reminisces about an event that actually happened to James. The writer agrees to go horse riding with 'Mr B.' and the fourth verse explicitly describes a sexual experience once the couple

94

had stopped, presumably to eat.

> I won't say much of what happened next,
> I own I was extremely vexed,
> Indeed, I should have been aghast
> If anyone had seen what passed:
> But nobody need ever know,
> That, as I leaned forward to stir the fire,
> He advanced before I could retire,
> And I suddenly felt to my great alarm,
> The grasp of a warm unlicensed arm,
> An embrace in which I found no charm;
> I was awfully glad when he let me go.

Can we learn about further intimacies, as outlined in a wistful verse from 'The Old School List'?

> There were two good fellows I used to know,
> – How distant it all appears.
> We played together in football weather,
> And messed together for years:

James's brother wrote:

While he was at school he worked hard at such of his studies as particularly interested him, and as hard as he thought practically necessary at those that did not. The consequence was that he distinguished himself greatly as an essay-writer and a student of history, and did not especially distinguish himself either in classics or mathematics.

An appraisal of James's similarly mixed fortunes at various athletic activities is recorded, but a clearer picture of him at Eton emerges from one of the contemporary students. Arthur Christopher Benson, the eldest of three sons born to the Archbishop of Canterbury, was enrolled at Eton in 1874, three years behind J.K. Stephen. Despite the difference in their ages and grades the boys became firm friends, and later Arthur (less famous than his younger brother, E.F. Benson, author of the *Lucia* books) wrote a volume of short biographies which include reminiscences of J.K. Stephen:

I do not remember my first actual sight of him, but he was so entirely unlike other boys that, once seen, it was impossible to forget him. He had a very big head with fine, clear-cut features, large and rather terrific eyes, a strong expressive mouth and a solid chin. He wore his hair, which curled slightly, somewhat long, and parted in the middle. The expression of his face was severe to grimness in repose – it was eminently a judicial face – though it lit up with an irrepressible smile. He gave the impression of enormous strength.

A contemporary of J.K.'s great-grandfather described that ancestor as 'a man of volcanic personality – and also a volcanic temper'. Interestingly, Benson writes about J.K.: '...and on the rare occasions when he lost his temper, the terror of the situation...' Clearly James's temper mirrored that of his volcanic ancestor. Incidentally, my family doctor told me that he is descended from the Stephen family, and another branch of the clan gave birth to one of the country's most notorious mass-murderers, a man who is still in prison. I have not mentioned names as I cannot confirm these details.

When J.K. left Eton in 1878 to study at Cambridge University he carried on a vigorous correspondence with the young Benson, who eventually followed his friend to Cambridge. At Cambridge, James soon gathered around him a coterie of university peers, a group who, according to Benson, 'deliberately made friends with several small boys who seemed inclined to be interested in the same things'. Even at Eton, James had been an idol of young lads for several reasons. 'He played the odd game of football ... with remarkable skill and endurance, he was extremely good natured, he did very little work, *he defied authority...*' [My italics.] As a schoolboy, J.K. also showed signs of a restless energy ('he was never still') and signs of individuality ('he was eccentric in dress'). In a short passage, Benson states sentiments about J.K. which Eddy might also have experienced in the company of his new tutor:

> I was not, I remember, exactly at ease with him, though I felt it was a great honour to be selected as his friend. I was always overshadowed by a sense of his cleverness, quickness, and ability, and was afraid of not being up to the mark in talk.

I can imagine Eddy writing those very words. The passage continues:

> He was of an emotional nature always, but found it hard to express his feelings: and I was aware in those days, especially just before the time came for him to leave the School, that there was some hidden flow of feeling about him, a heartfelt craving which he could not express even to himself.

Then Arthur added some pages later, '...he loved close and intimate relationships.'

From Benson's writing a clear picture begins to build up of a mysterious, eccentric, brilliant, highly emotional young man. There was also a sense of daring in the young J.K. At Cambridge University he broke the rules by running across lawns in full view of the Vice-Provost. He escaped punishment. At Eton he was once late for an important church service: this unpunctuality could have had serious consequences, so J.K. waited until all the main authorities had closed their eyes and bowed their heads in prayer. He then entered the chapel, walked silently up the aisle and took his place.

> It was exactly timed. Just as he [J.K.] slipped into place, Hornby rose refreshed, wholly unaware of the interruption, and perhaps a little puzzled by the broad smiles of the Collegers.

Other telling sentences are spread throughout Benson's recollections: '... he expanded in an atmosphere of delicate care and caressing affection.' 'He was a strong agnostic.' The writer then touches on his friend's royal appointment, mentioning Eddy, who by then, had received a title – Duke of Clarence – from Queen Victoria.

> Then he went for a while as tutor to the Duke of Clarence, and his time at Sandringham proved extremely pleasant and delightful: though I have sometimes wondered whether Jem Stephen's dry art of statement and somewhat impatient quality of mind fitted him to teach a prince of extraordinary amiability and sweetness, but whose intellectual tastes were of the simplest character. They were, however, firm friends: and Jem Stephen realised to the full, as none who knew the Duke ever failed to find, the warm affection and constant fidelity of his illustrious pupil.

We learn that Stephen once wrote a sonnet that alluded to Harvey, the discoverer of the circulation of blood:

> What are the habits of this crimson flood
> We reek with? Man had questioned many a year.

This was the eccentric man who became the tutor and the close companion of Eddy, the Duke of Clarence.

❧

J.K. quickly recognised Eddy's educational limitations. He wrote to Dalton saying '. . . he hardly knows the words to read . . .' yet despite this harsh criticism the two men became close friends, as Arthur Benson confirms. This friendship was recognised by Eddy's official biographer, J.E. Vincent: '. . . he [Eddy] was a member of the Amateur Dramatic Society, to which his by now intimate friend, Jim Stephen, belonged . . .'

Such a deep friendship holds no surprises: two handsome, charming young men from illustrious family backgrounds, both yearning for affection, both highly sensual, both with homosexual leanings. There could only be one possible outcome: a love affair, probably of considerable depth and passion. One can imagine James beginning to weave his spell over the royal pupil, perhaps by pointing out that kingship requires not so much intellectual power – one can always employ brilliant minds – but the very qualities of charm, compassion and friendliness which Eddy possessed in such abundance. Benson in his memoirs recounts how J.K. Stephen would clown around and his antics could quickly convulse an audience with laughter. Doubtless J.K., who liked to be the centre of attention, brought a sense of the ridiculous into Eddy's life, a dimension which the prince would not have previously experienced.

From Eddy's reactions, Stephen must have been aware that he was slowly gaining power and ascendancy over a future King of England. What dreams of glory may have built up in the ambitious tutor's mind? I have dramatised the contents of this book, and although it might be unusual to quote parts of a play in a text of this nature, the imaginary dialogue might serve to further illuminate my thesis. Here is part of the scene where J.K. meets Eddy for the first time.

JAMES. I look forward to being your companion – and your teacher, sir.

EDDY. I don't envy you your task, Mr Stephen.

JAMES. Why not?

EDDY. A long line of tutors have tried hard to educate me. They have all failed.

JAMES. Who said?

EDDY. Everyone – my father most of all.

JAMES. Really? And why has your education drawn such negative comments?

EDDY. Because I am stupid.

JAMES. Who said?

EDDY. Everyone – again, my father most of all. You will soon form a similar opinion.

JAMES. Will I? In what subjects have you failed?

EDDY. All of them. English, history, mathematics . . .

JAMES. And how often will you need to use those subjects? How often will you need to use maths? How often will you need to assess military spending? How many tailoring bills will you be required to check?

EDDY. None.

JAMES. Precisely. Such matters concern housekeepers, not royalty. No man should enter a court of law and, once in the dock, condemn himself before any charges have been read out. Yet that is what you have just done. And that is not your failing – that is the fault of those who have taught you. The education of a prince lies far beyond the alphabet. Your future will depend on statesmanship and so on. It is too early for me to access you in depth, but I have already noted your charm and your ability to listen, your sincerity, your lack of pretension – all positive, vital traits that cannot be taught. And no doubt other sterling qualities will emerge in time. Your tutors should not have squashed you with negative talk – they should have highlighted your strengths, and given you a solid basis of confidence. So that will be my task, sir, and I, unlike the others, will not fail you.

EDDY. (*stunned*) You are an excellent speaker, Mr Stephen. Unfortunately many years of experience will exert more power than your words. So many people have already convinced me of my stupidity, it would now be difficult to believe otherwise. I have seen negative thoughts in so many eyes; in so many silent expressions; in so many stances. My opinions are set.

JAMES. Nothing is set. Certainly not thought. Let me demonstrate – even that chair does not exist.

EDDY. It does.

JAMES. Tell me why?

EDDY. Because – erm . . .

JAMES. Yes? Go on – explain.

EDDY. The chair must exist because I can see it. I can sit on it.

JAMES. An object is not seen because it is visible. It is visible because it is seen. What colour is the chair covering?

EDDY. Red.

JAMES. To me it is blue. I am colour blind. So already we are not seeing the same object. You may admire the chair's design. I may hate it. A third person may like the design but not the wood. And so on. So the chair does not exist in a rigidly set form. It exists only in the way each person sees it. And what applies to a chair must equally apply to someone's mind. Even the mind of a prince. We must make you see yourself though my eyes, not through past gazes. Once we have done that you will like what you see. Maybe even love what you see. (*Eddy stares*) What is wrong?

EDDY. You – you frighten me, Mr Stephen.

JAMES. I'm not surprised. The idea that someone might change a lifetime's conception of yourself – might make you aware of your sterling qualities, might make you realise that you are an extremely pleasant young man, struggling under the leaden weight of royalty, let down by all your tutors – yes, that must indeed be frightening. So let's hope that soon I will terrify you. (*Eddy stares, stunned, then smiles*) Good. A sense of humour to heap on the other positive traits. Your character improves by the second. (*He smiles*) Now, have I stopped frightening you?

EDDY. You have made me feel clever just listening to you, Mr Stephen.

JAMES. Excellent. My programme is already having an effect.

(*Eddy stares at James who stares back. There is a long pause.*)

EDDY. Mama tells me you come from a long line of barristers.

JAMES. I do. Which is distinctly preferable to your background.

EDDY. Why?

JAMES. Unlike me, you are trapped by birth, sealed into your destiny without choice, a living butterfly pinned to a satin board. But no amount of silky softness can make up for such an imprisonment. Freedom is man's most highly prized concept. Men have fought and died for it. It is therefore perverse that the heir to the British throne is denied the right of a peasant. You have been imprisoned from birth, which is a terrible situation, and those around you have made a bad situation worse.

EDDY. Oh Mr Stephen —

JAMES. Dare I be so forward as to ask if you will use my Christian name? James.

EDDY. And will you call me Eddy?

JAMES. Eddy. (*They grasp hands and hold the handshake*)

EDDY. No one else has realised how trapped and lonely I've been. Until you spoke, I hadn't fully realised it myself.

JAMES. It is said that a man can only know another man's pain if he has experienced it. You are not the only man who is trapped and lonely, Eddy. I often feel that way myself.

EDDY. (*Surprised*) You do?

JAMES. Oh yes. (*Pause*) Why are you staring?

EDDY. Because you are so unlike any of my past tutors.

JAMES. I should hope so. They were failures. You are the success. It will be my task to instil that concept into your mind. I look forward to working with you at Cambridge. Eddy.

EDDY. Not so much as I look forward to working with you. James.

∽

J.K. Stephen accompanied Eddy to Cambridge, a University that J.K. had left only a year earlier. He would therefore have known many of the students and lecturers, including Oscar Browning. Browning, despite his overtly homosexual bent and despite the nature of his dismissal from Eton, had been engaged to teach history at King's College, Cambridge, arriving there in 1876. Browning had not changed his ways – he was known to be friendly with the rich and perverted Lord Houghton, who enjoyed holding orgies and was a famous voyeur, although, to be fair, W.E. Forster did say of Houghton, 'I have friends who would be kind to me in distress, but only one who would be kind to me in disgrace'.

Interestingly, I have a copy of a friendly letter written by J.K. to Lord Houghton, and this will play an important role in my final thesis. So, we have documentary proof that J.K. was on friendly terms with a perverted, sexually-charged peer, and it was into this kind of company that Eddy was to be led, as the reserved prince would have relied on his knowledgeable companion and friend to choose and make any introductions. All the prince's early contacts at university would have been vetted and approved by the new royal tutor. Eddy's entire life, from the first moment, had been controlled by outside forces: every decision had been made for him by a string of advisers, tutors, and, of course, powerful members of his family, not least Queen Victoria. Knowing that total control and supervision from a minder would have been routine for the prince, J.K. could have gained an easy and complete mastery over his royal charge, and Eddy would have appreciated being led and manipulated.

We have seen J.K.'s skill at dazzling an admiring cluster of younger men, and we know that he had the ability to dominate such a group, but James's power had been modest up to leaving university. He had, in the past, dazzled young boys with his football skill, and he would, in the future, start his own magazine and thus rule a small but select band of distinguished writers. But as tutor to Eddy, unimaginable power might lie at hand. J.K. Stephen must have given this fact much thought. There is no reason why the ambitious James should not have been planning a glittering future for himself as the power behind the throne once Eddy was King – a monarch fully trained to listen to Stephen's advice and guidance and to act on such wisdom. J.K. would have been in the position of a dictator to one of the world's most powerful men. Similar dreams of power have, throughout the ages, led to disaster.

J.K. while at university had been raised in an atmosphere of intrigue. Oscar Browning, in his memoirs, asserts that jostling for power and position at the university was normal practice, carried out in an atmosphere of corruption. And the above assertions are not based purely on speculation. Stephen's brother, H.L. Stephen, wrote that his friend Harry Wilson, a man who regularly corresponded with Eddy, was being lined up as the prince's private secretary. This proves that Eddy's close friends had already worked out suitable positions of power for themselves once the time came.

It was in this atmosphere of intrigue that Eddy moved, carefully guided and watched over by his new tutor. It is easy to imagine Stephen manipulating his royal charge, weaving his web of influence. However, in seeking to dominate, it is often possible for the person who plots to become ensnared. The aphrodisiac of complete control over an important person is addictive, and the breaking of powerful dreams can cause mighty explosions. Neither James nor Eddy could have known that the seeds for a string of terrible murders were being sown.

Chapter 12

Who? And Why?

There is now only one more Ripper player to examine in detail. But first, let me pose an important question. Is it possible that members of the Royal Family and the son of a distinguished father, can be linked, however indirectly, to five penniless East End prostitutes and to their subsequent murder? And if so, how?

One renowned theory, that of my late, close friend Stephen Knight, links Prince Eddy *indirectly* to the crimes. This basic assumption is correct, but the details of Stephen Knight's theory are wrong. Several writers have accused Prince Eddy of *direct* involvement. For reasons already stated I do not believe this to be true, but it has been, in the past, a widely-held theory.

Eddy became a direct suspect in 1970. Dr Thomas Stowell, CBE, was an experienced medical man, born in 1885. He was a specialist in industrial medicine and the holder of several honorary diplomas which gained him prestigious private and governmental posts – clearly a distinguished man; a man whose word one would tend to trust and believe. In 1970, Dr Stowell claimed to have read the private papers of Sir William Gull. Gull had been born the son of a barge owner and had been raised in straitened and humble circumstances. He was, however, clearly gifted and intelligent and applied himself diligently to medicine, winning prizes and honours before gaining a teaching post at the prestigious Guy's Hospital in London. Gull's path to honours and fame was made possible in 1871; he attended and helped to cure Bertie, when the prince was close to death from typhoid fever. Gull was swiftly promoted to the post of Physician in Ordinary to Queen Victoria.

Dr Stowell caused an international sensation when he wrote in *The Criminologist* that Gull's papers had contained confidential matters which hinted that Queen Victoria's grandson might have been Jack the Ripper. For me, the interesting fact is not Sir William Gull's surreptitious naming of the killer: the interesting fact is that Sir William thought he might know the murderer's identity at all. Why, when the entire London police force was apparently baffled by the murders, should the Queen's Physician, with little obvious link to the crimes, think he knew Jack's identity? Is this further evidence of high involvement? Nigel Morland, the founding editor of *The Criminologist*, claimed that during a meeting with Inspector Frederick George Abberline, the noted detective had told him not to look for Jack the Ripper at the bottom of London society but a long way up. This assertion would make it appear that Abberline knew the identity of Jack the Ripper. I'm certain that he did.

Stephen Knight sincerely believed that he had solved the Whitechapel murders. He maintained that Eddy had met and fallen in love with a Catholic shop girl, Annie Crook. The couple secretly married and a child was born. The Establishment learned of this liaison and took Annie Crook into custody, where William Gull performed a brain operation to make her forget her past. Mary Kelly, who had been engaged to care for the Prince's child, Alice, escaped with the little girl into the East End. Here she foolishly revealed the explosive secret to four prostitutes; the five ladies then decided to try and blackmail the Establishment. But the powers behind the throne decided that the English crown might not survive such a scandal if the truth became widely known and the women were all killed to silence them: death was the Establishment's assurance of absolute silence. I was closely involved (professionally) with Stephen Knight during the writing of his book and eventually dramatised the story. As my own theories occasionally skirt close to those of my late friend's, let me analyse the above statements.

1) Prince Eddy married Annie Crook. I consider this highly unlikely. Eddy was timid and terrified of his family, especially Queen Victoria. He was also used to being led and advised, and tended not to take the initiative himself. He would not, therefore, have secretly married a shop girl, and certainly not a Catholic shop girl, knowing what the consequences would be once his secret wedding was discovered. And with Victoria's network of spies he must have known that any marriage would eventually be revealed.

2) There is documentary proof linking Eddy to homosexual activities (his discovery in a homosexual club) and reports of liaisons with sailors during his long trips at sea, but no direct proof that he ever indulged in heterosexual couplings. He was reported to have been in love with several women, including his fiancée May of Teck, who eventually married his brother, George, but these feelings could have been merely cerebral. There is certainly no documentary evidence that Eddy was ever involved with prostitutes. Given his known sexual proclivities, his known circle of friends and his known character, a love affair with a woman which drove him beyond all control is highly unlikely.

3) Mary's flight with the child. Why escape to the East End, where she and her charge could easily be identified and picked up by the authorities? An escape to France, a country with which she was apparently familiar, would have made far more sense. And where would Mary

have kept the child in the East End? There is no record of her being with any infant in Miller's Court – quite the opposite. And why did she tell the other prostitutes her secret? Mary was an intelligent woman. In order to obtain money from this affair, she would have followed the code of all blackmailers; the basis of extortion is secrecy; to reveal any confidential information undermines the power of the blackmailer. Mary's friends were frequently drunk: Mary would have known as well as anyone else that drink loosens tongues. She would have been very stupid to share her valuable knowledge and to risk her secret becoming widespread.

My own theory will reveal that Mary Kelly did indeed try to extort money from the Establishment, but not through a secret involving Eddy: the secret involved Eddy's father, the Prince of Wales. Bertie was the Victorian royal most closely associated with sexual adventures and his philandering ranged far and wide. As we have seen, Bertie explored an amazing variety of sordid adventures under the influence of his wild friend the Marquis of Hastings, amongst others. Only a few stories from these vice dens were ever recounted, but the men's antics were guided by just one principle – female beauty. A young woman's riches, social standing or marital status were not of prime importance, only a lady's looks and figure.

The notorious Victorian rake, Frank Harris, used to tell Bertie dirty jokes, 'the filthier the better'. He recounts in his autobiography (privately published in 1920) some of Bertie's sexual adventures. Several of them are so outrageous they do not bear repeating. Harris tells how Bertie would indulge in sexual adventures in the back of cabs while being driven around London. The prince dallied in the bedrooms of various friends' houses, in clubs, and on one occasion while in Scotland, overcome by lust, he tumbled one lady friend in the open in the heather. But these high-jinks took place in the main with middle class or aristocratic ladies: could Bertie, even briefly, have been involved with an East End prostitute? Once again the answer is 'yes'.

The infamous pamphlet that mercilessly lampooned Bertie's taste for low life, *The Coming Of K*, written by a knowledgeable insider, A. A. Dowty, mentions the prince's eagerness to sample any fresh loveliness who caught his eye, and mentions Bertie's 'sampling of night life in the Haymarket'. There he would have met only common prostitutes. Upper-class men who delight in adventures with women far removed from their own social standing are not uncommon. (The same standard applies equally to homosexual men. Oscar Browning was drawn towards young, uneducated males, and was known to frequently entertain young carpenters and labourers, having them stay with him in his rooms at

Cambridge.) An America writer recounted his London experiences in a book that was published in 1870:

> For the past seven years, the Prince of Wales [Bertie] has been a prominent actor in almost every scene of aristocratic dissipation and debauchery which has been enacted in the English metropolis. He is well known in the couliesses of the Opera and has openly maintained scandalous relations with ballet dancers and chorus singers ... and he has surrounded himself with pimps, panders, parasites and blackguards of the lowest kind.

Men in Victorian times would have considered such antics the behaviour of a full-blooded male – much-admired heterosexual high jinks. Bertie's love of loose women continued throughout his life. To repeat, even when, as king, he was too old and too infirm to mount, a special chair was constructed for the stout Edward, to enable prostitutes to provide oral stimulation.

Given Bertie's wild behaviour and known enthusiasm for loose women, a link with Mary Kelly becomes a distinct possibility. But where could he have met her? At a wild West End party? Mary had confided to Joe Barnett that before arriving in Whitechapel she had worked in a high-class West End brothel. There is no reason why she should not have maintained contact with people and friends from the past. Research shows that Mary was not a coarse girl but a well-educated woman who had a temper and a wild adventurous spirit – just the kind of personality that might have appealed to Bertie. However, Bertie and Mary probably did not meet in the West End. During my researches, I have uncovered the extraordinary fact that Bertie, along with Sir George Chetwynd, Lord Richard Grosvenor and several other wild friends, rented a flat in Watling Street, bordering on the territory around which Mary solicited. (This flat and further details will form part of my final thesis.) This is a natural link between the prostitute and the Prince. While the Prince, or one of his wild friends, travelled incognito towards Whitechapel, they might easily have spied Mary, who would have been natural prey for such men. Did Bertie bed Mary in Watling Street? If so, did he impregnate her?

Bertie's wild behaviour, including infidelities with countless women, had become widely known over a long period and his lifestyle had gained general acceptance, but this acceptance would have been strained to breaking point by a liaison with an East End prostitute; consorting with a low-class woman – or even a high-class woman – would have raised the greatest of alarm among the Establishment if two complications had arisen: *pregnancy* and *Catholicism*. Pregnancy by itself was bad enough. There were many claims that the Prince had fathered illegitimate children, and, given the number of affairs into which Bertie plunged, that is not unlikely. It was strongly rumoured that Lady Susan Pelham-Clinton, who was a close friend of the Prince of Wales, had given birth to his child. One of the Lady's advisers is said to have kept Bertie regularly informed about the progress of Susan's pregnancy. But for the Prince to sire a child with a titled lady was one thing; for him to sire a child with an East End prostitute was a different, dangerous matter. However, the most explosive issue of all would be for a member of the Victorian Royal Family to sire a child with a Roman Catholic, low-class whore or not. That would be dynamite waiting for a match to be struck. It cannot be too strongly expressed how unpopular such a coupling would be in Victorian times.

An attempt in the eighteenth-century to emancipate the Catholics led to violent rioting in London led by Lord George Gordon. Both the Government and the magistrates were intimidated and troops had to be called out onto the streets. Hugh Walpole, writing from his house in Twickenham, recounted the riots in a series of letters:

> [On 8 June, 1780]: Lord Mansfield's house was just burnt down, and at night there were shocking disorders. [And on 9 June]: Yesterday was some slaughter in Fleet Street – they have exacted sums from many houses to avoid being burnt as Popish ... Kirkgate saw men and women lying dead in the streets under barrows as he came home yesterday ... whole families ruined, wives that tried to drag their husband out of the mobs.

During betrothal arrangements between Queen Victoria and Albert the question of Catholicism had been discussed. There was a rumour that the forbidden religion was not unknown in Albert's family tree so Victoria wrote anxiously to her beloved on 22 November 1839 asking, on behalf of Lord Melbourne (the then Prime Minister) for a short history of the House of Saxe-Coburg. Her letter continues:

> ... he wishes to hear this in order to make people here know exactly who your ancestors are, for a few stupid people here try to say you are a Catholic ... [Albert was not.]

Violent demonstrations against Catholicism had taken place during the 1850s; an Anglican vicar had been attacked for merely placing candles on his altar and dressing his choirboys in surplices; such actions were construed as being a step towards Catholicism. That was the strength of feeling against the religion. Even that extraordinary royal servant, John Brown, was occasionally heard to mutter, 'Nasty beggars, those Catholic clergy'. It is perhaps difficult to understand in this age the deeply-rooted fear of the Church of Rome by the nineteenth-century Protestant population; hatred had passed down from decade to decade, century to century, fed by a knowledge of the Church's unquenchable zeal (dating back to the Middle Ages and still not forgotten) for hunting down heretics and for crushing, if possible, all opposition to Catholicism.

Soon after Bertie was born the King of Saxony was ruled out as one of his godfather's 'because he was a Catholic', causing great offence to the Coburgs. In 1890, a betrothal between Eddy and the Princess Hélène d'Orléans was seriously discussed, but the lady was a Catholic. When the Prime Minister, Lord Salisbury, was asked whether Princess Hélène might retain her religion after marriage to Eddy, provided that any children would be raised as Protestants, Salisbury warned that the country's anger against such a union might endanger the position of the throne. Let me repeat the Prime Minster's authoritative decision for emphasis. The marriage of a Victorian royal, even to another royal, '*might endanger the position of the throne*' (my italics) merely because the high-bred lady was a Catholic. Even today Catholicism would impede a union with a member of Britain's Royal Family.

Given the above facts, it is clear that the Establishment would be alarmed in the extreme if it believed that Bertie could be linked to a pregnant Catholic East End prostitute. If this liaison leaked out, the Establishment would no doubt fear that the throne might be in danger – given the vacillating feelings towards the Crown in Victorian times. Indeed, the Establishment's fears are confirmed by no less a person than Queen Victoria herself. At her request, William Gladstone (another of Queen Victoria's Prime Ministers and an unpopular one with Her Majesty) wrote to tell Bertie that the throne of England was safe only so long as the nation had confidence in the personal character of the sovereign. Yet the nation clearly did not have that confidence.

In 1871 a pamphlet entitled *What Does She Do With It?* referred to Queen Victoria's rapaciousness. In late September 1871 Gladstone saw an advertisement for the pamphlet and remarked, 'Things go from bad to worse.' He then commented, 'The Queen is invisible and the Prince of Wales is not respected.' Clearly, from time to time, even the Government feared for the Crown's stability, as did the Crown itself. As late as February 1888, just months before the commencement of the Ripper murders, the *East London Observer* opined, 'There is grave reason to fear that a social revolution is impending'. Contemporary opinion at all levels signalled the deepest social discontent among sections of the population; moreover, the Queen's unpopularity took firm root after she had gone into seclusion following the death of Albert. There were six attempts on her life, culminating in an unemployed Scotsman firing shots at her on Windsor Station in 1882. On her few public appearances, Victoria was, from time to time, hissed or booed. The *National*

Reformer commented that: 'Her Majesty, by doing nothing except receiving her civil list, is teaching the country that it can get along quite well without a monarch.'

E.F. Benson, writing in 1933, summed up anti-monarchy feeling succinctly:

> ...the report [of a breach of neutrality in the Franco-Prussian War] fanned public feeling against them both [Victoria and Bertie], and there was widespread agitation for the establishment of a Republic in England. Further fuel was piled on from other sources of discontent with the monarchy: the Queen's continued seclusion, already extremely unpopular, was added to the blaze and speakers in newly-founded Republican clubs all over the country produced figures to show what the country spent on a sovereign whom her subjects never saw, and who must be laying by enormous sums contributed by taxpayers who received no benefit whatever from her existence. Bertie similarly had an income from the country of over a hundred thousand pounds; certainly he, unlike his mother, spent it all, and was supposed to be heavily in debt. But the manner of his spending was as objectionable as his mother's saving, for it was all poured down the sink of his private life, and went in gambling and in betting ... With a sovereign who was never seen ... and an heir-apparent who appeared too often where he should not, England would do very well to be rid of them. And all this was not merely gutter-talk; Mr Gladstone, the Prime Minister, told both the absentee mother and the too-frequently-present son that he was seriously disturbed about it.

Queen Victoria had periods of popularity with the masses, but these periods alternated with moods of the opposite humour. In 1870 Bertie was enveloped in a scandal which resulted in his appearance in a court of law – a scandal in itself. Sir Charles Mordaunt sued his wife for divorce. The indiscreet Lady Mordaunt had, in a fit of guilt, confessed to her husband that she had been unfaithful to him. The Prince of Wales was named among a string of lovers and he was subpoenaed to appear as a witness. As Bertie had indeed been engaging in frequent sexual intercourse with the lady (presumably dodging the other lovers) he was in a difficult position. However, in the witness box, under oath, he denied any improper relationship with the lady, thereby committing perjury. On this occasion Bertie was saved by Lady Mordaunt's father, Sir Thomas Moncrieff: with ruthless ingenuity he had his daughter certified as insane when she made the allegations. Temporary insanity was confirmed by leading doctors, the judge accepted this evidence, and thus Mordaunt lost his case. This is a blatant example of one member of the Establishment lying in order to save fellow members of the Establishment, even to the extent of vilifying a daughter and breaking the Hippocratic Oath. Plainly no sacrifice was too great for Queen and Country.

The Mordaunt case naturally increased gossip about Bertie's private life. It was alleged that he was heavily in debt to French money-lenders and that they were beginning to harass him for repayment. He was hissed at and booed during public appearances. On one occasion rotten fruit was thrown at him. As we have seen, cartoons began to lampoon the prince mercilessly, and it was not until a year after the Mordaunt affair that public sympathy was regained by the prince. He became seriously ill with typhoid fever and was thought likely to die. Bertie's recovery signalled a wave of popularity, but subsequent scandals, including a second appearance in court (in a slander case over cheating at cards) led to a further dimming of the public's affections.

In the 1870s virulent outbursts of Republicanism must have alarmed the many members of the Government who had warned about the dangers of such movements. One leading Republican declared that the monarchy was 'the master of fraud that shelters all others'. The death in 1883 of the much-favoured royal servant, John Brown, renewed speculation about his true relationship with the Queen. Persistent rumours that Victoria and John had been secretly married and that the union had produced a child did not add to the Monarch's popularity.

On 8 February 1886 a series of meetings and marches were organised to highlight, among other things, the plight of the unemployed. After parading through the heart of London the marches were to culminate in Trafalgar Square, where a mixture of leading Socialist and Marxist speakers would address the crowd. This meeting, which became known as Black Monday, led to a series of violent disturbances and a not unexpected confrontation with the police. Queen Victoria wrote to her Prime Minister, Mr Gladstone:

The Queen cannot sufficiently express her indignation at the monstrous riot which took place the other day in London, and which risked people's lives and was a momentary triumph of socialism and disgrace to the capital. If steps, and very strong ones, are not speedily taken to put these proceedings down with a high hand, to punish severely the real ringleaders, and to 'probe to the bottom' as Mr Gladstone has promised, the whole affair, the Government will suffer severely. The effect abroad is already very humiliating to this country.

If Queen Victoria was outraged by the 1886 disturbances, the serious riots one year later, known as Bloody Sunday, must have been even more distressing. In 1887, only one year before the Ripper murders, Sir

Charles Warren decided to ban meetings in Trafalgar Square, which had become a favoured venue for political gatherings. Socialists and Marxists drew large crowds to this central meeting place to listen to fiery messages of revolution. Many people decided to ignore Warren's ban and converged on central London, but were prevented from entering Trafalgar Square by baton-wielding police. Despite this the Square eventually filled up, and armed guards and mounted police were ordered into action against a crowd of around 100,000. In the ensuing battle hundreds of civilians were injured and two were killed. Memories of this battle soured relations between the working classes and the police for decades.

In 1888 the centenary of the French Revolution was approaching and the national newspapers were certain to comment on this insurrection. That thought may have alarmed the powers behind the throne. There was also the rise of Communism to contend with. Eleanor Marx was repeating her father's famous slogan:

> ...[Communist] ends can only be attained by the forcible overthrow of all existing social conditions. Let the ruling class tremble at the communist revolution. The proletarians have nothing to lose but their chains. They have a world to win. Workers of all countries unite.

These powerful words were reinforced by the blazing voice of George Bernard Shaw who, along with other committed and vociferous socialists, had pledged solidarity with the communists. Only one year earlier, in 1887, Lenin's brother Alexander – despite stirring speeches during his trial – had been executed in Russia for an attempt on the Czar's life. The Czar was, of course, closely related to the British Royal Family.

With such violent contemporary events and with disturbed social forces to brood over, the possibility of further insurrection in the land would have greatly alarmed the Establishment, and there are few forces more ruthless than a powerful State when it feels threatened and has to protect its own interests. It was in this atmosphere of massive discontent and civil strife, with a growing voice for Republicanism, that the Establishment found itself embroiled in 1888.

It is my contention that during this disturbed period, Mary Kelly, an East End Catholic prostitute, selected a reliable contact and announced to him that she was carrying the Prince of Wales's child. Given the above considerations, if the Establishment thought that there might be any reason whatsoever for believing this statement, it is easy to see that panic would have ensued throughout the corridors of Power. And given Bertie's record of sexual conquests, and given his extraordinary accommodation arrangements in Watling Street with his wild friends, there would be every reason to believe such a story. So – leaving aside the question of parentage, was Mary pregnant? Many recorded opinions say 'yes'.

On the morning following Mary's supposed death, Caroline Maxwell said that she remarked to Mary, after she had been sick, 'I pity your feelings'. Many people think this remark interpreted the nausea as morning sickness. The highly-regarded Ripper authority Donald Rumbelow, a former policeman, boldly states in his book *The Complete Jack the Ripper*:

> Kelly, not quite three months pregnant and probably feeling the effects of morning sickness, was generally too unwell to solicit for much custom.

A retired detective from New Scotland Yard, Arthur Butler, writing about the Ripper killings for *The Sun* in 1972, stated that he knew Mary Kelly had told acquaintances that she was pregnant and that she was getting rid of the child; that could have meant abortion; on the other hand, could it have meant adoption? Were arrangements already in place? However, it was established that the body found in Miller's Court was *not* pregnant, despite rumours to the contrary. General gossip indicated that the uterus of the corpse had been removed and taken away by the killer. This was not so, as Doctor Thomas Bond's autopsy makes clear; the report mentions the uterus. This would undoubtedly have been examined, and if the body had been pregnant this would been mentioned. (There would have been little point in mentioning that the body was not pregnant, as that was not an issue.) So was the body found in Miller's Court a substitute corpse? I believe that that was the case.

∽

Let us recapitulate:

QUESTION. Is there any evidence of an official cover-up during the Ripper crimes?

ANSWER. A considerable amount. The press remarked on an official cover-up several times. Vital witnesses were not called into court to give evidence, and facts were suppressed. Sir Charles Warren clearly and blatantly prevented the Goulston Street graffiti from being seen. During Mary Kelly's inquest the law was broken, official papers were not signed and the affair was rushed through in one day and closed with indecent haste.

QUESTION. What class of person would merit such an extraordinary bending of the law?

ANSWER. Only the very highest in the land, meaning a member of the Royal Family or possibly one or two very senior politicians. From this group, the only person known to be actively associated with the services of prostitutes was the Prince of Wales.

QUESTION. Given the above evidence of a cover-up by the authorities, is it possible that Mary might have met with Bertie, and might sexual relations have taken place?

ANSWER. Considering Bertie's known tastes, I can give an emphatic 'yes'. Given the use of the borrowed flat in Watling Street, near to Mary's soliciting area, a meeting with Mary, a capricious, unpredictable girl, is distinctly possible. Mary would have attracted the prince – Bertie was also capricious and unpredictable.

QUESTION. Would there be any need to protect the Crown from deep scandal by so drastic a measure as a cover-up?

ANSWER. Given the abundant evidence contained in this chapter regarding the Crown's precarious position, an official cover-up at any cost would be vital.

QUESTION. Is it likely that high authority would dare to sanction a manipulation of the law?

ANSWER. Yes. We saw an example of this manipulation during the Mordaunt divorce scandal and over Prince Eddy's clandestine homosexual affairs. Indeed, several times recently I have seen, in various newspapers, suspicions of a police cover-up in various scandals, even though in the twenty-first century we have a powerful, often intrusive investigative press, and probing television programmes. In the Victorian age the police had far less accountability than present-day forces. In 1888 East Enders knew little about politics; they did not even recognise their Royal Family in person. Authority and the upper classes, within certain limits, carried on as they pleased. In 1888 the Police Force had only been in existence for around six decades. This was enough time for it to become a law unto itself without becoming accountable for its actions. Recently a serving police officer (who has studied the history of the Police Force since its founding by Sir Robert Peel) said to me, 'Until 1972, no one – not even serving officers and certainly not the public at large – dared to question the decisions of the higher authority in the police force. Whatever was said or done went unchallenged.' Such unquestioned and dangerous power would have applied even more strongly in the nineteenth century.

✎

If Mary Kelly became pregnant soon after meeting Bertie, it need not have mattered whether the Prince, one of her clients, or Joe Barnett was the real father. Being intelligent, Mary would have realised the vast opportunities which involving Bertie in a plausible paternity suit could bring. The authorities' actions indicate that they believed Kelly's story, so let us, for interest's sake, consider all the various possibilities inherent in this situation.

1) Kelly, knowing Bertie's reputation, might have dreamed up a promising blackmail plot. The Prince was, of course, a prime target for extortion, and, in later years, there was at least one documented blackmail attempt, when indiscreet love letters to his mistress, the beautiful Frances, Countess of Warwick ('Darling Daisy') got into the wrong hands.

2) Mary might have attended a party at which the Prince of Wales was present without actually meeting him, but, from this experience, she dreamed up her pregnancy story.

3) Mary might have been to the Prince's East End flat and engaged in sexual intercourse with Bertie *without* becoming pregnant. In Victorian times, prostitutes must have been adept at avoiding pregnancy.

4) Mary might have been impregnated by one of her clients or by Joe Barnett, but with a stroke of cunning, after relations with Bertie, she might have devised a plan whereby she could convincingly claim that the child belonged to the Prince of Wales.

If Mary approached the Establishment in the hope of money on any of the above four pretexts, then she would have been guilty of blackmail. But, as we have already mentioned, it is a distinct possibility that Mary did indeed meet Bertie in intimate surroundings; if so, sexual intercourse would almost certainly have taken place and the prostitute might (perhaps deliberately) have become pregnant. In this case, if Bertie *was* responsible for impregnating Mary, then her demands for support would not have been blackmail in the accepted sense of the word. Any woman in a similar situation would have expected to be cared for lavishly. It is my contention that Mary *was* genuinely carrying a royal child and felt entitled to some support, as any woman would. So in what way could she have approached the Establishment with her demands?

Chapter 13

Montague Druitt

The last link in our Ripper puzzle involves Montague John Druitt. Druitt was born in Wimborne, Dorset on 15 August 1857, and, like J.K. Stephen, he came from an eminently respectable family. His father William was a highly-regarded surgeon and a Justice of the Peace who was described in the *Wimborne Guardian* as having been 'a strong churchman'. Might Montague have been raised in a repressed religious atmosphere? William married his wife Ann in 1854 and the union produced seven children – a first son (named after the father), then Montague, then five more offspring. Ann brought her own wealth into the partnership and the couple, with their seven children, lived in spacious comfort in one of Wimborne's finest houses.

Montague displayed intellectual ability early in life, when, aged thirteen, he won a scholarship to the prestigious Winchester College, whose students were known as 'Wykehamists' after the founder, William of Wykeham. At Winchester, Montague would have been subjected to the typical harsh regime which was prevalent at Victorian public schools. Conditions at Winchester during the 1820s were outlined by F.D. How:

> Chapel was at 6.00 a.m. Morning school at 7.30, after which an excursion had frequently to be made to the top of St Catherine's Hill, an apparently useless process to which the conservatism of Winchester clung, and which went by the name of 'Morning Hills'.

Strict discipline was maintained at the school during Montague's time. A contemporary describes Dr George Moberly (headmaster until a few years before Montague's arrival) taking studies in classical literature. He asked a pupil to translate a section of work by the great Roman poet Horace. The boy's efforts to read the verse, *Decende caelo et dic age tibia*, produced 'Come down from heaven and give us a tune'. Dr Moberly was outraged by this vulgar lack of learning and ordered the boy to be flogged. There was a set routine for this procedure. The boy was made to kneel down, his clothing rolled up as high as the waist, then a rod with four long apple twigs attached was used by Dr Moberly to administer from four to six lashes.

Pupils at Winchester were raised in a strongly religious atmosphere and they were made to submit to the infamous 'fagging' system. Flogging, both from the masters and from senior students, was prevalent. However the harshness of public school life did not seem to deter Montague: he achieved success in his studies, he was clever in debates, and he became an excellent and devoted cricketer. A memorable anecdote, found in Tom Cullen's book *Autumn of Terror*, records that Druitt: '. . . championed Wordsworth against his detractors, finding it a great merit on the part of the poet that he was a '*bulwark of Protestantism.*' (My italics.) After gaining distinction at Winchester Druitt was awarded a scholarship to Oxford; he graduated with a BA in 1880. After a break Montague decided on a career in law, which meant a further period of study. To underwrite his legal examinations for admittance to the Bar, Montague was forced to borrow from his father. From this borrowing there might be hints that the son did not find complete favour with his father; when William died he left an estate of over £16,000, a very large sum in the 1880s. The main assets were shared between Ann, the three daughters and William junior. Montague, along with two brothers, received very little; his share was an ungenerous £500, and deducted from this was the money Montague had been forced to borrow against educational expenses. This rider was a niggardly gesture on the part of his father, especially when one considers that in Victorian times it was considered mandatory for rich parents to pay for their sons' education.

Montague became a registered barrister in 1885 and a few months later he rented chambers. Several commentators (not paid critics but commentators, who, apparently, have never heard of circumstantial evidence) have opined that there is no evidence to show that Montague Druitt and J.K. Stephen knew each other. Well, J.K.'s two brothers had chambers very near to Druitt, who was at 9, King's Bench Walk; Harry Stephen was at 3, King's Bench Walk; Herbert Stephen had offices directly opposite King's Bench Walk. Further, J.K. had chambers very close to King's Bench Walk at Lincoln's Inn. It appears to be beyond some peoples' reasoning that two barrister brothers might know a potential rival who worked a few doors away from their office. I contend that they most certainly would. Isn't it likely that J.K. would visit his brothers from time to time? That places him directly outside Druitt's offices. Two young, attractive, homosexual men would only have needed to catch a glimpse of each other to become interested. The Stephens' father was a high court judge who would have been interested in all members of the legal profession. Yet apparently some people are convinced that J.K. Stephen would have been totally unaware of Druitt.

Furthermore, J.K. was Eddy's tutor. Those excellent researchers Keith Skinner and Martin Howell have uncovered an important fact. Druitt was invited to a ball that included Eddy on the guest list, which places the two men in the same room; J.K. Stephen tutored Eddy; that forms a link between all three men. Then again, I coupled the men on the strength of the Goulston Street graffiti. New evidence will outline why I find the graffiti such an important part of my Ripper investigation. Only the most obtuse would refuse to acknowledge that there are many facts that point towards Druitt and Stephen knowing each other.

Montague's legal career did not flourish, a not unusual state of affairs in the 1880s. A contemporary of Druitt, George R. Sims, a journalist and dramatist, wrote that only one in eight who were called to the Bar made a living from the law:

> ...the life of men who have come enthusiastic to the law and have utterly failed would fill as many pages as are contained in a complete set of law reports.

This is confirmed by my own researches. *London Souvenirs*, written in 1899 by C.W. Heckthorn, contains an anecdote on the above subject:

> Success at the Bar comes to barristers in the most capricious manner. In this profession, as in many other pursuits, modest merit but slowly makes its way. Manners maketh the man, but impudence an advocate; without this latter quality even high connections and powerful patronage often seems ineffectual. Earl Camden, the son of Chief Justice Pratt, was called to the Bar in his twenty-fourth year, and remained a briefless barrister for nine long years, when he resolved to abandon Westminster Hall for his College Fellowship...

Montague Druitt kept his chambers until his death, and although he was one of the many luckless barristers who received no briefs, and although he was without any appreciable inheritance from his father, Montague appeared to enjoy a comfortable lifestyle. He had had the foresight to provide extra earnings by taking a teaching job in a private school at 9 Eliot Place, Blackheath in 1881. It is clear, however, that his schoolmaster's salary did not allow the accumulation of savings, as, in 1882, he was borrowing against his meagre inheritance to pay for his legal training. The owner and Headmaster of the successful school at which Druitt taught was George Valentine. Unfortunately, little information about the school, and no information about Druitt's life while he taught there, can be unearthed: but we do know that in 1881 Druitt indulged his passion for sport by joining the Morden Cricket Club in Blackheath, where he became treasurer.

It is a generally accepted fact that Montague received no legal work whatsoever once he became empowered to practise law, but the invaluable Paul Begg discovered that the law lists of 1887 cite Druitt in employment as a 'special pleader'. Pleading was an occupation mainly undertaken by law students who were not yet fully qualified to practise at the Bar. The job mainly entailed advisory work and assistance in civil cases. In pleading, a writ outlining the harm which a plaintiff has suffered is sent to the defendant, who, in reply, returns his defence. In Druitt's time the position was between counsel and attorney; special pleaders no longer exist, but in late Victorian times the work provided a good grounding for students before they were called to the Bar. But Montague *had* been called to the Bar. Perhaps he was especially short of cash in 1887 when he took on work that was clearly below his abilities and his status as a barrister? Puzzlingly, Druitt was able to save a considerable sum of money while he was teaching. When he died in December 1888 his estate amounted to around £1,300, most of which he had presumably earned personally: the above figure assumes that he had about half of his father's legacy over after paying for educational expenses. Money was later added to the estate posthumously by his mother's will.

In late Victorian times £1,300 was a very considerable sum – around £93,600 based on today's figures, using the retail price index of £1 in 1888 equalling around £72 in today's money. Yet Montague's salary as a teacher would have been around £200 per annum, and we know that he was penniless in 1882, as he was forced to borrow against his inheritance.

Let us examine Druitt's savings more closely. The cheque for £16 found on his body might well have represented one month's wages – that would fit in with a salary of £200 per annum. There was, of course, his work as a pleader. I have tried to ascertain from a number of sources how much Druitt might have earned from pleading, but it has proved impossible to quantify accurately. The amount would have depended upon the nature of the case being tried, the eminence of the barrister involved, and, of course, on the number of jobs Druitt was able to undertake. The pay for such work would have been reasonably generous, but as Druitt was a full-time school teacher, with a considerable number of evening and weekend responsibilities at several sporting clubs, it is difficult to know how much time he could have spent at his extracurricular legal activities; surely not enough time to accumulate considerable savings? And, of course, had the pleading work been regular and lucrative, Druitt would have been able to give up teaching to follow his chosen profession.

We must now consider why Druitt took up pleading in the first place. The obvious reason would be that by 1887 he was short of money. So short that he was willing to accept work for which he was overqualified. There were rigid social barriers in Victorian times, and for a barrister to accept a pleader's job must have meant some loss of face. The fact that Druitt found and accepted such work indicates an urgent need for extra income during 1887. This would make sense. From the time that Montague had been called to the Bar he had had the expense of setting up his legal practice (very costly); the expense of maintaining chambers at King's Bench Walk; the expenses of day-to-day living; lodging expenses if he was not resident at Eliot Place; travelling expenses; clothing expenses, and expenses relating to his many sporting activities. Could this full financial load, along with considerable savings, have been achieved on the modest income of a school teacher? Almost certainly not; so it not surprising that Druitt accepted extra work of any kind to supplement his regular income. But this creates another puzzle. It is inconceivable that Druitt, even with the pleader's job, could have saved the equivalent in today's money of £93,600 during the last two years of his life. Therefore, the large estate left in his will should have meant that he was already financially comfortable in 1887, with considerable cash savings. If that was the case, why did he need to accept further, socially inferior, work? There seems to be no logical explanation for Druitt's fortune. Could there be sinister reasons behind his nest egg?

After the death of her husband the mental health of Ann Druitt began to deteriorate. By July 1888 she required full-time treatment for her problems at an asylum in Clapton, East London. It was only one month later, at the end of August, that the first Ripper murder was committed.

At the end of November 1888, Montague's career at Eliot's Place, Blackheath, came to an abrupt end when he was summarily dismissed from his teaching post by Mr Valentine. Reports of this affair are sketchy, and we have details of the dismissal mainly from testimony given by William junior at his younger brother's inquest. William told the coroner that after he had been informed that Montague appeared to be missing, he had gone to the school in Blackheath where he was told that his brother had 'got into serious trouble and had been dismissed'. Clearly William had heard of no trouble brewing in his brother's affairs, which would indicate that the dismissal was peremptory. The most common speculation for this discharge has been that Montague had an improper relationship with one of the boys, but this is only inspired guesswork. Druitt's previous record of behaviour does not indicate the likelihood of such conduct, although a sudden and forbidden uncharacteristic passion cannot be ruled out, and it is difficult to think of any other reason for so abrupt a termination of employment without, one assumes, any notice whatsoever. Shortly after his dismissal from the school Druitt was dead. The *Acton Chiswick and Turnham Green*

Gazette of 5 January 1889, gives a full account of events concerning Druitt's death:

> FOUND DROWNED. Shortly after midday on Monday, a waterman named Winslade, of Chiswick, found the body of a man, well-dressed, floating in the Thames off Thornycroft's. He at once informed a constable, and without delay the body was at once conveyed to the mortuary. On Wednesday afternoon, Dr. Diplock, coroner, held the inquest at the Lamb Tap, when the following evidence was adduced:- William H. Druitt said he lived at Bournemouth and was a solicitor. The deceased was his brother, who was 31 last birthday. He was a barrister-at-law, and an assistant master at a school in Blackheath ... witness heard from a friend on 11 December that deceased had not been heard of at his chambers for more than a week. Witness then went to London to make inquiries, and at Blackheath he found that the deceased had got into serious trouble at the school, and had been dismissed. That was on 30 December. Witness had deceased's things searched where he resided, and found a paper addressed to him (produced). The coroner read this letter, which was to the effect:- 'Since Friday I felt that I was going to be like mother, and the best thing was for me to die.' Witness continuing, said deceased had never made any attempt on his life before. His mother became insane in July last. He had no other relative...

There are several curious features in this report. Firstly, there is the statement by William that Montague had no other relative. This is patently untrue. Montague was one of seven children and he was the first one to die, so why did William, himself a solicitor, stand in a court of law and blatantly lie? And is there any significance in the statement: '...witness had the deceased's things searched where he resided...'? Might not William have been expected to search through his brother's things personally, or did he want an independent witness to find Montague's suicide note? The Gazette continued with a report on the finding of Druitt's body:

> ...Henry Winslade was the next witness. He said that he lived at No. 4, Shore Street, Paxton Road, and that he was a waterman. About one o'clock on Monday, he was on the river in a boat, when he saw the body floating. The tide was at half flood running up. He brought the body ashore and gave information to the police. PC George Moulson, 216 T said he searched the body, which was fully dressed, excepting the hat and collar. He found four large stones in each pocket in the top coat; £2.10s in gold, 7s in silver, 2p in bronze, two cheques on the London and Provincial Bank (one for

£50 and the other for £16), a first-class season ticket from Blackheath to London (South Western Railways), a second-half return Hammersmith to Charing Cross (dated 1 December), a silver watch, gold chain with silver guinea attached, a pair of kid gloves, and a white handkerchief. There were no marks of injury on the body, but it was rather decomposed. A verdict of suicide whilst in unsound mind was returned.

This appears to be a full and highly detailed report of the proceedings. Yet as Montague had been dramatically dismissed from his post, his sacking may well have affected the balance of his mind which could help to explain the suicide. He was dismissed from the school on 30 November, which was a Friday, obviously the day referred in his suicide note. It is, therefore, surprising that the coroner did not want to know why Montague had been dismissed, though one can understand William not volunteering such information if the details were sordid. As this was an article for a provincial newspaper, which would have been only too eager to deal in scandal, it is unlikely that the reporter would have failed to include details of Montague's dismissal if they had been discussed in open court. It has generally been accepted that Druitt died on 3 December, but, as the invaluable *The Jack the Ripper A to Z* points out, the death might have occurred on 1 December, a date which would be confirmed by the return ticket found on the body.

Druitt's known actions paint a strange picture of a man in a suicidal state of mind. After writing a note plainly indicating that he intends to take his life, Montague keeps in his pocket a large sum of cash and several cheques for impressive amounts. He dons his gold chain and silver watch and collects a pair of fine gloves. Then he walks to Blackheath Station and travels to London (Charing Cross). Here, if we accept the date of his death as 1 December, he must have bought a return ticket to Hammersmith. He then travels to Hammersmith and throws himself into the Thames, although there is a long stretch of the River only one minute's walk from where his journey from Blackheath had ended. And why did Montague travel into London to find a river in the first place?

I used to frequently visit friends at Blackheath; the reaches of Greenwich are not too far distant. If Montague had walked across the heath and down Croom's Hill, he would have reached a long stretch of the Thames into which he could have jumped. There is an unreal air about a person who, having decided to commit suicide, dresses himself in all his finery, keeps very large sums of money on his person, then takes two train journeys (buying a return ticket on one of them) to his death. Even given the fact that an unbalanced person's actions cannot be explained, a long, solitary walk seems a more likely choice for a man with deep suicidal urges than several train journeys to a specific spot. As the diligent and intelligent Ripper researchers Martin Howells and Keith Skinner comment:

> ...are we to assume that he [Druitt] wished to prolong his life just long enough to jump off his favourite bridge? The hypothesis is ludicrous, and yet if we are to accept William's statement, that is what we must believe. At the very least, we can see how imperative was the coroner's need to ascertain the last person to see Montague alive; the fact that he did not even try, when a report about this barrister's death was being prepared for the Home Office, is highly suspicious...

Precisely. Here is further evidence of irregular conduct in a court of law, and once again the death of a subject linked to the Ripper murders was not fully investigated. Why?

The first positive indications that Druitt might be involved in the Ripper murders came from Sir Melville Macnaghten. He was clearly fascinated by the case and wrote extensively on the subject, as we have seen from the highly-placed police officer's comments in Chapter 4. Macnaghten stated that: '...the Whitechapel murderer had five victims and five victims only...' There are two available versions of Macnaghten's confidential report on the murders, one version still on Scotland Yard files and one version which was copied by Sir Melville's daughter, Lady Christabel Aberconway, from her father's original notes. After discussing the case of a popular suspect, Thomas Cutbush (who enjoyed lightly stabbing ladies around the buttocks), Sir Melville wrote:

> ...I may mention the cases of three men, any one of whom would have been more likely than Cutbush to have committed this series of murders:-
>
> 1) A Mr M.J. Druitt, said to be a doctor and of good family, who disappeared at the time of the Miller's Court murder, and whose body (which was said to have been upwards of a month in the water) was found in the Thames on 31st Dec. – or about 7 weeks after that murder. He was sexually insane and from private info I have little doubt but that his own family believed him to have been the murderer...

M.J. Druitt was, of course, a barrister, but he came from a medical background and Sir Melville was writing some years after the events (in 1894) from memory. It is quite clear that his suspect was Montague. And equally clearly, the remark 'from private info' means that Sir Melville had been told more than he was prepared to reveal: what could that have been, and why was he not prepared to reveal it? Sir Melville's second choice falls on 'Kosminski, a Polish Jew', and his third candidate is 'a Russian doctor, Michael Ostrog'. However, by 1914, the year in which Sir Melville's memoirs were published, the two latter suspects had been dropped and his opinion had focused sharply on to one man:

> I incline to the belief that the individual [Jack the Ripper] who held up London in terror resided with his own people; that he absented himself from home at certain times, and that he committed suicide on or about the 10th November, 1888.

Despite the incorrect minor detail (Druitt did not live at home) and despite the incorrect date in the memoirs (December would have been more accurate; Montague died in the first week of that month), it is clear that Sir Melville was referring to Druitt. Macnaghten's proud boast of 'working from memory' would account for the errors. So we must wonder again what the highly-placed policeman's 'private info' could have been? And why would he not reveal it? There was no compunction about discussing the case in detail in every other respect. Who was being protected?

Sir Melville was not the only one to suspect Druitt. William Bachert, who, by 1890 had taken over the chairmanship of the Vigilance Committee, continued to pester the police over the Ripper case. There are claims that, after being sworn to secrecy, Bachert was told that the murderer had drowned at the end of 1888. Why were the authorities so certain? In 1924, Sir Basil Thomson, who had access to the records of Scotland Yard, stated that the police believed Jack to have been an insane Russian medical student 'whose body was found floating in the Thames immediately after the last of the outrages.' This is clearly a garbled version of Druitt's death.

J.F. Moylan, writing about Scotland Yard in 1929, stated that there was public anger against the police and the CID because of their failure to arrest Jack the Ripper. It is now certain that the murderer, Mr Moylan maintains, '. . . escaped justice by committing suicide at the end of 1888'. Clearly Druitt was a favourite police suspect, but this was kept secret from the public for a great many years. Hargreave Lee Adam, a former member of the CID turned crime writer, wrote in the introduction to his 1930 book *The Trial of George Chapman* that three leading policemen, Dr (later Sir) Robert Anderson, Major Henry Smith and Sir Melville Macnaghten had all told him that the police knew the identity of the Ripper. Macnaghten added that he had documentary proof of the killer's name but he had burned the papers, which, if true, is the most extraordinary behaviour for a policeman in his position: but then, as we shall see in the final chapter, an inordinate amount of official material that referred to Jack the Ripper was burned. And what was the evidence that convinced Sir Melville Macnaghten that Montague's own family suspected their relative? Why was that evidence not stated in court during Montague's inquest? William, the brother, a solicitor trained in the ways of law, had ample opportunity to speak out.

As we have seen, the whole ambience of Montague's last journey was that of a man travelling to a pre-arranged meeting, probably somewhere in Hammersmith; could he therefore have been murdered? And if so, by whom, and why? One further puzzle: the cheque for £50 found on the body, translated into today's money would equal around £3,600. Who gave Druitt a cheque for such an amount and why did the authorities not probe the matter and find out where the money came from? With all the bank details to hand it would have been a straightforward matter to investigate. It is unlikely that a part-time job as a lowly pleader would have provided such a large sum. Even the £16 cheque represents almost £1,155 today; and Druitt was carrying today's equivalent of over £216 in cash – in all, a sum of almost £5,000 in today's money was on Druitt's body when it was recovered from the River Thames. Why does a man, who is on his way to commit suicide, stuff his pockets with such an enormous amount of money? Indeed, Druitt's life and death contain many mysteries still to be examined. First, for clarity's sake, let us once again list the main points in this complicated story.

‿

On Friday, 31 August 1888, in the middle of the night, a middle-aged prostitute, Mary Nichols, was murdered and mutilated. She was found lying sprawled on her back on a London pavement. Although people were spending fretful nights in houses overlooking the murder site, no unusual sounds were heard. Nichols, before her death, had boasted about her new bonnet.

One week later, another middle-aged prostitute, Annie Chapman, who resided mainly at an address only a few minutes' walk from Nichols's favoured doss-house, was discovered at dawn in the back yard of a common lodging-house. Annie had been murdered and mutilated. Her pocket had been cut open and rifled, and its contents had been laid out beside her body. Although the yard was in constant use, both day and night, no one saw the murderer at work and no cries for help were heard.

Three weeks later, the body of Liz Stride was found huddled in a passageway leading to Dutfield's Yard, its throat slashed from ear to ear. A witness, Israel Schwartz, testified to the police that he had seen an initial attack on Liz; she had been thrown to the pavement by a man outside Dutfield's Yard, but Schwartz was frightened away by a second man, possibly a look-out. Why did Liz struggle with a young man? She was soliciting to meet male custom. Despite this vital and unique evidence, Schwartz – possibly the only man ever to have seen the Ripper about to begin work – was *not* called to give evidence at the murdered woman's inquest. Why? In his statement to the police Schwartz claimed to have seen two men in the street while Stride was being attacked. Even if the men were not together (I believe they were) surely full details should have been circulated? They were not. Why? And why did Schwartz, after one newspaper interview, disappear, never to be heard of again?

Stride was seen being attacked at 12.45 a.m.; she was murdered close to 1.00 a.m. What happened to her and where was she in those missing fifteen minutes?

Forty-five minutes or so after the discovery of Stride's body, a second murder victim, Catharine Eddowes, was found dead and badly mutilated, lying on her back on the pavement of a London square. Eddowes was known to use the name 'Mary Kelly' from time to time. On the day before her death Catharine was many hours late for a meeting with her lover. She disappeared penniless and sober at 2.00 p.m. and for over six hours there were no recorded sightings, despite massive publicity after her death. Yet Catharine had obtained enough alcohol during the afternoon and early evening to inebriate her. Did she get the money for drink from soliciting? If so, why did someone not see her touting for custom?; all the other prostitutes had been spotted in the middle of the night. If Catharine had found clients during the six hours of her disappearance, where could she have taken them? She had no lodgings. She was arrested at 8.30 p.m. and taken to Bishopsgate Police Station. There, after some hours in custody, and despite the fact that the police themselves had warned women not go out at night, the duty officers at Bishopsgate Police Station released the penniless Catharine into the heart of the Ripper territory at 1.00 a.m. Did the police expect her to walk the streets all night? Surprisingly, after being released from custody in the early hours, ill and presumably suffering from a hang-over, possibly still unsteady on her legs, the middle-aged woman did not turn in the direction of her partner's lodging house to try and get in touch with him, although she had remembered her earlier broken promise, 'to be back soon': instead, she headed towards Mitre Square, and somewhere along the way she met Jack the Ripper. Mitre Square was a respectable business centre. Why would Catharine have been so far from home in such an area? No one heard a sound nor saw anything suspicious during this fourth Ripper murder. Jack, as usual, had melted away.

After the double murders the police became uncooperative. As one paper reported; 'The police are extraordinarily reticent with reference to the Mitre Square tragedy.' A second paper said; 'The police apparently have strict orders to close all channels of information to members of the press.' Why? Even embarrassment at their lack of success should not have forced the authorities to clam up; they should have been explaining how much effort they were putting into the murder investigations. The actions of the Metropolitan Police Commissioner, Sir Charles Warren, were extraordinary. Graffiti, which could have yielded vital clues, was discovered over a piece of blood-smeared apron thrown away by Jack. The writing was washed away, either personally by Warren, or on his orders. The police chief then hid copies of the graffiti on closed files, although the message should have been presented in court. Warren then wrote to the Home Office lying about the positioning of the message.

Almost six weeks after the double killings, a fifth murder occurred in 13 Miller's Court, part of a London lodging house. Here the victim, named as Mary Kelly, was slashed beyond recognition. (Although credit was unheard of in the East End, Mary had been offered extended rental credit – which is inexplicable.)

The corpse in Number 13 had been mutilated, eviscerated and partially skinned. Apart from a cry of 'murder' (which might not have referred to the affairs in Miller's Court), no sound was heard. No suspect could be pin-pointed and no arrest was made.

On the morning after the fifth murder, the supposed 'corpse' was sighted by three independent witnesses many hours after her supposed death. One witness, under oath, (Caroline Maxwell) swore that she had had a conversation with Mary Kelly, although Kelly was supposed to have been murdered by this time. The inquest on the Ripper's final victim was presided over by an experienced ex-police surgeon, Roderick MacDonald, who was well versed in the rules of procedure on such occasions. Yet the enquiry headed by MacDonald broke several basic legal requirements. Vital facts concerning the injuries of the victim and the weapon used to inflict those injuries were not ascertained. Little notice was taken of Mrs Maxwell's sensational sighting of Mary Kelly after her supposed death, and Maxwell was not recalled to give further evidence. The inquest was rushed through at breakneck speed; it opened and was closed in one day. This speed meant that there was insufficient time to trace Kelly's Irish relatives, who could possibly have helped identify the mangled remains found in Miller's Court. Kelly's lover of 18 months, Joe Barnett, said that he could only identify her by the ears and the eyes; but the ears had been partially sliced away which surely would have made identification almost impossible. And with the face slashed to pulp it must have been difficult to see the eyes mixed amongst the mashed flesh. After the inquest, official papers relating to the affair were not signed by MacDonald. Despite the highlighting of these inadequacies by national newspapers, no new inquest was called.

As soon as Kelly's inquest was closed, an important witness, George Hutchinson, approached the police and said that he had seen a man pick up Mary Kelly on the night she was supposedly murdered. Hutchinson then gave an incredibly detailed description of Kelly's companion – a man who might have been Jack the Ripper. Inspector Frederick George Abberline, the officer in charge of the basic Ripper investigations, thought that George Hutchinson's evidence was important, but the police did not reopen Kelly's inquest in order to examine this new material officially.

Sir Charles Warren had been responsible for the use of bloodhounds in the murder investigations, although it must have been obvious to the dullest of minds that in a dirty, smelly, overcrowded area such as the East End, no dog could ever be successful in tracking a particular odour. The dogs proved useless, yet despite that failure, the final murder victim (and the murder site) remained unattended for most of the morning, while the advisability of calling in dogs to Miller's Court was debated. Warren must have been informed about the final murder immediately. He must have known that policemen were waiting for orders about the use or otherwise of bloodhounds; he must have known that the murder site had not been entered while the men were waiting for his orders. Yet instead of issuing instructions to sort out the chaos, Warren resigned. As it turned out, this was the last Ripper murder, and immediately it was over, *Warren resigned!* It later transpired that no bloodhounds were available to be brought to Miller's Court even if they *had* been needed.

At the inquest into the death of Montague Druitt vital facts were again withheld from the proceedings. Sir Melville Macnaghten said that he had been given private information which led him to believe that Druitt's family believed Montague was the killer; the family would presumably be in a position to know the truth of this matter, and clearly they had succeeded in convincing a highly-placed police officer that their suspicions were well founded. Yet Macnaghten took the matter no further, which is distinctly odd. William Druitt, on hearing of his brother's disappearance, did not go to Montague's lodgings personally, but delegated the task to outsiders, who found a suicide note. This stated that Montague thought he had been going insane since the Friday [three days earlier] – yet his family believed him to be Jack the Ripper, which means he should have thought that he was mad for about four months. At the inquest into Montague's death, no efforts were made to find witnesses to the deceased's final hours. No attempt was made to find out why he was dismissed from his teaching job, although this could have had vital bearings on his death. There was no attempt to discover the source of the very large amounts of money that the body was carrying. The victim's brother told blatant lies to the court by claiming that there were no other brothers or sisters. Yet these questionable events brought no murmur of protest from the authorities. Why?

Druitt's suicide also raises many questions. I have been assured that suicides frequently dress in their best clothes, but why the very large amount of money; why the *return* railway ticket; why the long and unnecessary journey to a distant part of the River Thames to end his life? Could Druitt's death have been murder and not suicide? If so, who would have wanted him dead? And why? And indeed, why should a young, educated man venture into the dangerous East End in order to kill five penniless, defenceless prostitutes?

This set of circumstances is so strange and bizarre a story it would hardly be accepted as a work of fiction, yet the above details are strictly factual. We must now attempt to weave a scenario that can provide a solution to this extraordinary set of facts. No doubt a few midnight anoraks on the Internet will start caterwauling. Let them, instead, try to find a scenario that fits the many puzzling facts connected to this case, as I have done. It will not be easy.

Chapter 14

Do the Suspects fit the Crime?

In the final chapter of this book I will reveal my thesis about Jack the Ripper's identity, and explain *why* these terrible crimes took place; 'why?' is equally as important as 'who?' in the Ripper mystery. However the actual *modus operandi* of the five murders can only be based on informed speculation, based on facts which are known about the case.

As a starting point, let us accept that Mary Kelly had indeed been made pregnant by the Prince of Wales – probably during high jinks in the Watling Street flat used by Bertie and his upper-class cronies. Unless she were careful, it might be difficult for a prostitute to know who had impregnated her; did Mary, therefore, deliberately entrap the Prince?

Once Mary's plans were laid she would have been faced with the problem of approaching the Establishment; an Establishment which, when faced with a Catholic prostitute who might be able to prove that the Prince of Wales had bedded her, would have panicked – even without the claim that she was pregnant from her royal encounter.

What role did Montague Druitt play in the murders, along with a partner in crime? How did the apparently pleasant young barrister become involved in so sordid an affair? To answer that question we must remember that Mary Kelly mixed with a wide range of social classes. She was known to have been taken to France by a rich lover and she was known to have had many West End contacts. If she had been bedded by the Prince of Wales she may also have been bedded by his aristocratic friends. With her range of associates there is no reason why Mary should not have learned of, or even met, Montague Druitt, perhaps through some society or school function.

As I'm convinced that Kelly did approach the Establishment she must have used some link to do this; as Druitt was involved in the murders it is a reasonable speculation that he was that link: he was the man Mary approached with her delicate problem. Montague was highly accessible. He had contacts in cricket clubs, in the legal profession and, of course, being a full-time school teacher, he would have a had great many contacts with the parents of his pupils. It was also well-known that J.K. Stephen had been the tutor and friend of Eddy, heir to the English throne. Might Mary have known, perhaps through socialite gossip, that Stephen was acquainted with Druitt, giving her direct access to royalty?

As we have seen, it was entirely possible that Montague Druitt and J.K. could have met through the proximity of their offices – two young, attractive, homosexual men instantly drawn to each other – possibly on first sight. Could they have bonded deeply enough to join together in a partnership that needed daring and total trust?

Male allegiance and loyalty is found in many parts of society. Such a bonding between men of all sexual persuasions appears to be an inherited form of tribal behaviour. Men's clubs abound. In 1991 a famous West End Club voted to continue to uphold their century-old rules – men only, no women. Many of these clubs are essentially masculine places where the mutual support of various members is unwaveringly maintained by a rigid, frequently tacit code of conduct. Public houses were (and still are) another kind of favoured regular male meeting place. It is only comparatively recently that the presence of women in public houses has become accepted by male drinkers.

Then there is the most influential loyalty of all, the old school tie; that will chain young males to each other in an absolute allegiance. Men who were educated together in celebrated public schools will frequently protect their peers' interests, no matter what the crime and no matter what the consequence. We can see this ethic clearly demonstrated in a famous spy cadre, when privileged men banded together in secret and betrayed their country but kept an unwavering loyalty to each other. James Kenneth Stephen was raised in an environment that encouraged this kind of loyal behaviour; at university he had been a member of the Apostles.

The Apostles group was a Cambridge University-based secret society, one important enough to be the subject of a book by Richard Deacon. This collection of like-minded young men was a traditional and recognised part of life at Cambridge University but its workings were cloistered and its agenda secret. However, the Apostles' unofficial motto was 'the love of man for man is greater than the love of man for woman', which is very revealing, although many of the more recent members of this society have been indisputably heterosexual.

H.F. Wilson (who, after leaving the university, retained a lively correspondence with Eddy) and J.K. Stephen were both members of the Apostles, and both were close friends of the Duke of Clarence. James was raised among secret intimate male relationships, and there is no reason to believe that Montague, considering his education, was not equally versed in similar ties; all Victorian public schools had analogous traditions. George Broderick, remembering his days at Eton during the 1840s, writes of '. . . a strange and subtle instinct of honour . . . which was an unwritten code of conduct at the College'. James was an Etonian and Montague a Wykehamist, but both men would have understood the public school code of loyalty and honour – more so given a strong bond of sexual attraction.

There are other points to consider. James Stephen and Montague Druitt had remarkable similarities:

1) Both men came from the same social background.
2) Both men came from families which, up to that date at least, had a history of mental illness. (James's father and Montague's mother and grandmother suffered from periods of insanity.)
3) Both men were trained in law.
4) Both men were renowned for their debating skills.
5) Both men were skilled and enthusiastic sportsmen.
6) Both men had the same sexual proclivities if Sir Melville Macnaghten's assertion that Montague was 'sexually insane' meant, as Victorians usually meant by that phrase, that he was homosexual.
7) Neither man attained the eminence which early talent had indicated.
8) Both men were involved in murder.

But how did two such advantaged and presumably pleasant young men become involved in a series of revolting and savage acts of homicide? And would such educated and refined minds be likely to rampage around the East End committing barbaric acts? To answer the second question first – even the most apparently sane and refined of minds can commit callous acts of cruelty, often as a considered matter of duty.

It does not require any specialised training or knowledge to be able to recognise the double standards of normality and barbarity that can exist comfortably side-by-side in the most apparently civilised of minds. No doubt the men who conducted the Spanish Inquisition considered themselves fine, upstanding citizens, loving family men, happy to play with their children and take part in all civic duties, yet these devout men would torture and inflict indescribable cruelties on their victims in the name of religion and love. Examples of political terrorism are too numerous and too well-documented to need repeating. Absolute loyalty to a cause appears to paralyse the human conscience. As we have recently and tragically seen, pleasant young men from all cultures will plant bombs with not a jot of remorse or sympathy for the consequences of their actions on their victims or on themselves.

∞

Let us return to the narrative, reiterating that we can only, at this point, attempt informed speculation. Mary has now solved the problem of how best to approach the Establishment – through Montague Druitt. His chambers at King's Bench Walk EC4 could be easily reached on foot from the East End.

So this is my reconstruction: Mary Kelly calls and sees Montague at his chambers, where she breaks the news about her pregnancy and the alleged father of the expected child. Mary would have asked for Druitt's professional advice, but being smart, she probably would not have left a forwarding address. Mary would only have pledged to call again after Montague had had time to consider her case. Montague, realising the enormous repercussions which this information could have, goes immediately and sees J.K. Stephen, who was a noted friend of royalty. James would have been readily accessible either at his parents' home in De Vere Gardens, Kensington, where he lived, or at the West End offices of *The Reflector*. This was a magazine which J.K. had founded, an enterprise on which he lavished his entire attention. The magazine was to be printed on the best possible paper, and its contents would be either political or literary.

Druitt, although he was not a noted royalist, might well have met, and possibly liked, Eddy. I make no apologies for constant repetition, given so complicated a story – so I again point out that Martin Howells and Keith Skinner's book reveals the astonishing information that Eddy was invited to a ball at Wimborne, with Druitt's name on the guest list. That puts the two men in the same room. Indeed, the excellent *The Ripper Legacy*, make a very solid case for Eddy and Druitt being friends; part of a group of the same sexual persuasion who banded together in great secrecy; secrecy was essential as homosexuality caused such horror in the Victorian era. Keith and Martin point out a number of other links between Eddy and Druitt. (For instance, one of Druitt's brothers served in the same regiment as Eddy's equerry.)

So Druitt visits Stephen and relates his startling news. It is easy to imagine the fury aroused in James's sick mind on hearing about Mary Kelly's royal pregnancy. His first thought would have been directed towards the consequences that such a situation might bring about if it were to become public knowledge. Did James visualise a public uprising? Or, more likely, did he think of the possible destruction of his own dreams and ambitions? The Crown, as we have seen, was widely unpopular in many quarters during the 1880s, and a royal scandal of massive proportions may well have toppled the monarchy. Such a fall would have smashed James's own considerable ambitions to be the force behind Eddy, once he had become king. James would have seen the possible disintegration of the things most dear to him – the State, the Crown, his beloved friend, and his own glowing future – all threatened by a worthless woman. Any illegitimate child would be a half-brother or sister to Eddy, and this child would link, by blood, the Royal Family to a Roman Catholic East End prostitute. A tidal wave of anger would have swept through James Stephen's sick mind. We have read A.C. Benson's account of this man's terrifying fury as a young, healthy fellow. We need only read through *Lapsus Calami*, a collection of Stephen's poems, to realise the inherent violence in the man. We know for certain from medical reports still on file at St. Andrew's Hospital, Northampton, that J.K.'s mind was beginning to become unhinged in 1888. James's troubles were reputed to have started with an accident to the head from which he never fully recovered, although experts have expressed doubts that this accident would be any more than a contributory factor to the severe mental problems that followed. In the foreword to *Lapsus Calami* James's brother writes:

> In the winter of 1886-7, while paying a visit at Felixstowe, he accidentally received a very severe blow on the head. He did not lose consciousness but was badly cut. The wound healed, but I do not think he ever enjoyed perfect health again.

Following a line of reasoned speculation based on facts, are there any pointers which indicate that J.K. Stephen was mentally disturbed shortly before the murders? There are definite indications that this was the case. At the end of April 1888, about four months before the murders started, James closed his magazine. From the text of his final editorial, it is quite clear that the man's mind was troubled. Most writers on the subject of *The Reflector's* demise state that this was caused by financial pressure. J.K. sets out a range of possibilities to explain the magazine's closure. Revealingly, he keeps on referring to the magazine's demise as his own.

Was it towards the end of April when Montague brought news of Mary's bombshell? Excerpts from J.K.'s last editorial in his magazine (April 21st 1888) may prove instructive: I have a strong suspicion that J.K. Stephen was obliquely accusing Bertie, the Prince of Wales for what was about to happen. It is certainly the most extraordinary diatribe.

> Ladies and gentlemen, it is with a mixture of regret and satisfaction that I inform you that this is in all probability the last time I shall address you. One never knows for certain what is going to happen; ... moreover, it is not unpleasant to sink mysteriously into that unknown abyss from which (such as I am) I not less mysteriously arose. *Mystery is a mighty thing*; [my italics] ... from trifles grave consequences sometimes spring ... out of the ashes of the dead Reflector may arise a marriage, *a murder* or the regeneration of mankind. [My italics] ... (accursed calendar, you cannot harm me now) ... I do not pretend – I will be frank with you – that the King of Terrors has claimed either the publisher or the editor as a subject ... 'But why, sir, have you come to this sudden decision?' Aha, my friends, do not press me too nearly ... Prudence and diplomacy seal my closing lips ... Anyhow I owe an account to no living man

or woman, and 'the rest is silence', as another moribund gentleman is reputed to have exclaimed. Not quite silence either. I know that some of you, who are more nearly unemployed than I could wish you to be, will not spare my memory the probings of inquisitive speculation. Questions will be asked, and answers will be given. *Even in the jaws of death I smile, superior to the conjectures of others on a problem whose solution I am about to carry undivulged into a world whence no questioner returns to enlighten his companions in ignorance.* [my italics] ... Others, perhaps, will more charitably infer that, although not a ruined man, fearful of sheriff's officers, *and apt to toy significantly with deadly weapons in hours of solitary despondency*, I am, nevertheless aware that the limit of expenditure which I am willing to incur is within measurable distance, *and that I prefer instant death, while my proportions are still bulky, and my printing and paper beyond reproach, to the horrors of a lingering end* ... [my italics]

There then follows an extraordinary passage addressed to the 'Postmaster General'. Clearly there had been a contretemps about postal rates, but could the 'Postmaster General' be an oblique reference to another person? In the next passage, which is placed three-quarters way through the long, final editorial, an underlying message is loud and clear:

But hold: there are a few whose guesses on this melancholy problem have a personal character, and to them a word in season may be spoken. Yes, sir: you the Postmaster General; I mean you. Skulk not behind the pretence of being too much occupied to give ear to what I say; you shall not escape being gibbeted before my readers. Doubtless you think that your unjust refusal to recognise that I, too, am a newspaper, has either drained my coffers dry, that your wine and wheel-taxing colleagues may revel in half-pence which belongs by right to me, or has blasted my faith in mankind, and destroyed my interest in life. I will not undeceive you, tyrant: *even if you hereafter should govern colonies, or perhaps sway the destinies of an empire, even though you continue to be my representative and that of my betters in the Commons House of Parliament, this weight shall hang for ever around your guilty neck for anything that I will do to remove it.* [my italics]

That is an extraordinary passage. Would the Postmaster-General, Henry Cecil Raikes, ever govern colonies or sway the destiny of an Empire? Not if his past record was anything to go by. And he was not an MP.

Raikes, born in 1838 at Chester, stood for election to Parliament in

1865, contesting his home town seat. He lost. In 1866 he contested an election at Devonport and lost. In 1868 he finally became an MP winning the seat for Chester, but he lost that seat again in 1880. Two years later Raikes once more became an MP, representing Preston, but less than a year later he resigned the seat. Raikes became Postmaster-General in 1886 and died five years later in 1891. Clearly the Postmaster-General, with such a chequered career, would never '*govern colonies*' or '*sway the destinies of an Empire*'. But Bertie would. Clearly James was not referring to postage anymore. So what was on his mind? The key words are: '... this weight shall hang for ever around your guilty neck.' What weight? Mary's recent declaration of pregnancy? And the added words. '... this weight will hang around your guilty neck for anything that I will do to remove it' speak for themselves. James is clearly writing on several different levels. A further passage from the final editorial states: 'My death will, perhaps involve the non-appearance of some literary gems...' James's writing is full of phrases such as 'mystery; death; horror'. His final editorial finishes with the words:

> In conclusion, I can but wish you all such species of good fortune as may be to your taste, and declare that for myself I crave the only blessings which can now avail me aught – a kindly epitaph, and reluctant oblivion. I am, Ladies and Gentlemen (or shall I say I have been?) Your obliged, humble Servant, The Reflector.

These are extraordinary words that betray a maelstrom of emotions. In this writing I can find several hints which say that Mary's bombshell may well have been dropped towards the end of April 1888, and no reason to think that this was not the case. We must also consider the strange fact that the murders, apart from one, early on a Friday morning and one on a public Bank holiday, occurred only at the weekend. Michael Harrison, in his book *The Life of the Duke of Clarence and Avondale 1864–1892*, reveals that James was in Wales on weekdays during the period when the Ripper murders occurred. Could this account for all the murders taking place only towards the weekend period, dates when Stephen could be in London?

After winding up his magazine in the summer of 1888, James was appointed (by his father) Clerk of Assize for South Wales, giving him light circuit duties – duties which, by all accounts he did not carry out efficiently. Medical notes indicate that Stephen's mental collapse began around this period. (J.K. was committed to St Andrew's Hospital, Nothampton in 1891.) Laurence Humphrey MD, the noted doctor who attended James at the hospital (where James eventually died in 1892), diagnosed that his patient had been suffering from mental disease since 1888. The year of the Ripper murders. Throughout his stay in the mental hospital James thought that a warrant had been issued for his arrest. Why should he think that he might be arrested? Even although the man was by this time insane, the fact that he felt so constantly guilty and in fear of retribution is interesting.

∽

The potential threat to the Establishment that Kelly posed could have elicited a strong response from the most normal and controlled of minds, and, as we know, J.K. Stephen's mind was far from normal during the summer of 1888. This is well documented by A.C. Benson (J.K.'s schoolfriend), who writes:

> ...he accepted a legal appointment – a Clerkship of Assize – which gave him light circuit duties and a competence. But now his behaviour began to be marked by a curious eccentricity. It all seemed so deliberate, and his mental powers were so preternaturally acute and brilliant, that it was supposed and hoped that it was a passing phase. He became very restless in mind, taking up such pursuits as drawing and even music, for which he had no aptitude whatever. I remember his showing me a number of water-colour pictures of the most grotesque kind, which he assured me were portraits; *one in particular, of a female figure in a long brown coat sitting on the rail of a stile, in a kind of twilight, with a low moon in the distance, and a curious suggestiveness about it.* [My italics.]

Mary Nichols was murdered on the second day of the moon's last quarter, and the night was fine. She was wearing a long brown coat.

As has been mentioned, James's reaction to possible danger to the Crown would be a complex one, with the over-riding consideration of ambition mixed with his passion for Eddy. Absolute proof of this deep-seated feeling (on the part of James at least) is available, but first, let us consider the circumstantial evidence – J.K's poetry. In the lampoon '*The Coming of K.*' -- 'K' was the symbol used to represent Bertie. Did it stand for 'king', although Bertie was not yet crowned? I made a startling discovery connected with the letter 'K', but for the time being I will just accept the symbol as referring to royalty. Among James's poems is an ode that also uses the letter 'K'. Could this poem, with its distinctly erotic language, have been based on experiences shared between Eddy (K) and Stephen? The second verse is headed by the words 'Placid K.' Few were more placid than Eddy.

TO A.T.M.
See where the K. in sturdy self-reliance,
Thoughtful and placid as a brooding dove,
Stands, firmly sucking, in the cause of science,
Just such a peppermint as schoolboys love.

Suck placid K.: the world will be thy debtor;
Though thine eyes water and thine heart grow faint,
Suck: and the less thou likest it the better;
Suck for our sake and utter no complaint.

In stanzas three and five, it may be that James was egotistically mentioning himself with the words, 'Near thee a being, passionate and gentle, Man's latest teacher, wisdom's pioneer' and – 'Lo! with a voice unspeakably dramatic, Lo! with a gesture singularly fine...' A.C. Benson relates James's over-dramatic but effective acting performances. And extraordinary images seem to suggest oral sex:

(Delicate soft impalpable sensations,
Born of thy palate, quiver in his brain)

(He makes at last a lucid and emphatic
Statement of what is in that mouth of thine)

To complete the poem, here are stanzas three to eight:

Near thee a being, passionate and gentle,
Man's latest teacher, wisdom's pioneer,
Calmly majestically monumental,
Stands: the august Telepathist is here.
Waves of perception, subtle emanations,
Thrill through the ether, circulate amain;
Delicate soft impalpable sensations,
Born of thy palate, quiver in his brain.
Lo! with a voice unspeakably dramatic,
Lo! with a gesture singularly fine,
He makes at last a lucid and emphatic
Statement of what is in that mouth of thine.
He could detect that peppermint's existence,
He read its nature in the book of doom;
Standing at some considerable distance;
Standing, in fact, in quite another room.
Was there a faint impenetrable essence
Wafted towards him from the sucking K.?
Did some pale ghost inform him of its presence?
Or did it happen in some other way?
These are the questions nobody can answer,
These are the problems nobody can solve;
Only we know that Man is an Advancer:
Only we know the Centuries revolve.

(*The Reflector*, 1888)

There is passion in the above poem, but might the friendship between Eddy and J.K. have weakened by 1888? In 1885 Eddy had been drafted into the 10th Hussars as a lieutenant; his father was Colonel of the regiment. During this period Eddy maintained a spirited correspondence with H.F. Wilson but there is no record of any letters between Eddy and J.K. Stephen. Any correspondence might, of course, have been destroyed. An alarming amount of written material belonging to characters associated with Jack the Ripper was subsequently burned. Perhaps James, in his torment, might have thought that by taking dramatic action in the Kelly affair he would demonstrate his continuing love for Eddy in no uncertain manner, and so strengthen the ties of friendship once more? James would mastermind the removal of Kelly and then maybe Eddy would learn of – and appreciate – the danger that J.K. had been willing to face in order to protect the Crown? Of James's love there can be no doubt: solid proof of that deep affection was clearly demonstrated by his reaction to Eddy's untimely death from influenza-related pneumonia on 14 January 1892. As soon as he heard of the demise James refused to eat, and, over the following weeks, starved himself to death.

So, to return to a reconstruction of events: Montague has now related Mary's story to J.K. Stephen; we have already considered Stephen's reaction. Obviously his first move would be to recruit Druitt into the murderous plans which must have formed in his mind. Given James's hypnotic personality and gift of overpowering persuasion, involving Druitt as a support is likely to have required little effort, but was there also the added bait of money? Montague would have had little to lose, protected by the powerful forces of State, and he had much to gain. We have seen that by 1888, Druitt's legal career was moribund and he was trapped in a schoolteacher's post in an unimportant South London school, forced to take part-time legal work below his capabilities: not a happy outcome for a man whose early achievements promised a glittering future. In addition, around April, his mother's mental health was showing signs of deterioration. Ann Druitt had attempted suicide in early 1888, and, later that same year, in July, she was placed in the Brooke Asylum, Clapton, where she was certified insane.

Beside these family worries, Montague had, as we have seen, considerable financial commitments. The idea of combining help to the Establishment with a large reward would have been seductive. This could account for Montague's puzzling wealth discovered after his death. As for James – he could combine his love of State and the monarchy (and of Eddy in particular) with his misogyny. This hatred of women is clearly expressed in much-quoted stanzas from two of J.K. Stephen's poems, both published in February 1891.

A THOUGHT

If all the harm that women have done,
Were put in a bundle and rolled into one,
Earth would not hold it,
The sky could not enfold it,
It could not be lighted nor warmed by the sun;
Such masses of evil
Would puzzle the devil,
And keep him in fuel while Time's wheels run.

But if all the harm that's been done by men
Were doubled and doubled and doubled again,
And melted and fused into vapour and then
Were squared and raised to the power of ten,
There wouldn't be nearly enough, not near,
To keep a small girl for the tenth of a year.

(Granta Feb. 1891)

and

IN THE BACKS

As I was strolling lonely in the Backs,
I met a woman whom I did not like.
I did not like the way the woman walked:
Loose-hipped, big boned, disjointed, angular.

After a long, unflattering description of the woman, her clothing and her possible character, the poem ends with the lines:

I do not want to see that girl again:
I did not like her: and I should not mind
If she were done away with, killed or ploughed.
She did not seem to serve a useful end:
And certainly she was not beautiful.

(Cambridge Review, Feb 1891)

There is little ambiguity in the above stanzas regarding Stephen's feelings towards women. The decision to kill Mary Kelly would certainly fit this man's personality. He was a fellow of massive self-confidence who tended to disregard authority even while still at school. He was a man of wild passion and great physical strength; a man with theatrical urges, and a misogynist. When such a man saw all that he loved and respected threatened by an East End prostitute, murder would be an almost inevitable course of action.

A first move would be to check the basic truth of Mary's story. Was Bertie in London around March and April, 1888? He was, and moreover, he was celebrating heavily. 10 March 1888 marked Bertie and Alexandra's silver wedding anniversary. There was a State Ball at

Buckingham Palace and a family dinner party at Marlborough House. Queen Victoria, after leaving this function, drove through the West End to see the illuminations. Such an anniversary would have been the ideal occasion for Bertie's friends to give him the kind of entertainment that he loved most – wild parties, possibly at the Watling Street flat, naturally without his wife. Alix's deafness would have contributed to her preference for quiet nights in the bosom of her family, a choice that must have suited Bertie very well.

So let us assume that Bertie and Mary Kelly met and intimacy occurred. As we have seen, the attractive prostitute might well have been in the habit of robbing sailors during the course of sexual bargaining. This was common practice. So could Mary have stolen a memento from Bertie for later use against him? I believe that this was indeed the case. Mary had a cool, calculating nature, and the opportunity to gain proof of her association with the prince would have been too good an opportunity to miss.

But if the death of Mary Kelly was the murderer's sole objective, and many writers have believed that it was, why were four other prostitutes killed? Here we must delve deeply into the realms of speculation. Could the four earlier murders have been a clever smoke-screen? If even a hint of Mary's story – linking her sexually to Bertie – had leaked out, and she had then been mysteriously murdered, gossip might have quickly flared up and inflamed the East End. (The Los Angeles riots of 1992 were a contemporary example of how quickly insurrection can arise and engulf a city). But if Mary's death appeared to be only one in a string of unrelated murders, no particular attention would be drawn to it. This seems tenable, yet there is a flaw in such an explanation. As Stephen Knight pointed out, the murdered women all lived within a minute's walk of each other. This is a list of their last known addresses:

MARY NICHOLS
The day before she was murdered,
Mary was staying at: 56, Flower and Dean Street
LIZ STRIDE
On the day before she was murdered,
Liz had been at: 52, Flower and Dean Street
CATHARINE EDDOWES
On the day before she was murdered,
Catharine had spent the afternoon at: 55, Flower and Dean Street
ANNIE CHAPMAN
On the night she was murdered,
Annie had been trying to pay for a bed at: 35, Dorset Street
THE FINAL MURDER TOOK PLACE AT: 29, Dorset Street
(13 Miller's Court was the back part of this house)

This was no random selection. The five victims of these attacks all lived very close to each other, three in one street, two in another street, both streets almost adjoining. There were, according to Metropolitan Police estimates, around 1,200 prostitutes in Whitechapel in 1888; obviously not all of these women would have lived around Dorset Street. Many lived in the other East End areas which comprised Bethnal Green, Mile End, Bromley-By-Bow, Limehouse, Spitalfields, Old Ford, Shoreditch, St George's in the East, Poplar, Whitechapel, Stepney and Bow.

Now if the five Ripper victims had not known each other, and had lived in different districts, but had been murdered on the one spot, then the murders could possibly have been random: there would be nothing to link the women to each other, except the fact that a murderer had become fixated by one small area, and killed any woman who happened to be in that place at a suitable time for murder. But the five women we are discussing all lived almost next door to each other, they knew each other, they would have talked together and they were all killed by the same method – with a knife; three were named Mary (counting Catharine's alias), and two of the women used the name 'Mary Kelly'. This makes the odds astronomically high that the Ripper murders were not random killings. *The women were hunted down as part of a pattern.* However, this fact creates a new puzzle. What would be the purpose of hunting down a group of penniless, pathetic prostitutes? My theory alleges that Kelly was demanding money to support an unborn royal child, and, as we have already mentioned, if this were the case, Kelly was intelligent enough not to involve four alcoholic, gossipy prostitutes. So if the murdered quartet did not share a deadly secret with Mary Kelly, what grouped them together as women who needed to be eliminated?

It might be advisable at this juncture to ask whether there is any indication that Kelly was expecting a large sum of money. If Mary had *not* been expecting money, it is difficult to understand why she had been given three months' credit on the rent of her room – a favour unheard of in the East End when sick, middle-aged women were turned out in the middle of the night because they did not have four-pence. To reiterate, could the young, attractive Mary have paid her rent by offering sexual favours to the landlord, Mr McCarthy? From all accounts, McCarthy was a respectable businessman, married with four children. This outward respectability might not preclude such an arrangement, but as we have seen, it was his wife, Mrs McCarthy who collected the rents, and she was a stickler for prompt payment. So Mary must have been able to convince the woman that she would soon have an ample amount of cash. Maybe she showed Druitt's business card to Mrs McCarthy and convinced her (without giving any details) that a large settlement was soon due, as, indeed, Mary might well have had every reason to believe? I will return to this scenario shortly. For now, let us consider if there was any particular reason why the murders began with Nichols?

∽

Once Kelly had contacted Druitt there may well have been a long delay while the truth about her story was tested. If she had claimed to be pregnant around the beginning of April, it would have taken some time for the condition to become obvious. Perhaps the Establishment needed proof of Mary's condition, considering her demands a possible, baseless plot. The Victorians did not have sophisticated pregnancy tests: proof could only be discovered by physical signs.

Was it perhaps this final proof of the prostitute's pregnancy – a swollen stomach – notably evident around July, that roused Stephen to his first bout of murderous fury? Or did he receive a doctor's report to that effect? Did tortuous, but unsuccessful bargaining with the sly and tough Mary Kelly take place? At some point it must have become clear that murder was the only solution to the Establishment's problem. Then it would have been easy for J.K. to track her down. He might have had Mary followed after a visit to Montague, but most likely he would have used powerful friends who had influence with the East End police (to whom Kelly was well known) to discover the prostitute's address; given the high-level cover-up, some trusted members of the police force must have been involved in the affair.

Once J.K. was convinced that murder was necessary it would not have been difficult to talk Druitt around to the same point of view. He might even have persuaded Montague that he had personally obtained agreement, tacit or otherwise, from leading members of the Establishment, and perhaps he had. But probably the most powerful persuasion offered to Druitt was that of money. Druitt's large estate would confirm this view.

Once murder had been decided as a solution by the two unbalanced young men, plans and logistics had to be worked out. Two pleasant-looking, well dressed, clean young men would have been highly visible in the East End of London, but that could easily be overcome. Nondescript clothing would not be difficult to arrange, and this would appeal to James's sense of theatre: as we have seen, the murders have a distinctly theatrical character. The display of the mutilated bodies was itself obscenely theatrical; the corpses were laid out as though for view, one woman with her possessions neatly arranged on the ground. There was an element of 'look at what I've done' in Jack's grotesque games – and we know from documentary evidence that J.K. enjoyed being the centre of attention, displaying his many talents at various educational establishments. Such a personality may well inject a theatrical element into his crimes. J.K. fits perfectly the psychological portrait of the murderer; a murderer who knew that he was being protected.

∽

The two men must now have worked out detailed plans for their proposed crime. A rumour that Jack the Ripper used a coach has been current for a number of years, but a coach and groomed horses would have been as much out of place in the slums of Whitechapel as well-dressed young men. The one form of transport that would not raise a second glance would be a horse and cart, the cart perhaps covered by a tarpaulin under which a change of clothing, wet towels, and even a long knife could be hidden. In the days before motorised travel such a method of transport could be easily purchased, and there was a plethora of stableyards throughout London. In the light of this theory, might it be significant that Mary Nichols's body was discovered lying outside the gates of a stableyard in Buck's Row and Liz Stride near to stabling facilities in Dutfield's Yard? If several of the victims had been lured onto the back of a cart where they were strangled while being driven through dark areas, then no sounds of murder would have been heard. This would explain the absolute silence of the attacks: no cries, no grunts, no scuffles as the unfortunate women fought for their lives.

This is my thesis on the first murder: on the night of 30/31 August 1888, J.K. Stephen, his mind dangerously unbalanced, set out with Montague Druitt on a journey to the East End. At this moment Druitt would also have been suffering from intense mental strain, since only a month earlier his mother had been declared insane and placed in an asylum. Driven by a mixture of conflicting emotions, the couple, having discovered Kelly's address, must have travelled to the East End to search her out, with murder on their minds.

Let me surmise. In the yard at Buck's Row (site of the first murder), the two men could have stabled a horse and cart with equipment hidden under a tarpaulin. After harnessing the horse, Druitt and J.K. drive to Dorset Street in search of Kelly. At Mary Kelly's address, Stephen dismounts and goes into the Court to check out the scene. At this moment Kelly might have glanced out of the broken window and seen a stranger staring at her premises. After her plotting Mary might have been expecting trouble. With this in mind, suspicious and intelligent, she decides to test the stranger. She pulls on a bonnet and maybe a distinctive shawl, and leaves her lodgings to go to her local bar, the Britannia, on the corner of Dorset and Commercial Street. On her way to the bar Mary must have realised that she was being followed. As we saw in Chapter 7, the prostitute, when in trouble, was in the habit of changing clothing with friends. In the Britannia Kelly could have met a regular drinker, Mary Nichols, and persuaded her to change clothing. How was this done? Here is a further short scene from my play.

〜

MARY NICHOLS. (*Going over*) Mary darling – got a penny I can lend?

MARY KELLY. I don't – but I might be able to help you to earn some money.

MARY NICHOLS. How?

MARY KELLY. Borrow my new clothing. See if it attracts custom. Try my bonnet on. It's new. The very latest fashion.

MARY NICHOLS. Ooh, the hat is so pretty. Here, this isn't another set-up, is it? We all know what you're like for robbin' and rollin'. Always someone asking, 'Where's Mary Kelly?'. In this lot, they might mistake me...

MARY KELLY. So what? What if the cops are out looking for me in this bonnet and shawl? What would they find? You. No harm done.

(*She ties the bonnet on Mary*)

That should attract trade.

MARY NICHOLS. (*Doubtful*) Well...

MARY KELLY. Right. Give the clothes back.

MARY NICHOLS. Hold on. The shawl is lovely and warm and the bonnet so smart. It's true what they say – 'Clothes maketh the man'. Okay. Ta love.

(*Nichols moves to the pub door, leaving the parcel*)

Look after me fashion clothing. I won't be long. I should soon earn a few more gins wearing this outfit. (*She exits*)

〜

Nichols's hat was certainly a recent acquisition. We have that information from the doss-house deputy from whom the penniless Nichols tried to cadge accommodation on the night she was murdered. He said that he had not seen the hat before, and the victim's last reliably recorded words were: '*I'll soon get my doss money. See what a jolly bonnet I've got now*' – words that clearly indicate recent ownership of the hat. How else would Nichols have received her bonnet, if not by loan? We know that she was penniless; no one gave expensive presents in the East End; if Nichols had stolen the hat it would have been pawned to buy drink; as we've seen, John Kelly even took the boots off his feet to pledge them. And Mary would not have bought the head-wear; money has only one purpose for an alchoholic – to buy drink. On the day she died Nichols confessed to her friend, Ellen Holland, that she had earned her doss-house money three times but on each occasion the cash had been spent on gin. An alcoholic will spend money on drink before he or she will pay for lodgings, buy food, and certainly before they will buy clothing. Indeed, if Nichols had owned the bonnet while the pawn shops were open earlier in the day it would, no doubt, have been pledged. Facts indicate that she received the head wear only a short time before her murder.

To continue the scenario: Nichols, proud of her new outfit, leaves the Britannia. Up to this point in time no Ripper murders had taken place so Nichols would not have been feeling nervous. J.K. and Druitt see the hat and shawl (which they associate with Kelly) leaving the public house. Although Nichols was a few inches shorter and a bit slimmer than Mary Kelly, Victorian clothing was voluminous; layers of material reached from the chin down to the ankles, and if one looks at old photographs of the poorer women, their clothing was often similar. High fashion was not known in the poorer parts of London – long, black outfits were. Finally, a peaked bonnet would hide the face, especially in badly-lit streets. It would have been easy to fool the two men; to them, the distinctive outfit was Mary Kelly, either returning home or going to solicit. The murderous duo now follow Nichols. Most likely J.K. Stephen (as the men would have assumed that 'Mary Kelly' knew Druitt from their previous meetings) jumped from the cart and trailed his prey on foot, still thinking that he was following Kelly. The 'hat and shawl' would not have far to go, as the Britannia was close to Flower and Dean Street.

After a brief visit to the doss-house, Nichols was back on the streets. One wonders why she even tried to get lodgings without money in her pocket; she must have known the strict doss-house rules better than anyone.

James now only had to follow Nichols into one of the many dark side streets. An approach by a stranger would, of course, be a regular occurrence. Did J.K. ask, 'Is your name Mary?' It was, of course. In the badly lit, or even unlit street, late at night, with his prey wearing a peaked bonnet, it would have been difficult for Stephen to judge the woman's age or looks, although, as has already been mentioned, Nichol's father and a journalist both remarked that she looked at least ten years younger than her real age when they saw her in the mortuary. Moreover, in Stephen's state of manic fury, rational thinking would have disappeared. There are certainly examples of this kind of murder – for instance, Lord Lucan was accused of killing his children's nanny in mistake for his wife.

Bargaining would have been speedy. The cart was near and Nichols might have been delighted at having a comfortable trysting place, nestled among canvas as opposed to standing up against a wall. Druitt, assuming he had met the supposed victim, must have kept his face muffled and looked straight ahead to hide his features. Nichols would have climbed eagerly on to the back of the cart with J.K. and allowed herself to be partly covered by the tarpaulin. I repeat, as no Ripper murders had taken place by this date she would have had no fear. As Druitt drove off, J.K. (who, as A.C. Benson confirmed, was physically very strong) would have strangled her into a state of unconsciousness. It would not have taken long for Druitt to drive to Buck's Row and into the stableyard. People living nearby would have been so used to the sound of horses' hooves they would not have noticed a late-arriving cart, any more than people nowadays living near a multi-purpose garage would notice the late arrival of a car.

After pulling into the stableyard and checking that no pedestrians were approaching, the men could have easily rolled Nichols's body from the back of the cart, after which James might well have been overcome with feelings of repulsion and loathing for his victim. Still unaware that he had attacked the wrong woman, and appalled by the thought that a royal foetus that could bring ruin and disgrace might be nestling in the crumpled heap at his feet, Stephen (while his partner stabled the horse) viciously cut Nichols's throat, then lifted her skirt to slash at the vagina, the focus of his hatred and disgust. Had the murderers seen any pedestrians approaching they could easily have dodged back into the stable-yard. This killing had been achieved in silence and perfect safety. Their job completed, the duo would have returned home either by taking a train from Whitechapel – although they would have had to wait for the rail services to begin at around about 5.00 a.m. – or they could have walked back to Druitt's chambers in the Temple. Or maybe they had a safe house not so far from the scene of the crime – the Watling Street flat?

Over the weekend, it would have become clear from the copious press reports that they had murdered the wrong woman, but Stephen's reaction to this mistake is more likely to have been fury than remorse.

On the Sunday evening, 2 September, James would have left London for his Assizes in Wales, and Montague would have returned to his teaching post. Meanwhile, Mary Kelly would have been deeply disturbed. She could have had no absolute proof that the murder was personally connected to her; the killing of Nichols while wearing Kelly's clothing might well have been a curious coincidence in the violent East End, but Kelly must have had her suspicions. Erring on the side of caution, might she have boldly called on Druitt during the week? Kelly might have decided that there was only one way in which she could protect herself, apart from running away, and it would have been difficult for a penniless prostitute to dig up her roots and move. Anyway, the lure of substantial sums from the Establishment would have kept her in place; and Mary might have felt that she had the upper hand; at that time, she probably did. So did she, for protection, tell Druitt that she had stolen a memento from Bertie? She may well have done so. We know that Bertie carried mementos. Lillie Langtry, one of Bertie's many mistresses, delighted in giving friends souvenirs, as she recorded in her autobiography *The Days I Knew*. The beautiful Lillie even named the shop from where she purchased her gifts, and records the delight of the young Eddy when it was his turn to receive a memento from her. Mary would have been feeling invulnerable as she explained to Druitt that Bertie's stolen item, along with its history, had been passed on to a friend and neighbour for safe keeping. Did she name that friend as Annie Chapman? If Annie was subsequently attacked then Mary would be absolutely certain that she herself was the target for murder, and she could have made further plans for her safety. Once more a short extract from my play is used to highlight my thesis.

(*Mary in her room begins to wipe down the wall behind the bed with a sponge. There is a knock on the door.*
Mary dries her hands. Opens the door.)

MARY KELLY. Liz Stride. Darling. Come in. You got my message at the Ten Bells?

LIZ STRIDE. It's never good news when you're so welcoming, Mary Kelly.

(*Liz enters the room. She is a tall, thin, confident, intelligent woman. Her manner, even when sharp, is not unpleasant.*)

Why did you ask me to call?

MARY KELLY. How about Mary Nichols being done in at the weekend?

LIZ STRIDE. The girls talk of nothing else. Did you hear the details? Poor Mary was stretched out in Buck's Row, throat cut from ear to ear, her skirt up, belly slashed, everything on show.

MARY KELLY. The bastard that killed Nichols got the wrong one. He was after me.

LIZ STRIDE. Gerr off.

MARY KELLY. He was. That's why Mary was found with her dress pulled up. They were looking for valuables. They must have known that all us East End girls keep any valuables in a purse around our waists.

LIZ STRIDE. Nichols was penniless.

MARY KELLY. I said – they were after *me* – after *my* valuables.

LIZ STRIDE. What valuables have you got? You're always as skint as the rest of us.

MARY KELLY. When they found nothing, they slashed Mary's stomach, as if to say, 'That's where babies come from'.

LIZ STRIDE. What are you talking about?

MARY KELLY. Never mind.

LIZ STRIDE. Why do you think anyone would want to murder you?

MARY KELLY. In the Ten Bells, Mary Nichols insisted on borrowing my clothes. When she left the pub, a man, who'd been stalking me, began to follow her.

LIZ STRIDE. Coincidence.

MARY KELLY. That's my one worry. Anything can happen to any one in the East End. So Mary's murder might have been a coincidence. I don't think so, but it just might. I need to be certain – although I still believe they were after me.

LIZ STRIDE. Why would anyone be interested in you?

MARY KELLY. You'd be surprised. To make certain, I'll set a trap for the bastards. And that is where you can help.

LIZ STRIDE. (*Cynical*) Oh yes? How, precisely? (*Loud knock*)

MARY KELLY. (*Frightened*) Who's that?

LIZ STRIDE. Open the door and find out. (*Another loud knock.*) You are terrified of someone. What's been going on?

MRS MCCARTHY. (*Offstage.*) Open the door, Mary.

MARY KELLY. Oh Jesus, it's only the landlady. This hatchet-faced old cow could chop firewood with her chin.

(*She opens the door and speaks warmly*)

Mrs McCarthy. Come in, darling. I've just put the kettle on.

MRS MCCARTHY. I don't want tea, Mary. I want rent. One week in advance.

MARY KELLY. Mrs McCarthy – just for once . . .

MRS MCCARTHY. You know the rules. Absolutely no one lodges without advance payment. You have a room to yourself, with its own front door.

MARY KELLY. And I just love the place to death, even with the wood worm and the damp. They add such character to the room. But right now, my boyfriend Joe is out of work. And I don't have much time to follow my trade, and I've got special expenses.

LIZ STRIDE. Such as?

MARY KELLY. I can't say, but – take a chance on me, Mrs McCarthy.

MRS MCCARTHY. I'm sorry. I'd like to help, but . . .

MARY KELLY. Hear me out. I have a nob over a barrel. I wish I could tell you the whole story, but I can't say a word until my case comes up. I've been consulting a barrister. (*The word is effective.*)

MRS MCCARTHY. A barrister? A proper one?

MARY KELLY. Look. (*She hands over a business card.*)

MRS MCCARTHY. 'M. J. Druitt. Barrister'. What beautiful printing. What a beautiful card.

MARY KELLY. Lord Druitt is one of the best.

LIZ STRIDE. He's a Lord?

MARY KELLY. Yes. And his father's an Earl.

MRS MCCARTHY. Oh my.

MARY KELLY. The family dine with the royal family regularly. So of course, they know how to deal with the nob that I'm suing.

(*She covers her mouth.*)

I mustn't say any more. I've said too much already.

MRS MCCARTHY. (*Impressed*) I've never known anyone who's consulted a barrister before – let alone an Earl.

MARY KELLY. His mother's a Countess. They are all so distinguished. Yet you've never met anyone nicer. You really must come and meet

Lord Druitt once my case is over, Mrs McCarthy. He and I are getting – well, let's say – very friendly.

MRS MCCARTHY. (*Giggly*) My goodness. You'll have us all dining at the Palace with the Queen, soon.

MARY KELLY. Don't think that couldn't happen. Eventually this nob will have to pay me a fortune. And I mean a fortune. That's Earl Druitt's opinion, not mine.

LIZ STRIDE. I thought he was 'Lord' Druitt.

MARY KELLY. You are ignorant, Liz. The title of a Lord and an Earl are interchangeable. Of course, Lord Druitt will take a cut of my money for himself, but there'll be plenty to cut into. So I'll do you a favour Mrs McCarthy – I'll offer you and your husband a hundred per cent interest on any money owing.

MRS MCCARTHY. You must be on to a good thing, when a titled barrister is involved – giving you his card and all that.

MARY KELLY. It's just a question of finalising the deal. As the Earl said – I'll soon have so much wealth I'll be tipping the tradesmen sovereigns.

MRS MCCARTHY. He said that?

MARY KELLY. His very words. I tell you what – I'll guarantee you two hundred per cent interest on any rent owing and a twenty guinea bonus. That may sound fantasy, but if you knew who I've got my claws into, you'd understand.

(*Pause.*)

MRS MCCARTHY. I always knew that you'd make something of yourself, Mary. How long will this all take?

MARY KELLY. A fortnight or so. Or maybe a bit longer. But it will be worth waiting for. Don't kill the golden goose, Mrs McCarthy.

MRS MCCARTHY. Well. (*She considers*) It's always nice to give a youngster a helping hand.

MARY KELLY. You're so generous. (*She hugs Mrs McCarthy.*) You won't regret this once I'm loaded.

MRS MCCARTHY. You're a real character, and no mistake. A titled barrister. Well, I never. I'll try and persuade Mr McCarthy. (*She exits.*)

MARY KELLY. That'll need four words. 'Do it, or else. ' I think he shaves her while she powders his nose. (*Liz laughs*) At least I can be sure the greedy, avaricious old bitch will keep her mouth shut. If she had a route map to heaven in her hand, she wouldn't tell her own grandmother the way.

LIZ STRIDE. Just what are you up to, Mary Kelly, you sly bitch? And what was that load of rubbish?

MARY KELLY. Sorry?

LIZ STRIDE. You must think I'm as stupid as your landlady. 'Lord' –

'Earl' Druitt, indeed. When did a member of the gentry work? They don't have to.

MARY KELLY. There's always the odd exception, Liz.

LIZ STRIDE. What's going on, you lying bitch?

MARY KELLY. Well, I *am* seeing a barrister. And I *will* be getting loads of money.

LIZ STRIDE. Who from? (*Mary smiles and touches her nose*) And what's this favour you want?

MARY KELLY. I borrowed a few trinkets from a titled nob.

LIZ STRIDE. Oh not again. We've all warned you. Pinch from the poor. They're too skint to fight back.

MARY KELLY. I like the excitement. And if this one comes off, it will be the jackpot of all jackpots. That's why I'm consulting a barrister. But meanwhile, I have a few trinkets that the nob wants back, so could I pretend you're safe-keeping them for me?

LIZ STRIDE. Like buggery. What do you take me for?

MARY KELLY. (*Glancing out of the window*) Jesus. Liz. Look. That man in the shadows on the other side of the court. (*Liz goes and stares.*) Careful. Don't let him see you looking. He's the one who did Nichols in.

LIZ STRIDE. You can't know that.

MARY KELLY. I do. He's the one who was following me, then he followed Nichols when she was wearing my clothes. So it's a reasonable assumption to think the worst. Unless he's just trying to put the frighteners on me? Let's set a trap and find out.

LIZ STRIDE. What are you talking about?

MARY KELLY. Who could I say is safe-keeping my trinkets, if you won't help?

LIZ STRIDE. Your boyfriend, Joe.

MARY KELLY . No, I don't want him involved. Who else?

LIZ STRIDE. Who lives next door?

MARY KELLY. Annie Chapman.

LIZ STRIDE. The obvious choice, then. But talk to Annie before involving her in something dangerous.

MARY KELLY. There's no danger. It was easy enough to mistake Mary Nichols for me, in the dark, wearing my clothes and with a wide-brimmed bonnet hiding her face. But no one could mix me up with short, fat Annie. Get out there and strike up a conversation with that gitt. Let him pump you – and make sure he learns that my valuables are being kept with Annie Chapman.

LIZ STRIDE. I'm not getting involved in your dangerous games.

MARY KELLY. You'll be involved the moment that bastard sees you leaving this room. They're trying to scare me. They'll find that easier said than done. (*Liz goes to argue*) When I'm rich, I'll guarantee to get you out of the East End. That is a firm promise. Come and live with me in the West End if you like. We've always got on well. So . . . ?

LIZ STRIDE. (*After consideration*) Who could resist that? Where are the valuables that are causing such a fuss?

MARY KELLY. Never mind. You set the trap, then we'll see if the mice come out to play. In fact, I'll sew up muslin in a bag, and ask Annie to keep it for me. I'll tell her it's valuable. A real test.

LIZ STRIDE. Look, Mary . . .

MARY KELLY. Don't let me down, Liz. Help me just this once, and you will benefit beyond your wildest dreams. I promise gold the like you've never seen before. Go on – talk to that shadow out there. Will you? For me? Yes?

Liz Stride considers carefully. Mary waits anxiously for her reply.
Lights out on the 'Rough Room'.

ော

Mary's escape from death, and her games, hiding the stolen trinket, could have been construed as a challenge by J.K. A man of his inflated ego would have been driven into a manic fury by such hubris from (to his way of thinking) an East End slut. And he may well, in this deranged state, have been suffering from delusions of grandeur, an aberration whereby the person feels totally invulnerable and above all law and authority: the Ripper's behaviour did indeed indicate such a state of mind, as a distinguished Australian psychiatrist, Dr Anthony Orsmond, pointed out to me. Certainly, backed by the power of the Establishment, James would have felt invulnerable.

Let us now return to my version of events before Annie Chapman's death. If Kelly had indeed spun a cunning plot to protect herself by naming the unfortunate Annie Chapman, then the unbalanced and infuriated James, on his return to London from Wales the following weekend, could easily have determined on a further murder. He might have decided that Annie must also be murdered – then searched. If he could retrieve Bertie's goods much of Mary's power would be taken away. Maybe James reasoned that if the killing was savage enough, Mary Kelly might be so stunned and frightened she would be terrified into silence and obedience. Such reasoning is not new. Primitive tribes have long used this method to keep members of their communities under strict control. In the past, several native American tribes, in secret initiation ceremonies for boys passing into manhood, used to perform acts so terrifying and dramatic that the youngsters were shocked into a state of permanent fear of the elders. Masks used during this type of tribal ceremony are frequently grotesque and frightening. The brutality of the

Ripper murders display the same basic intent to terrify.

To return to my theory: the week after Nichols's killing, J.K. Stephen and Montague Druitt were once again in the East End and Annie Chapman was now their target. We know that Annie was turned out of the doss-house around 2.a.m. She was seen by a night-watchman, John Evans, as she turned into Paternoster Row. Frederick Stevens, a fellow lodger at Annie's usual doss-house, reported to the newspapers that he had been drinking with her (probably in the Britannia) in the early hours of the morning, before her murder. Was this after she had been turned out of her usual lodgings? If so, it looks as though Annie had been lucky and found a client and had decided to spend the money on drink – a typical decision for an alcoholic as we have seen. Did the murderers, while hunting for Annie, re-enact the Nichols affair? Let us again speculate. J.K. Stephen might have tracked Annie down to The Britannia in the early hours. Glancing through the door he could have asked a woman who was leaving whether Annie Chapman was inside. The woman might have pointed out J.K.'s intended victim. As soon as she left The Britannia Annie could have been followed.

The time of her death was officially estimated to be around 4.30 a.m., although with imprecise Victorian medical calculations there are variations on this time, but it is clear that several hours have to be accounted for. Maybe another client turned up, and Annie then indulged herself with another drink. Maybe, feeling ill, she reported to an all-night infirmary, either for further treatment (pills from previous infirmary visits were still on her body when she was killed) or in the hope that they would take her in. The unfortunate woman must certainly have been feeling dreadful.

Whatever happened, I am sure that J.K. and Druitt were not far behind, waiting for the chance to kill her. Finally J.K. would have found the right opportunity; when no pedestrians were around Chapman was approached. As she was feeling unwell (and little wonder, she was near to death from natural causes) she might have declined an offer to climb onto the back of the cart. But a convenient yard was close at hand. This venue would not have worried (and might even have helped) James. After the murder, he needed space to search the body and the clothing. *The Times's* view, that '... the assassin, if not suffering from insanity, appears to be free from any fear of interruption while on his dreadful work' was near the mark. Careful planning had replaced the need for luck. With Annie lying dead on the ground at his feet, James could now search the body for any souvenir that Kelly might have entrusted to her friend for safe keeping.

Poor people tended to keep valuables on their person, although they seldom had anything worth hiding; so why would the killer waste time, and court the threat of discovery, if he was not looking for something specific? None of the other victims had their goods examined. A quick examination of Annie's pocket yielded no result, so, in a further display of rage, arrogant contempt and self-confidence, J.K. carefully arranged Annie's few pathetic trinkets on the ground. We know that Annie was penniless earlier in the evening. If she earned money from a client, it would have been at least four-pence, if not more. Or did J.K. personally provide the polished farthings that were found at Annie's feet – perhaps with the royal portrait upward – a tilt at Bertie? To repeat, several writers have cast doubt on the coins, yet at the inquest of an unrelated murder victim, a police witness stated: '. . . for underneath the body was found a bloodstained farthing . . . the assumption is that it was given to the deceased in the same way as similar coins were passed upon the Hanbury Street victim [Annie Chapman] as half-sovereigns . . . in that instance they had been brightly polished.'

Finally, as a further display of rage and disgust, and maybe as an attempt to signal to Mary Kelly the kind of fate she might possibly expect, the organ most central to the Ripper affair, the uterus, was cut out and taken away. This would have been a clear warning to the pregnant prostitute.

It has always been assumed that Jack cut away the vital organs from his victim then stuffed them into his pocket or into a bag, but this method of transporting human tissue would allow blood to seep from it, which might be noticed by any number of people. According to my thesis, James had only to wrap the bloody pieces of flesh in a piece of oilcloth, perhaps reinforced by newspaper or a towel, then slip his dreadful souvenirs under the tarpaulin on the back of the cart. His own bloodstained clothing could have been changed at the stableyard, or even under the tarpaulin, his task unseen during the dark ride through unlit side streets. Blood could have been wiped from his hands by a damp towel also kept on the cart. This explanation would solve the mystery of Jack's legendary invisibility.

As we have seen, a cover-up by the authorities must have started as early as the inquest into Annie Chapman's death. We are now faced with the problem of Mary Kelly's reaction to these grim proceedings. We know from Joseph Barnett's testimony that Mary was frightened not only by the murders (the whole East End population was paralysed with fear for the same reason) but also of 'someone'. Here is Barnett's evidence again.

CORONER. Have you heard her [Mary Kelly] speak of being afraid of anyone?

BARNETT. Yes, several times. I bought newspapers and I read to her everything about the murders, which she asked me about.

We also know, through a friend of Kelly's, Lizzie Albrook, that Mary wanted to leave the country. Clearly, without funds, this was not possible, and Kelly was trapped. She had still not received any money from the Establishment and she was in serious debt to her landlord. Despite her fear, the alluring prospect of cash and great comfort must still have loomed large in her mind – riches for the taking, if only she could keep her nerve and outwit her adversaries.

∽

Is it possible that at this juncture in the proceedings Queen Victoria interfered, and that this interference provided a new complication? The Queen took a great interest in the Ripper murders, as her notes on the subject to her then Prime Minister, Lord Salisbury, show. The following theory can be only supposition – much of the Ripper solution has to be – but I am selecting facts that will fit in with the baffling, and apparently inexplicable scenario. We are dealing with facts, so there has to be an answer (no matter how outlandish) to the puzzles.

That Victoria had spies everywhere is a solid fact. She knew all the Court intrigues and all the gossip, knowledge that caused one of her exasperated ministers to ask, 'Where *does* she get her information from?' It is almost certain that news of an illegitimate royal child would quickly come to the Queen's attention. Any such baby would be Albert's grandchild, by blood if not by ties of marriage, and Victoria's passion for her dead husband still raged. Given this continuing passion, the idea that a direct descendent from Albert might be killed, even before birth, would have aroused the Queen's fury, and this could be a fearsome emotion. Victoria had been known to sweep her dressing table clear during one of her uncontrollable rages. Did the Queen insist that Kelly's foetus be fully conceived and delivered? Such insistence would fit in with the Queen's other actions toward her dead husband – actions that could hardly be called mentally balanced. Each day Albert's bed was made up, even his chamber pot was scoured. Victoria, when faced with problems, would 'consult' her dead husband by holding one of his treasured possessions and waiting for his thoughts to be directed to her from heaven; such behaviour borders on the psychotic. Victoria's unhinged passion for Albert – and no doubt for his blood-line, may well have overcome possible feelings of hatred and disgust for the child's mother.

We must now consider how the Establishment would have viewed the Queen's interference. The high authorities most likely to be concerned with the matter were the police commissioner, Sir Charles Warren (who was certainly part of a cover-up); Sir William Gull (whose notes indicated that he had private information about the murders); Inspector Frederick George Abberline (who was in charge of the ground forces during the murders, a man who hinted that he knew the killer's identity); and possibly the Prime Minister, Lord Salisbury, as the holder of the highest office in the land. They would have had their own safety to consider if insurrection swept the country, and, as we saw earlier, a pregnant Catholic prostitute represented a great threat to the State – and thereby to themselves. It had so far proved difficult to murder the cunning, intelligent Kelly, and now such a course of action was being forbidden by Queen Victoria, at least until her grandchild had been delivered.

Even if Mary just disappeared, and if she did indeed possess proof of her liaison with Bertie, then awkward questions might have been asked. And once the child was born Mary would be even more dangerous. The prostitute held powerful cards in her hand and she must have now been treated with a new respect by the Establishment. The best plan would be to try and consult with Kelly – to lure her onto their side, then she might be persuaded to help during this crisis.

My own choice as a negotiator for any deal would be Sir William Gull. Having been born in humble circumstances he presumably had the 'common touch' and he certainly had the best interests of the Royal Family at heart. A contract between Mary and the Establishment might have been in the process of negotiation when a new complication arose. Catharine Eddowes, who frequently called herself 'Mary Kelly' (Kelly being the surname of her common-law husband), started to spread the news that she knew the identity of Jack the Ripper. A much-delayed reward had been offered for information which could lead to the serial killer's arrest, and this money naturally attracted Catharine. As we saw in Chapter 5, the Superintendent of a casual ward related (in an October interview with *The East London Observer*) how Catharine had told him she was about to claim the reward money; she knew Jack's identity. Such a claim would almost certainly have been repeated to other people.

Once news of this statement became known (even if Catharine was mistaken or only boasting) the Establishment might have been worried that Mary Kelly, perhaps while drunk, had hinted at, or had actually discussed, her deadly information. This, like many other Ripper mysteries, can only remain the subject of speculation, but it fits the known facts.

To recapitulate: Queen Victoria has forbidden the killing of Kelly while she is carrying a royal child with Albert's bloodline. Then news reaches the Establishment that a woman is claiming to know the identity of the Ripper; that might mean she knows the reason behind the killings. A dilemma. J.K. Stephen now decides, either unilaterally or with the consent of the powers behind the throne, that Eddowes must be silenced. I see no reason why Stephen, when he had free time, should not have personally wandered around the East End during daylight hours, picking up gossip and information. As I have written earlier in the text, Paul Begg mentioned to me the puzzle of 'the unidentified stranger' seen with Mary Kelly in Miller's Court two days before her death. This stranger was described by Thomas Bowyer as being smartly dressed, aged around 27 or 28, with 'very peculiar eyes'. Could that have been J.K? Had he by now met and bewitched Mary Kelly with his charm, power and handsome looks? Had he persuaded Kelly that she had as much to lose as anyone if Eddowes talked? Did he persuade Kelly to change sides? Once again I have been tempted to include a scene from my play as the dialogue has clarified the situation for several friends and contacts.

> SCENE TWO. *Lights rise on the study. Montague and James sit facing across the desk.*
>
> JAMES. Kelly is late.
>
> MONTAGUE DRUITT. Maybe she won't come?
>
> JAMES. Why shouldn't she?
>
> MONTAGUE DRUITT. Annie Chapman's murder might have paralysed her with fright.
>
> JAMES. That was the object of the exercise. Now the whore knows what she is up against. And what might happen to her if she doesn't co-operate with us. As I said recently to Eddy, 'Terror can make a splendid road block.'
>
> (*Pause. James goes to the door and looks out into the corridor.*)
>
> No sign yet. In a strange way, I'm looking forward to meeting this brazen-faced whore.
>
> (*Pause*)
>
> MONTAGUE DRUITT. If she comes.
>
> JAMES. If she doesn't, we'll have to go out and find her. I've promised Sir William Gull that I'll retrieve the prince's stolen goods. And I will.
>
> MONTAGUE DRUITT. I don't know how you can be so sure.
>
> JAMES. I am sure because it is my wish, so it will happen.
>
> MONTAGUE DRUITT. If only I could be that confident.
>
> JAMES. Not only must I retrieve the stolen goods – I must also get Kelly working on our side for a short time.
>
> MONTAGUE DRUITT. That would need a miracle.
>
> JAMES. Then I must work a miracle.
>
> MONTAGUE DRUITT. Not even you...
>
> JAMES. It is essential that the whore helps us overcome this new danger.
>
> MONTAGUE DRUITT. You mean the woman who is going around saying she knows who the killer is?

JAMES. Yes.

MONTAGUE DRUITT. That might be idle talk.

JAMES. On the other hand, maybe it isn't.

MONTAGUE DRUITT. My fear is not that someone has already talked. I'm afraid that Chapman's murder might have frightened Kelly too much. Instead of shutting her up, it might *start* her talking.

JAMES. No. The whore will keep her mouth shut.

MONTAGUE DRUITT. Why? Because you wish it?

JAMES. No, because, number one – we've terrified her. And even more importantly – because a blackmailer's power relies on secrecy.

MONTAGUE DRUITT. Kelly might prefer to lose her power rather than her life.

JAMES. She won't suspect that she is going to lose either. Sir William, of course, is adamant that she will.

MONTAGUE. Maybe Kelly has worked that out. She's an intelligent woman.

JAMES. Greed will overcome her fear. You'll see – when Kelly arrives –

MONTAGUE DRUITT. If she does...

JAMES. I will snare her into our camp.

MONTAGUE DRUITT. Never. I'd take a large bet against that.

JAMES. How much? (*There are noises off stage, then a tap on the door.*) Here she is. I knew she'd come. I feel quite excited.

James steps into a corner. The door bursts open.

Mary Kelly appears. Without warning she flies at Druitt, failing to notice James.

MARY KELLY. You murdering bastards. Even a week after Annie Chapman's death, my flesh feels pumped up with fear and rage. If the murder and mutilations were designed to terrify me, then by Christ they have. I'm so dazed every step drains energy from my body. For a week I've stayed locked in my room, frozen with terror. (*The furious Kelly leans across the desk, fingers clawed.*) I should scratch your bloody eyes out.

(*James moves sharply forward.*)

JAMES. Sit down. And don't bring your gutter-snipe manners into this office.

(MARY KELLY *whirls around, startled by James's unseen presence, and the authority in his voice*)

MARY KELLY. Who are you?

JAMES. We were sorry to hear about Mrs Chapman's death, but it had nothing to do with either of us.

MARY KELLY. Lying bastard.

(*James bends close and hisses.*)

JAMES. (*Icy*) Do not be offensive. I repeat – your friend's death had nothing to do with Mr Druitt – or me.

MARY KELLY. (*Stunned by James's authority*) Perhaps not personally, but I'd bet some of your nob friends were involved.

JAMES. That is a libellous statement. What proof do you have for such a serious allegation? You could find yourself under arrest for making remarks like that.

MARY KELLY. (*Turning*) I've had enough of you bastards.

JAMES. Does it ever occur to you that we might have had enough of you?

MARY KELLY. I should have known that someone like me couldn't win against the likes of you. So. If I can't get support for my child from his posh father I'll drag the baby up myself. A nice life a royal baby will have in the East End.

JAMES. We are prepared to pay you. Handsomely.

MARY KELLY. I'll believe that when I see it.

JAMES. On my word as a gentleman – you'll get paid.

MARY KELLY. So will you buy back my royal trinkets?

JAMES. No.

MARY KELLY. I knew it. You bastards are all talk.

JAMES. You will get paid when the stolen goods have been returned. We will not give in to blackmail. (*Mary throws a parcel onto the table.*)

MARY KELLY. Here. Dumping these was one of my reasons for calling. I don't want my throat cut over a few lousy trinkets. I know that your lot murdered Annie to get back the goods in that package.

(*James examines the contents*)

They're all there. Including the official seal. Satisfied?

MONTAGUE DRUITT. So Mrs Chapman wasn't minding the valuables after all? You had them. Did you put the false story around?

MARY KELLY. Never you mind. Now you've got the things back you won't hear anything further from me. So just leave me alone and I'll leave you alone. And God help the royal child.

(*Kelly goes to the door. As she reaches to open it, James clamps her hand. Mary turns, frightened.*)

MARY KELLY. Let me out.

JAMES. Don't be frightened, Mary. Neither my friend nor I are violent. Now that you have returned the stolen goods – now my associates no longer have a threat hanging over their heads – you will get the support you have been demanding.

MARY KELLY. When? I'm desperate. I'm pregnant – I owe rent – I owe money on the slate all over the place. I need cash now.

JAMES. Shall we give the lady something on account, Montague?

MONTAGUE DRUITT. Why not?

JAMES. Very well. Here is a sovereign.

MARY KELLY. That won't even start to pay off my debts.

JAMES. Then I'll add another. (*He does so.*) Soon there will be a pot of gold.

MARY KELLY. When?

JAMES. When you've joined my associates. When you've helped them.

MARY KELLY. Helped you lot? After what's happened? I wouldn't lift a finger. (*Her temper starts to rise again.*) All I'm getting are promises. I'll make my own way. Bugger the lot of you and good riddance. (*She turns.*)

JAMES. (*Barring her way.*) Mary – you don't understand what an important woman you have become.

MARY KELLY. For the last time – leave me alone – you've got your things back – so bugger off.

JAMES. The mother of English royalty wields great power. I must be frank – it's not so much you that concerns my friends – it's the unborn baby.

MARY KELLY. That makes sense. I thought it odd – the toffs allowing one of their own to be dragged up in East End filth. I'd expected a nice house in a nice area.

JAMES. That is the least you will get. And there will be far more. Soon you will become part of the aristocracy. Your child will underwrite such an elevation.

MARY KELLY. Honestly?

JAMES. On my honour.

MARY KELLY. I knew it. I dreamt it. I've always felt that I was destined to be something special. The trouble is, I wouldn't trust either of you as far as I could throw you.

JAMES. How can we prove our sincerity?

MARY KELLY. You can't.

JAMES. Those blackmail items that you stole...

MARY KELLY. 'Blackmail?' Asking a rich nob to support his child?

JAMES. Very well. (*He picks up the package.*) Here are the things you borrowed. Your protection returned. Could we show our faith in a more solid form?

(*Pause.*)

MARY KELLY. What's the catch?

JAMES. There isn't one. I'm putting myself back in your power. Soon you will be part of the Establishment, so what have we to fear? What have you to fear? You cannot doubt our sincerity. You are carrying royal blood – that makes you a woman of great importance. You must see that – you are an intelligent woman. And a beautiful one. You must know that soon your child will be the passport to a change in your fortunes, taking you from East End squalor to West End luxury.

MARY KELLY. Oh Christ, how I would love to get back to all that.

JAMES. And you shall. Soon you will have a house, a carriage, fine clothing – soon you will be attending glittering West End parties.

MARY KELLY. Your words are setting me on fire, Mr . . . ?

JAMES. Mr name is James Stephen. Will you do me the honour of calling me 'James'?

MARY KELLY. I'd give anything to go to a posh West End do once again. Scent instead of stink. Elegance instead of violence. I could still turn heads with the right clothes and a bit of money to spend on tarting myself up.

JAMES. That is obvious. With grooming, you will be the belle of the ball.

MARY KELLY. (*Softly*) Would I ? Would you like to see me in a tight-bodiced, velvet dress, all cleaned and groomed and powdered?

JAMES. Now you're setting *my* blood on fire. Add a diamond clip holding up your hair and the imagery would make me tremble.

MARY KELLY. So you can imagine me as I might be?

JAMES. Very clearly.

(*There is a sudden spark between the couple. Kelly speaks softly, her voice emotional.*)

MARY KELLY. Once I have money, I know exactly the hair style that you would like. (*She stares at James.*) I don't know how you've done this, but within minutes you have made the past totally unimportant. Even poor Annie is unimportant. She was so ill she would have been dead soon anyway. Maybe I did her a good turn setting her up – not much pleasure in struggling through an East End winter only to die in the Spring. The future you've opened up for me, Mr Stephen . . .

JAMES. . . . 'James',

MARY KELLY. Sorry. Your words have totally swallowed the past for me. Will I really be taken back into high West End society?

JAMES. I don't see how a woman as beautiful as you could doubt it.

MARY KELLY. (*Softly*) Do you really think I'm beautiful?

JAMES. Exceptionally so. You remind me of a younger version of my mother, and no one could be more attractive than that.

MARY KELLY. What a lovely thing to say. (*Pause. The couple hold eye contact.*) In my new life, would I be protected from anyone in the West End with a grudge against me and a long memory?

JAMES. In your new position you will be invulnerable. You will be more important and more powerful than many titled hosts. No one would dare to raise a finger against you.

MARY KELLY. Only a few minutes ago I was stuffed full of terror, now I'm stuffed full of hope. Pictures of the future – horses, carriages, houses – have wiped away every doubt. I'd need posh clothes. Money.

JAMES. As the mother of royalty you will be fully provided for.

MARY KELLY. But when will this start?

JAMES. Once you have earned our trust. You might have let us down already.

MARY KELLY. How?

JAMES. Do you know a Catharine Eddowes?

MARY KELLY. Of course.

JAMES. We have a network of efficient East End informants. Apparently Mrs Eddowes is going around saying she can give information leading to the killer's arrest. And she seems very confident.

MARY KELLY. I haven't said anything.

JAMES. Are you sure? I know you drink, and that can loosen the tightest of tongues. (*Mary looks frightened.*) Informants tell us that Eddowes is saying she can help the police solve the killings.

MARY KELLY. The loose-mouthed bitch. She could cause no end of trouble – for all of us. And I have my baby to think of now.

MONTAGUE DRUITT. Exactly. Might Eddowes start revealing what she knows?

MARY KELLY. Not the important stuff. She's a canny bitch. But we need to act quickly. Where is she?

MONTAGUE DRUITT. The lady returned from hop picking this morning.

MARY KELLY. I'm beginning to understand your colleagues' way of thinking. You have to protect yourself in any way possible. Your mates are good at wiping people away. Why shouldn't the same thing happen to Eddowes?

JAMES. (*horrified*) You mean – another murder?

MARY KELLY. You may be shocked, but your violent colleagues won't be. They can give Eddowes the usual treatment – shut her mouth for good.

JAMES. We can't condone violence.

MARY KELLY. Your friends can. My solution would solve a lot of problems.

(*Long pause, as James strides around, deep in thought.*)

JAMES. You know, Montague, Miss Kelly is right. When you think of all that is at stake – not least to Miss Kelly and her unborn royal child. They must be protected from danger at all costs. And I suppose, being rational, the killing of a dangerous, worthless woman is not too bad, if it protects people like Mary.

(*To Mary*) If I can persuade our associates to carry out your plan, we would need your help.

MARY KELLY. Anything you want. (*She stares at James, examining his handsome face.*) I'll have to get Eddowes on her own – quickly – before she can say anything damaging, James. I'll have to get the bitch drunk, and she can put it away. I'd need more gold.

JAMES. I will make arrangements at the appropriate time. After getting Eddowes drunk, you will have to deliver her to a pre-arranged spot, and help us lure her onto a cart. Then our friends can deal with her.

MARY KELLY. No problem.

JAMES. May we shake hands on the deal?

(*He holds out his hand. Mary takes it. She holds the grip and stares at James. She is clearly smitten.*)

JAMES. What beautiful eyes you have.

MARY KELLY. Do you really think so?

JAMES. Look in a mirror if you don't believe me. Look at the full lips – the perfect bone structure. You are very beautiful.

MARY KELLY. Wait until you see me all dolled up.

JAMES. I look forward to that.

MARY KELLY. Goodbye, James.

(*She goes to pick up the souvenirs. James beats her to it.*)

JAMES. You don't need these now, do you? After all, they do rightfully belong to the Prince of Wales.

MARY KELLY. Yes. (*She turns.*)

JAMES. If holding on to them makes you feel safer, by all means . . .

(*He gestures*)

MARY KELLY. (*Still dazed*) No – keep the stuff. I trust you.

JAMES. (*Moving close and staring into her eyes*) Thank you for that, Mary. You don't know how much your trust means to me.

MARY KELLY. If there is anything else that I can do, let me know.

JAMES. I will.

MARY KELLY. I so look forward to our next meeting.

JAMES. And I.

(*Mary moves to the door, then turns and stares at James. She exits. James turns to Druitt in triumph.*)

JAMES. She is in our web.

MONTAGUE DRUITT. Amazing. I would never have believed it. You can hypnotise people with your words, James. The woman has fallen under your spell.

JAMES. A one-sided affair. I hate women in general and Kelly in particular. If my hate for her could be weighed, the tonnage would tilt the world. I will enjoy leading the whore on with tales of a glittering future. Making her believe that I lust after her, when, in fact, the feel of her body against mine would make me vomit. Once Miss Kelly is tangled in our web, Montague, she will be in for a surprise. Such a surprise. Indeed, one might say the surprise of her life.

(*Lights out on the study*.)

∽

As is apparent from the above dialogue, I strongly suspect that Kelly was, by now, on the side of the Establishment. It is not difficult to imagine her being seduced by her new power and by her meeting with men such as Sir William Gull, J.K. Stephen, and Montague Druitt. There is a natural tendency for underlings to believe and trust implicitly the word of someone in a position of the highest authority. To be told that Queen Victoria was taking a personal interest in the safety of the child and its mother would have been a powerful drug. Kelly must have been convinced that the child was her passport to safety and luxury, in which case she would have been only too willing to help out in any way she could. The need to commit a new murder might have provided the authorities with an opportunity to trap Kelly.

Are there any pointers to Kelly's involvement in the later murders? As we have seen, she was, amazingly, allowed to run up a huge debt in the months before her 'death' (or disappearance) which means she was probably able to convince her landlords she was expecting cash. The former CID officer turned crime writer, Hargrave Lee Adam, wrote in his introduction to *The Trial of Dr Lamson*, published in 1912, 'If you wish to discover the motives of a cunning person, you must apply common sense to his actions. Every man has a motive for his smallest action; if his actions are not governed by custom and habit, then he has an ulterior motive.' Interestingly, Mary Kelly stopped going to her usual haunt The Britannia about one month before her own 'death'; that is around the time of the double murder of Stride and Eddowes.

Maybe Kelly was made to believe that it would be best for everyone, herself included, if, at some point, she should 'disappear'. Maybe clever talk by clever people convinced her that if her own identity could be exchanged with that of someone else, she could then melt away into a life of luxury and ease. And maybe she did just that. Here it is useful to repeat the strange fact that not one member of her family turned up before or after her funeral, despite proceedings being delayed while a search was made for them. I have seen a suggestion that maybe the family could not afford the journey, but surely they would have identified themselves to the authorities? Then any newspaper or even the police would have been willing to arrange financial matters. Did the family know that Mary had been spirited away, while maybe not knowing the reason behind her disappearance?

There has to be some explanation for this totally baffling scenario –

a 'dead woman' holding a conversation and the subsequent disappearance of her family. Many writers and authorities have claimed that Mary Kelly was the key to the Ripper affair, and it is indeed an extraordinary coincidence, much remarked upon, that two women using the same name should be targets of the killer. Perhaps J.K. (as in the scenario from my play) convinced Mary that if Eddowes really did have knowledge of Jack's identity as she claimed, and freely talked about it, then she would be a danger not only to the Establishment but to Kelly herself? Certainly recruiting Kelly into their murder plot would have been a most cunning move on the part of the Establishment. If she could be persuaded to help in silencing Eddowes, then that complicity could be used as counter-blackmail. Kelly, trapped, would have to tread even more carefully and cautiously. Death by hanging for the crime of murder was commonplace in Victorian times.

Considered detachedly from a modern viewpoint, such planning might seem complicated, but one has only to recall modern instances of State plotting to realise that a scheme to involve Kelly in murder was relatively straightforward. A fairly recent example of State plotting that leaps immediately to mind is the removal of an exile by the Bulgarian authorities. Georgi Markov, a forty-nine-year-old defector, while walking along the Strand, was stabbed by the tip of a specially prepared umbrella which inserted a deadly pellet of poison into Markov's leg, causing his death. That sounds more like a fictitious method of assassination, hard to believe, but it actually happened. Then there is the history of the Watergate affair, and the many puzzles surrounding the assassination of President John Kennedy. We all know about the on-going inquiry into the death of Diana, Princess of Wales; many people believe, rightly or wrongly, that that was State murder, and there are many unanswered questions on the death of Marilyn Monroe. When powerful people in government have much to lose, State plotting, of the kind that involved Mary Kelly, has proved, over the years, to be fairly routine.

As we have seen, Catharine Eddowes's behaviour on the day of her death was distinctly unusual, a day during which she disappeared without trace for around six hours. Catharine and her partner John Kelly appear to have been a devoted couple, despite personal defects, so why did she lie to John on the eve of her death? And why did she not go straight to him after being released from custody in the early hours of the morning?

As I have already mentioned, it might be reasonably expected that someone would have reported seeing Catharine around before her arrest. No one did. She just disappeared into thin air, then reappeared out of nowhere in Aldgate High Street. It must therefore be assumed that she drank in someone's house, or in an area where she was totally unknown. But going out of the area was out of character. East Enders had their favourite watering holes to which they tended to stick. So where did Eddowes go to get drunk?

It is my belief that she was with Mary Kelly, who, setting her friend up for death, must have pumped alcohol into Catharine until she was paralytic; then Mary left Eddowes in Aldgate, ready to be picked up by the murderers on their horse and cart. But Eddowes began to cause a disturbance. Tom Cullen, in his book *Autumn Of Terror*, records that she was acting like a fire-engine. So the local police got to her before the murderers could pick her up. Alternatively, a highly-placed contact at Bishopsgate Police Station might have been drafted into the arrangements, with Catharine's arrest being deliberately engineered by the authorities. Mary Kelly, under instructions, might have deliberately left her friend on a policeman's beat. Under this arrangement, the murderers would have known exactly where Eddowes was and when they could get at her. Policemen on the beat and even coroners would have followed any instructions from their superiors without question and without needing an explanation for the orders. In Victorian times workers did as they were told in a chain of command that passed downwards from the top echelons.

Whatever actually happened, it is certain that Catharine did not spend a normal day in the hours before she was murdered, and her movements and motives are still shrouded in mystery. There is no reason to think, when Catharine told John at 2.00 p.m. that she would be back no later than 4.00 p.m., that she did not believe that herself. Whatever Catharine was planning, wherever she intended to go, she must have calculated that several hours – between 2 and 4 o'clock in the afternoon – would be sufficient time to complete her business. Clearly it was not. Intriguingly, once in police custody, Catharine, when asked her name, said she was called 'nothing', but in the office before her discharge she gave the name Mary Ann Kelly.

As we have seen, Eddowes was released from Bishopsgate Police Station in the early hours of 30 September at exactly 1.00 a.m. – a precise timing that hints at a possible pre-arrangement. Catharine's arrest had been witnessed by one of her friends who reported the event to John Kelly. He immediately, and sensibly, assumed that the police would detain Catharine for the entire night, so he did not worry about her continued absence. Even a lowly market porter had enough common sense to believe that no woman would be released in the middle of the night into Whitechapel. The police force (in general) was desperate to prevent any more murders, especially as their lack of progress in catching the killer had reflected very badly on the force's efficiency, so they constantly asked woman not to go out alone at night. But that same force, in the early hours of the morning, released the penniless Eddowes into the heart of the Ripper's territory, as though positively inviting further violence from the killer. Why?

Let us return to my version of events. After Mary Kelly had become embroiled in the conspiracy she must have been given sufficient money to cover the expenses of a day's carousing: maybe she took Catharine to an out-of-the-way drinking place where neither of them were known. Or was Kelly invited to use the Watling Street flat? She had already been there for sex with Bertie. That would make sense if Kelly had been recruited by the Establishment; and what stories might she have spun to her friend Catharine? Dreams of riches if they both unmasked the Ripper perhaps – any lie would do while Catharine drank herself into a trap.

The police, or even the police-surgeon and the coroners Roderick MacDonald and Wynne Baxter, would only have needed a set of instructions from higher authority on how to proceed; to repeat – an explanation for that course of action would be neither expected nor given. So, after approximately four hours in custody, Eddowes on gaining her freedom would have been, along with every other East End woman, suspicious of an approach by a stranger. Catharine's clear intent (indicated by her words, 'I'll get a damn fine hiding when I get home') was to head for the lodgings of her common-law husband. And this objective could have been achieved with just a few minutes' walk. Part of the plan, therefore, must have been for Mary Kelly to meet Catharine 'accidentally' on her release from Bishopsgate Police Station. Common sense tells us that a woman, on a cold night, who remembers her promise to hurry home, a woman suffering from a hangover and Bright's Disease (which causes lethargy), must have been waylaid to have ended up in Mitre Square, in the opposite direction to, and some distance from, her lover's lodgings. Being hailed as she left the police station by the lady-friend who had supplied her with drink for the whole afternoon would be a very plausible explanation for Catharine's actions after being released from custody; and that delay, which prevented her from reaching the safety of her lover's lodgings, would have set her up as an easy target. Meanwhile Kelly, by allowing herself to be used as a decoy, would have been enmeshed even further into the web that the Establishment was weaving.

It was reported that the police officer on duty watched Eddowes leave the station after her release. He saw her turn to the left, away from Flower and Dean Street. This action would fit in perfectly with the fact that someone may have called to her as soon as the station door was shut behind her. Mary, I believe, had been waiting for her victim.

We must now try to work out the killers' timetable on the night of the double homicide. It would appear, from the timing of the murders, that James and Montague were back in the East End at around half-past midnight on 30 September 1888, both prepared for violent action.

It is highly likely that Stephen and Druitt changed their stableyard throughout the ten-week Ripper operation. They would not wish to become known in any one area, so it would have made sense to move venues to different locations, perhaps several times.

Dutfield's Yard provided limited stabling facilities. It is therefore possible that by late September Stephen and Druitt were using the yard for their operations. No one would have made any enquiries about, or paid much attention to, a couple of indifferently-dressed young men. In the yard horses would have arrived and departed constantly and no one would have linked Stephen or Druitt to the murders. Let us try and follow the scenario through, using part of Israel Schwartz's statement to the police as a rough guideline. 'He saw a man stop and speak to a woman who was standing in the gateway [where the murder was committed]. The man tried to pull the woman into the street . . .'

The murderous duo must have gone to their new stabling quarters at Dutfield's Yard, where the pattern of murder suddenly changed. If Hargrave Lee Adam is correct, there has to be an ulterior motive for that change. The Stride murder is different from the other four homicides in two main respects. Firstly, the body was not mutilated, and secondly, the place of the murder was not a deserted spot. Indeed, the area outside the working men's club and around Dutfield's Yard in general was fairly busy on the night of the double murder, which means that Jack took a definite risk, which was not characteristic; he was even spotted about to begin work by Schwartz. So what made him change his usual working pattern – that of only killing in dark, deserted places where there was minimal chance of being seen? Obviously he was forced, for some reason or other, into a murder which, unlike the others, he had not planned. What could that reason be? Could it be that, unlike Nichols, Chapman or Eddowes, Liz Stride recognised her killers? There had to be some reason for Jack to kill in a relatively busy street with so many people coming and going. And Liz Stride's actions show fear towards at least one of the men, which means she recognised danger. Why?

We should also note that Schwartz's description of the two men seen during the struggle with Stride could easily fit Stephen and Druitt. '. . . the first man who threw the woman down:- age about 30; ht., 5ft 5in; comp., fair; hair, dark, small brown moustache . . .' [There are photographs of Druitt in which he has grown a small moustache.]

'...second man: age 35; ht., 5ft 11 in. comp. fresh: hair, light brown;...'

To repeat Schwartz's words yet again, as they are so important: 'The man tried to pull the woman into the street...' But why should Liz Stride resist a personable man's advances? She was waiting to be propositioned. If Liz had not been frightened, there would have been no need for Druitt to use force. A prostitute confronted by two fine-looking young men would have been more than willing to go into a dark corner with them. We know that Stride had decided to defy fate and solicit late at night in the Ripper's territory, so she was obviously not the nervous type. And Victorian theories depicted the killer as a solitary, depraved man, stalking the streets alone. There was no hint in newspapers of the time, in interviews or in published police reports, that more than one man might be involved. Liz, therefore, should have had no reason to suspect and so repulse two customers. Many young fellows would have wanted sex and that was the commodity which Liz supplied, so why did she resist and scream? If the men had ignored her advances, that in itself would not alarm her: many men doubtless did. So what was all the fuss about?

If Stephen and Druitt had pre-planned Liz's murder, they would have continued their *modus operandi* and lured Liz on to the cart without any commotion, to be taken to a dark, deserted place. The prostitute would have been only too delighted to have quietly melted away with what seemed to be two personable young fellows, so clearly some fore-knowledge about the men alarmed Liz, and her reaction to that alarm forced the normally cautious murderers to take unnecessary risks.

It is interesting to note that, according to Israel Schwartz's evidence, the man watching was peacefully lighting his pipe. J.K. Stephen smoked a pipe – he even wrote a poem dedicated to 'The Grand Old Pipe', which includes the line, 'My pipe was my one consolation'.

As I have suggested in my dramatic version of the scenario, Liz Stride might have seen Stephen or Druitt. Clearly something about the men who approached her outside Dutfield's Yard frightened her. She knew *something* about them – she realised they were dangerous. The intriguing possibility that the men knew Liz's name was raised by my first editor, Roderick Brown.

Let us yet again examine part of Israel Schwartz's invaluable state-ment. 'The man who threw the woman down called out, apparently to the man on the opposite side of the road, "Lipski".' We must ask our-selves why? The man on the opposite side of the road clearly was not a casual passer-by, as Schwartz tells us that the man stood '...lighting his pipe'. People who watch a violent incident do not casually light up tobacco while observing the drama. But why would the attacker call out

'Lipski' to his confederate? This was a term of abuse for Jews. Now Schwartz, who spoke no English, appeared to know the word 'Lipski', so he may well have been subjected to the insult. Mr Brown acutely observed that 'Liz Stride' called loudly and quickly, may well sound like 'Lipski' to foreign ears, especially to a man who spoke no English and who, perhaps, half-expected to hear such an insult.

A friend, William Pearson, the distinguished writer of *Tornado Down*, went a step further along this line. William suggested that 'Lizzie' was even closer to 'Lipski'. So was it a case of the wrong place at the wrong time for Liz Stride? Were the killers calling at Dutfield's Yard to collect their cart when they inadvertently met Liz Stride, who recognised them? Did Schwartz hear 'Lizzie' or 'Liz Stride' being called out, either word easily translated to the alarmed foreigner's ears as 'Lipski'? On his return from chasing Schwartz, Stephen must have found that his friend had already silenced their prey by strangulation to stop her screaming. The autopsy report stated that Stride had been asphyxiated prior to having her throat cut. But perhaps, just as J.K. returned to the entrance of Dutfield's Yard, he noticed that Mrs Mortimer (who testified the timing) had appeared at her doorway.

The men now had to get rid of the inert body. Stride was not originally part of the murder plot but she now had to be killed, as, once Liz had regained consciousness, her knowledge would make her dangerous in the extreme. But she could not be murdered on the spot for obvious reasons; someone could appear at any moment from the Working Men's Club; a woman was standing on the pavement a few doors away – this is a busy place. There is an easy solution to the problem. The cart is close at hand. Hoisting the body between them (she would look like a drunk being helped if anyone appeared), Stride was taken down the dark, unlit passageway towards the cart. Given a couple of minutes either way in witnesses' timings, the hour would be almost exactly 12. 45 a.m.

Once the murderers had the inert body on their cart, further difficulties appeared. Joseph Lave testified that he had left the Working Men's Club and walked about for five minutes to get some air. He had then groped his way back along the dark passageway. Fortunately for the murderers, Lave did not stay in the yard for very long. Stephen and Druitt were in a hurry – to get to the prearranged meeting place and pick up Catharine Eddowes and her decoy, Mary Kelly; and now, as it was getting so late, they could not risk taking the body with them in the hope that they would find a suitable dark and deserted place in which to kill and dump Stride. But they would not wish the cart to be seen by Mrs Mortimer – perhaps they could be traced from their stabling arrangements? One of the men, probably Druitt, therefore went to the end of the passage to peer out, unseen, into Berner Street. After a few more minutes, at 12.55 a.m., Mrs Mortimer went indoors. Druitt must have hurriedly returned to the stables, where Stephen was now on the cart, ready to drive away. The coast is clear, so the men drive from the stable into the yard, and, with the pressure of time, they decide to dump and murder Stride in the dark of the passageway.

Now it is Druitt's turn to murder. He has to climb down from his side of the cart and help to roll the body on to the ground, before quickly slitting its throat. To the two men Stride would not have represented a human being but merely an object that threatened the most important forces in their lives – the State, the Monarchy and Prince Eddy. The couple, like many other fanatics, would have felt no remorse, only complete justification for their brutality. This reconstruction provides a complete solution to the missing fifteen minutes between Stride's attack and her actual murder. The theory also explains Stride's injuries – injuries which differed from those of the four other Ripper victims, who were probably killed by J.K. Stephen. A short, broad knife with a bevelled edge was used to kill Stride: the other victims were dispatched with a long, narrow-bladed weapon. Clearly both men were armed. The body had fallen onto its left side (as it may well have done after being rolled from the cart in a cramped space) rather than on its back, as in the other murders. Dr Phillips, who examined the body, believed that the slash to the throat began on the left side. Stride was found with her head facing the wall. Phillips's observation would tie in with Druitt standing over her and drawing his knife straight up across the throat.

Such differences in the style of murder led Edwin Thomas Woodhall (who wrote *Jack the Ripper: or When London Walked in Terror*), and Chief Inspector Walter Dew (in his memoirs) to protest that Stride might not have been a Ripper victim. The lack of mutilation on her body has given rise to further speculation in this direction, but the mutilations were, I believe, Stephen's special trade mark. Colin Wilson, the noted crime writer, in his *Casebook of Murder*, has opined that it was the womb that fascinated the Ripper. And so it would be with J.K. Stephen, considering the trouble Bertie's amorous activities had caused. But there wasn't time to deal with Stride in the normal, obscene manner. The men's original rendezvous was with Catharine Eddowes, and they could not appear covered in blood, so with their unintended victim there was only time for a straightforward murder. During the killing of Stride, which would only have taken Druitt seconds, the horse and cart would have blocked any interruptions from Dutfield's Yard, and singing from the Working Men's Club would have drowned out any noises. Louis Diemschutz drove right past Mrs Mortimer's house and she heard him, but the murderers would have driven away from number 36, the noise of their cart being drowned out by the community singing.

The killing of Stride must have wrecked the mens' tight schedule. It would have been a few minutes before 1.00 a.m. when Stephen and Druitt drove away from Dutfield's Yard, and rounded the corner of Berner's Street, just as Louis Diemschutz, in his pony and trap, was rounding the opposite end of the street, shortly to find the murdered body of Liz Stride, her throat still oozing blood.

Meanwhile, as prearranged, Mary Kelly had waylaid Catharine Eddowes after her release from custody. They would have chatted, Catharine probably complaining about her detention and maybe mentioning the 'damn fine hiding' she would get from John for being so late home. If, after waylaying her victim, Mary had walked Catharine slowly towards Mitre Square (any direction to keep the woman engaged) Mary could easily have kept her friend chatting for a few minutes until, as planned, Druitt and Stephen drove past. Mary would now wave to the two men as though they were old friends. She tells Eddowes that she knows the men, she knows their likes, and she knows that they pay in sovereigns, not shillings. As Eddowes is hopelessly late anyway, and as it might mollify John if she were to arrive home with a handful of money, it would not have required much talk to persuade Catharine to climb on to the back of the cart with Mary, alongside Stephen: and, as the cart trundled off towards Mitre Square, Eddowes, waiting for her embrace among the canvas, was, instead, quickly choked into unconsciousness. Did J.K. then slit the woman's throat? After which Mary, shaken, blood on her clothes from Catharine's wounds, climbed out of the cart near to Dorset Street. This sequence of events would solve another abiding Ripper mystery, one that has already been mentioned in Chapter 6, and is now considered anew.

Major Henry Smith, Acting Police Commissioner for the City of London, had been awakened and told of the murders and of the graffiti at Goulston Street. He hurried to the site only to discover that Sir Charles Warren had washed the chalked message from the wall. The Major then continued his own investigations. He sleuthed around the East End and eventually found a sink near Dorset Street where blood-stained water was still gurgling down the drain. Major Smith remained convinced that he was only minutes behind the Ripper. But Eddowes's body had been found much earlier. Did Smith think that the murderer would have lingered in the area, covered in blood, only bothering to wash when the police had been fully alerted and were wandering around Whitechapel in large numbers? Many writers have commented on the fact that, as the sink was remote, and set back from the street, the Ripper must have known the territory well. But Mary Kelly *LIVED* in

Dorset Street. Given the long delay, a much more likely explanation is that *Mary* was responsible for the bloodstained water which Major Smith found still gurgling down the sink. It is highly likely that, once indoors, Kelly noticed a piece of her own clothing was bloodstained. Few East End Victorian houses had their own water supply, so Mary might well have slipped out and rinsed the blood from her clothing in the public sink; this would link her even more strongly to the murder of Eddowes, while they were both together on the back of the cart.

The invaluable Paul Begg has explained to me that there is now some doubt about Major Smith's testimony as his memoirs have proved unreliable. Still, it is unlikely that so distinguished a policeman had any cause to lie, so errors can be put down to the long delay between the murders and the writing of the memoirs.

After dropping off Kelly, Druitt and Stephen would have driven to the secluded Mitre Street, where the body could have been carried the few yards into Mitre Square before being dumped in a dark corner, thus solving the magical appearance of the corpse during the few minutes when the square was not under police observation. With Druitt on the lookout, Stephen could have completed his butchery on the body, or did that take place on the cart after dropping off Mary Kelly? The above scenario would explain how the Ripper managed to move so quickly between the two murder sites (Berner Street and Mitre Square) meeting, murdering and mutilating Eddowes without being seen or heard. The men would then have driven off leaving everyone baffled and perplexed about the timing and the mysterious appearance of the mutilated corpse. The feat was a conjuring trick, seemingly impossible if one does not know how it was done. With all available policemen swarming around Berner Street and Mitre Square, the couple could have melted away into the night on their cart, leaving behind them a baffled, bewildered, distraught and terrified populace.

And so, with the extraordinary double killing, a further myth was added to Jack's reputation. Incidentally, a daring robbery had taken place near Mitre Square at the same time as the Ripper killings. Mayhem truly ruled in the East End that night.

After leaving the scene of their crime, did the men drive to the invaluable Watling Street flat? And did J.K. then borrow chalk from the school master Druitt for his unnecessary but daring return to Goulston Street? Return he certainly did.

∽

By this stage, possible witnesses and those who might embarrass the Establishment had been eliminated to some degree, but the central problem still remained – Mary Kelly. Her condition was, by now, probably noticeable, although with layers of voluminous Victorian winter clothing the pregnancy might still not be obvious in public. I believe that with Queen Victoria insisting the child be born, events would have needed to move swiftly, and this need for haste perhaps contributed to James's lurid, absurd, but, no doubt to his sick mind, brilliant plan – what to do with Mary Kelly.

∽

Ripperologists have always been faced with the over-riding difficulty of explaining away the violent events at Miller's Court. A body, its face slashed beyond recognition, was identified as that of Mary Kelly by her boyfriend. Then, some hours after her supposed death, Kelly was seen and recognised by three independent witnesses, one of whom had a conversation with her. As I have asked several times – how can so bizarre a scenario be explained away? The above events have been recorded many times with few explanations being put forward: an acceptable solution is hard to find, but for factual happenings there has to be an explanation, and I must try to provide one.

Before doing so I would like to discuss a most interesting argument against my theory in that excellent magazine *The Ripperologist*. A contributor, Mark Banner, put forward an intelligent, constructive scenario well worth discussion. I do not know Mr Banner's background, but I have seen several of his Ripper articles and his incisive, probing but open mind impressed me: I was not lucky enough to see an article in *The Ripperologist* by another writer, Bill Beadle, who apparently put forward the theory that trying to work out the time of death from the onset of rigor mortis is fraught with difficulties – even in today's more enlightened times. Mr Banner now took over, and he stated that, if Dr Bond's assessment of the timing of Kelly's death (based on the onset of rigor mortis) had been incorrect, she might indeed have been seen by Mrs Maxwell and the two other witnesses before she went home – and was then killed by the Ripper.

Dr Thomas Bond, as we know, calculated that the body had been dead for about 12 hours. The doctor was experienced in forensics and I see no reason to doubt his opinion; Bond must have known the temperature of the room (heat affects the stiffening of the body), something modern researchers can only guess at. However, the *Ripperologist's* article was so novel, intelligent and cogent, that it was worth further consideration. At least this theory acknowledged the facts, and did not airily conclude that because there is no easy explanation to the sightings of Kelly, a simple, 'Mrs Maxwell and two other witnesses all made mistakes' will suffice.

I spoke to a doctor from a leading London hospital's forensic laboratory. He explained to me that in certain people stiffening does not take place at all, while some bodies become rigid more quickly than others –

rigor mortis appears to have no set rules, so the new theory might indeed have provided an explanation to one of the major and most baffling Ripper puzzles.

Let me set out the new theory in detail and consider the facts before hypothesising on them.

Mrs Maxwell testified under oath that she saw Mary Kelly standing on the corner of Miller's Court between 8.00 and 8.30. a.m. on the day after her supposed death. The couple spoke to each other. A Maurice Lewis then testified that he had seen Kelly around 10 a.m. at The Ringers and an unnamed girl also testified to seeing Kelly between 8 and 8.45 a.m. So if the new theory is correct, what time in the morning did Mary arrive home to meet her death? Based on the above witnesses' timings it could not have been before 10.10 a.m. at the earliest.

Given this scenario, the killer now has to arrive unseen at Miller's Court in broad daylight. He must gain admittance to Mary's room shortly after her return. He has to kill his victim and perform complicated mutilations, which must have taken a considerable time. He has to light a fire and burn voluminous Victorian clothing, knowing that a young, attractive prostitute might have any number of callers at such a time in the morning, and anyone could have looked into the room through the broken window. And all this dangerous activity had to be crammed into the space of thirty-five minutes at the most – the body was discovered at 10.45 a.m. We should also consider that all the other Ripper murders took place during the night. Why would Jack suddenly change his *modus operandi*? Especially since carrying out the Miller's Court murder mid-morning, when the area would have been crowded, made the attack dangerous in the extreme. Yet I was impressed that a solution based on *facts* had been worked out.

So, according to the new theory, the killer, having finished his work by mid-morning, now had to climb through the window – the door is reputed to have been blocked by a piece of furniture – why else would the police break it down? Jack then had to leave a busy court in broad daylight, wearing heavily blood-stained clothing, and no passer-by saw anything mysterious.

When I presented the above counter-arguments, the clever critic replied that the killer might have stripped naked during the murder and mutilations. Having finished his terrible butchery Jack had only to wipe away the worst of the mess, pull on his clothing, peer from the window to check that the coast was clear, then make his escape. That is possible – just – although why Jack did not remove the furniture from behind the door and leave that way cannot be explained. And even if the door had not been blocked – no one seems to know either way – Jack still had to enter the busy court in broad daylight. However, my final point in this argument must remain with Dr Bond's autopsy. As the new theory maintains that Mrs Maxwell's testimony is indeed correct, then it must also be accepted that Mary was seen being sick. Why, therefore, a short time later, did Dr Bond find the remains of a partly digested meal in the stomach of the murdered woman in Mary's room? That part of the autopsy could not be contested. The partly-digested meal provides further strong proof that the body was *not* that of Mary Kelly. The fact that a stranger's clothing was burned in Miller's Court – Mary's clothes were found in the room – provides further impetus to my theory.

There are other points to be considered from the same perceptive source. It was pointed out that if Mary Kelly had indeed been seen, the police should have tried to trace her final movements. But they *did* trace her final movements – up to the time of her supposed death. Then the Coroner, Dr Roderick Macdonald, after a peremptory enquiry, chose to ignore Mrs Maxwell's testimony; he didn't seem to know about the other two witnesses' sightings. The court accepted without question that the body was that of Mary Kelly – despite evidence to the contrary, and the inquest was closed.

Mr Banner is, of course, perfectly correct. Further sightings of Kelly after her supposed death should have been investigated. That is more evidence of a cover-up. Mary Kelly officially died in the early hours of 8/9 November, so why should the police investigate the movements of a dead woman? That was the brilliance of the whole plot, which seems extreme, yet fits in with the known facts – making truth appear stranger than fiction. J.K.'s wild reasoning made sense. If Mary Kelly, on the sovereign's unbalanced orders, could not be killed, but if she could also not be allowed to live, why not have the best of both worlds – life and death – a figurative murder? If Kelly did not officially exist, if her death were to be so sensational that every person in the land would discuss it, then later talk and gossip that Mary was living in luxury while she awaited the birth of Bertie's child would have been treated as nonsense, no matter how intense or how informed the speculation. Everyone would know that Mary Kelly was officially dead and dead women do not give birth to children.

Stephen, in his unbalanced state, would have found this plan feasible and clever, as indeed it proved to be. And with his forceful personality and clever use of language, he probably had little difficulty in selling his plan to both Kelly and Druitt. Probably both would have received plausible offers of great wealth. It is easy to believe even the most outlandish promises from people of power and prestige, who are usually thought of as honourable people, especially in Victorian times. Druitt and Kelly would have been made to believe that they were now honoured members of the Establishment, and, as such, they would have worked vigorously towards any end which their masters dictated. Druitt would have needed little convincing, and for Mary, the idea of being destroyed then reborn as a new woman with no ties of family or low-class East End friends must have had a strong appeal; especially if she were led to believe that Queen Victoria was taking a personal interest in her and her royal offspring. The idea that the Establishment would not want her trailing friends, or even family, from her old life into the higher echelons of society would have made perfect sense. Even today, the idea of completely wiping out the past and of changing one's role in life for a position of money, power and privilege would appeal to many people. Within the last few decades a former British cabinet minister, John Stonehouse, attempted to create a new character and life for himself by leaving the now legendary 'heap of clothes on a seashore'.

Once the tasks of Druitt and Mary were over it is my belief that both of them were then murdered; death would have been a guarantee of silence.

Kelly's actions before her own 'death' would tie in with preparations for a disappearance. Let us re-examine some of those actions.

After living with Joe Barnett for over a year, Kelly must have known her lover's character. She must have known that Barnett would object to her bringing prostitutes back to the cramped one-bedroom flat: she must have known that such actions would drive Joe away; yet, as we saw in Chapter 7, that is precisely what she did. Why would Mary want to drive Joe Barnett away? Maybe because she wanted to hide her pregnancy for a while longer? Although Mary tended towards stoutness, her condition, at around six to seven months, would, I assume, soon have been starting to show. On the other hand, although I am no expert on pregnancy, I remember a friend who, even very late in her pregnancy, showed little sign of her condition. Her husband would joke that she had only swallowed a grape. And I have read several reports of women giving birth to children without even knowing they were pregnant. So the condition is clearly variable.

I believe that Mary started bringing women back to her room because she was setting up a charade – indicating that she had personally chosen the prostitute who was to die in her place.

On the night of her supposed death, when, after the double killing of Stride and Eddowes, most prostitutes with any common sense (and Mary was not short of that) had stopped soliciting in the middle of the night, Kelly, according to George Hutchinson, strolled around the East End in the small hours with impunity, although we know she was terrified of the Ripper.

There are several reports of Mary mentioning her lack of money directly before the Miller's Court murder. Such complaints make me suspicious that she was trying to hide the opposite state of affairs. *All East Enders* were continually short of money; it was a fact of life, and there would be no need constantly to draw attention to it. Yet on the night of her 'death', Mary spoke to a young woman (reported only as Margaret) and said that she had no money and intended to 'do away with herself'. She then met George Hutchinson and said, 'I must go and look for some money'. This sounds urgent, but as she had her lodgings, and as she had had plenty of alcohol, why would she want money in the middle of the night?

Earlier, in the small hours, she had gone to her room, ostensibly with a client, where she began to sing loudly for about an hour. In her state of pregnancy Mary would probably have been uninterested in sex, and her actions seem to indicate that sex did not take place. The singing was obviously not a regular occurrence because it upset a neighbour, who was tempted to complain.

Then Mary went out again, when clearly she should have gone to bed. Once back on the streets, shortly after giving every indication that she was extremely drunk, Mary soberly solicited around Commercial Street, where she had a lucid conversation with George Hutchinson, and where she met up with another man. (Was this Druitt or Stephen?) These events have an air of exhibitionism about them, as though they were being staged in order to create a dramatic effect. A particular scene was being set.

Could George Hutchinson, that purveyor of detailed information to the police and to the press, possibly, maybe even unknowingly, have been a part of the plot? Hutchinson, at various times, mentioned a gold chain, a horseshoe shaped tie pin and a large seal with a red stone. Was he signalling that an objective (regaining Bertie's possessions) had now been achieved? Certainly a 'large seal with a red stone' might be the kind of official object, an object of great importance, that Bertie would carry.

The book *The Ripper and The Royals*, has Melvyn Fairclough and Joseph Sickert enterprisingly interviewing George Hutchinson's son Reg, a gentlemen then in his seventies. Reg reported that his father had information about the crimes but wouldn't reveal it. However, George believed that the Ripper crimes were, 'more to do with the Royal Family than ordinary people', which is extremely interesting. Reg also said that his father had been given a hundred shillings but George would not say why. Reg naturally stressed his father's excellent character and I have no reason to doubt otherwise. George may well have followed instructions without knowing the purpose behind the orders, and, no doubt, as an honest working Victorian man, he would have been glad of the money – no questions asked, and who could blame him? But the above scenario certainly fits in with my thesis.

For the final part of the drama, as I see it, we must assume that Mary Kelly callously left her chosen sacrifice – possibly someone who facially resembled her – asleep in Miller's Court. She let in Stephen (and perhaps Gull, who, as a doctor, would be able to completely destroy the body's identity) at some time between 2.00 and 4.00 a.m., then left the premises, maybe to wait on the cart, rolled up safely in the canvas. Or was she left in the care of Druitt, the Watling Street flat proving invaluable yet again? That makes more sense.

But the murder and mutilations at Miller's Court must have taken a considerable time, probably longer than had been anticipated; at 5.45 a.m. a resident of Miller's Court heard a man's footsteps leaving the court. Kelly, after her long wait, must have found that the tensions of the night, and the events that she knew were taking place in her rooms, too much to bear. And perhaps – just perhaps – she might have been experiencing some remorse at the thought of her friend's fate. It is easy to imagine that such mental pressures might become overwhelming, so I suggest that Mary, unable to overcome the craving for a drink (the public houses were open by this time), gave a watchful Druitt the slip in Watling Street and went to a local public house. The original intention might have been to visit the bar for one quick gin. Her 'murder', taking place indoors in the middle of the night, could not be precisely timed, so it would not matter if she were spotted. But for a lady who liked alcohol, and especially for a lady who was suffering from intense stress, one quick gin led to several more. With the comfort of alcohol (and Mary could now afford as much as she liked) she could quickly have lost track of time – maybe even of reality. Events of the night might have appeared, through the curtain of drink, to be a nightmare from which she would eventually awake. Whatever the explanation (and the above scenario seems most likely), Mary's craving for drink overcame her common sense and she went to her local public house where she was seen; having tasted alcohol she stayed much longer than was wise.

The murderers, their dreadful work completed, would have returned to the Watling Street flat only to discover that Mary had disappeared. The men must have been covered in blood, so initially they would have had to clean up and probably change their clothing, then they would have gone looking for Mary. She, in the mean time, dazed by stress and drink, and not thinking rationally, now returned to Miller's Court, perhaps expecting to find Gull and Stephen waiting for her there. This action, as we have seen, was backed by contemporary press reports: to recapitulate, *The Times* on 10 November 1888, stated that a tailor, Maurice Lewis, said that he had seen Kelly leave her room then return to it at 8.00 a.m. on the morning following her 'death' (no heavy object behind the door). This statement would be consistent with the above scenario. But Mary's actions were incautious to say the least. I can only assume that after she had entered her room the dreadful sight on the bed must have sent her into shock. Few people, even hardened characters such as Kelly, could witness the sight of a former friend literally slashed to pieces, without some kind of extreme reaction.

Half an hour later Mrs Caroline Maxwell had her reported conversation with Mary. Given that both the witnesses, Lewis and Maxwell, might have been slightly inaccurate in their recall of time, it is possible that Mary spent between 15 to 25 minutes in her room with the mutilated corpse. It is not beyond the bounds of possibility that shock and drink caused her to faint. Then, after recovery, but still overcome by alcohol and the night's events – all on top of her pregnancy – she rushed outside and was sick, which is hardly surprising. Then the conversation with Mrs. Maxwell occurred. To repeat:

MAXWELL. 'Why don't you go to The Ringers and have a pint.'
KELLY. 'I've been there and had it, but I've brought it all up again.'

So we have it from Kelly's own lips that she had indeed been in *The Ringers* public house. Yet there was a mutilated corpse in her room that had been dead for many hours. It would now have been essential for Mary to think quickly. She was in a dangerous position – the Establishment could prove her part in the murder. Maybe she suddenly realised that she had been trapped but, buoyed by alcohol and dazed by shock, beyond caring, she went out drinking once more – the last sighting of her was around 10.00 a.m.

The killers, now cleaned up, might have known Mary's usual haunts. After finding their prey with difficulty they must have quickly spirited her away and taken her to a safe place where the baby could be born. Gull was in charge of an asylum where his word was law. Was Mary taken there? After that, her fate would be completely in the hands of the Establishment.

The authorities now had in their power a woman who did not legally exist, and therefore, a woman whose baby would not exist. All other legal niceties would be completed by the law. A hasty inquest with a sympathetic coroner was rushed through. The corpse was declared to be that of Mary Kelly. Witnesses were swiftly dealt with; any awkward evidence was ignored. The affair was hastily, and irrationally, completed within a day. But, perhaps, with the last vestiges of duty lingering in his mind, the coroner, Roderick MacDonald, could not bring himself to sign a legal document that put his final stamp of approval on the proceedings. Negligent conduct in court – breaking the law by failing to establish the precise wounds and the weapon that caused death – this was certainly professional misconduct, but, in the circumstances, could be overlooked. However, a signature on a legal document has always been viewed with the utmost seriousness. Perhaps Roderick MacDonald's conscience was not entirely corruptible. The case of Mary Kelly was now finally closed, and the threat to the Establishment had, in the most spectacular fashion, been averted.

Perhaps the new Ripper puzzle should be – 'What happened to Mary Kelly?' Some months after the final killing a woman's torso was found under a railway arch in the East End's Pinchin Street. The legs and head had been hacked off and the womb was missing. Legend has attributed this murder to the Ripper. Was this the fate of Mary Kelly? Every nuance of the complicated Ripper events will, of course, never be known, but my resolution of the affair does explain away many of the abiding mysteries:

1. The silence of the murders and the actions of the authorities.
2. The mystery of Mary Nichol's new hat.
3. The rifling and laying out of Annie Chapman's possessions.
4. The difference of the wounds that killed Liz Stride.
5. The missing 15 minutes between Stride's attack and her murder.
6. Warren's actions over the Goulston Street graffiti.
7. Mary Kelly's unheard-of credit.
8. The strangely detailed information supplied by George Hutchinson.
9. The blood in the sink at Dorset Street.
10. The timing of the double murders.
11. Catharine Eddowes's mysterious wanderings, before her arrest and after her release from custody.
12. And, strangest and most puzzling of all, the reappearance of Mary Kelly, on the morning after she was presumed dead.

∽

There has been much speculation about the reason for the Ripper file remaining open at Scotland Yard until 1892, four years after the last Ripper murder was committed. The reason for that fact is clear and convincing. *J.K. Stephen died in 1892.* But let me repeat, the evidence presented so far regarding J.K. Stephen and M.J. Druitt being involved in the murders is circumstantial. Although so many of the facts provide a powerful case of guilt against the two men, there is no incontrovertible proof. I now want to try and supply that proof: I am certain that J.K. Stephens and M.J. Druitt were a combined Jack the Ripper team. The following chapter will explain why I can sound so positive.

Chapter 15

The Ripper Revealed

I believe that the Goulston Street graffiti is vital to the solution of Jack the Ripper's identity. While reading editions of J.K.'s previously mentioned *The Reflector*, the magazine he founded, edited and partly wrote, I discovered that J.K. enjoyed playing word games. Indeed, he appeared to have a passion for this diversion. This is hardly surprising – many Victorians enjoyed such pastimes. Without television or films for entertainment this was the heyday of music around the piano – along with parlour and word games. I consider J.K's literary bent to be highly important. Here is an acrostic that he offered his readers in *The Reflector*:

> 'The Mirror Of Mankind – though some folks quiz it,
> What the Reflector says it is – but is it?'
> 1) Our occupation – nay our whole existence,
> 2) What we attain by talent with persistence,
> 3) Fit audience for the wise; yet if not mended
> 4) It leads to this, and then the matter's ended.
> 5) Even to the far Gordan our rumour runs,
> 6) And where in Erie sinks colonial suns,
> 7) Who but the Daily News would care for numbers?
> 8) This is our Number – multitude encumbers,
> 9) Polished and true, the eye its image meets;
> It lures the birds to death and saves the fleet.

In my experience no magazine or newspaper has ever printed a puzzle, especially a difficult puzzle, without giving the solution, either in the same – or in a later edition. J.K. Stephen, in his entire magazine output, gave no solution. I wondered why?

Various attempts by myself, several experts and a group of erudite, puzzle-loving friends – including members of MENSA – tried hard to solve the above acrostic, but we all failed. Clearly this was a deeply cryptic puzzle, and, after vast effort, I eventually gave up all hope of solving it. Then, after my previous book was published, a letter from a reader, Lynda Finney, arrived: she informed me that she had solved the acrostic. I was deeply sceptical, but, to my extreme surprise, I believe this to be the case; I found Lynda's work ingenious. Before revealing the clever solution I would like to mention that I have received many queries about the exact form of an acrostic. To take the above example: the first two

lines, published in inverted commas, (*The Mirror Of Mankind...*)
hide a clue that refers to the whole solution. To arrive at that clue a
cryptic puzzle must be solved from each line; the answers are then written in a column and the first letter of each word in this column provides
a word that is a clue to the main puzzle at the top of the column. So each
line of J.K's general acrostic is a separate puzzle, except for the last two
lines, which, given the semi-colon, are clearly a continuous thought.
This complex explanation is easier to understand if it is demonstrated.
To do so, I have used Lynda's ingenious work, which she has kindly
given me permission to reproduce.

1) Our occupation – nay our whole existence; *ANSWER Living.*
   (By our occupation we earn our living – indeed living is, 'our whole
   existence'.)
2) What we attain by talent with persistence; *ANSWER Income.*
   (Self-evident.)
3) Fit audience for the wise; yet if not mended; *ANSWER Vigilance.*
   (A wise man is always vigilant; yet if that vigilance is broken...)
4) It leads to this, and then the matter's ended; *ANSWER Extinction.*
   (If vigilance is broken it can lead to extinction, and then the matter
   is ended.)
5) Even to the far Gordan our rumour runs; *ANSWER Rand.*
   (... 'to the far Gordan' can mean to the edge of the word. If we go
   to the edge of 'Gordan' we get 'rdan.' This is an easy anagram for
   'rand', which means the far edge (frequently used as an unploughed
   border around a field). Therefore 'rumour can run to the edge – to
   the very limit – to the rand' – which we know to be true.)
6) And where in Erie sinks colonial suns; *ANSWER Pelee.*
   (Pelee Island is situated on the Canadian side of Lake Erie. Here, 'in
   Erie' sinks the colonial sun.)
7) Who but the Daily News would care for numbers? *ANSWER Octo.*
   (The *Daily News*, presumably, cares for the number of sales the newspaper makes. After removing the Daily News, who else would care? A
   doctor's occupation is caring. And does 'doctor' also imply its alterna-
   tive meaning – 'to tinker with'? If we do just that and remove the first
   and last letters of the word 'doctor' [DR – the usual abbreviation] we
   find in the remaining letters 'octo' – the Latin number for eight.
   Therefore we find that [D]octo[R] cares for a number – 'octo' – the
   number eight.)
8) This is our Number – multitude encumbers; *ANSWER One*
   (Each person is number one – add to that and the multitude becomes
   encumbered – burdened.)
9) Polished and true, the eye its image meets;
   It lures the birds to death and saves the fleet. *ANSWER Light*

(Light travels straight and true, and allows the eye to meet its image. One of the strongest images of light is the lighthouse. This could lure birds to its beam, dashing them to death during a fierce storm, but that same light would save the fleet.) Therefore, the cryptic clues reveal:

Living Income Vigilance Extinction Rand Pelee Octo One Light
The first letter of each solution, put together, reads: *Liverpool*.
The opening lines of:

The Mirror Of Mankind, though some folks quiz it,
What the Reflector says it is – but is it?'

is the main clue to the solved word, '*Liverpool*';

A pool can be a mirror (though some folks might question that). Each person (mankind) could be described as someone who lives – a liver – therefore the liver could be reflected in a pool. '*Liverpool.*' A 'Reflector' (is J.K. referring to his own magazine?) might also be a mirror of mankind.

I was, and still am, amazed at Lynda's perspicacity and ingenuity. J.K. Stephen, having been appointed Clerk of the Assizes for the South Wales Circuit by his father (nepotism plainly in evidence), was, during the summer of 1888, in that part of the country from time to time. Wales is separated from Liverpool by a narrow stretch of water – the River Dee – the two places have always been within easy reach of each other. Interestingly, as we have seen in Chapter 6, puzzling Jack the Ripper letters, headed 'Liverpool' and citing a Liverpool address, are recorded in a book by J. Hall Richardson, a popular Fleet Street reporter who worked for the *Daily Telegraph*. Before discussing these, let us further examine the infamous Goulston Street graffiti.

The double murders occurred in the early hours of 30 September between approximately 1.00 a.m. (Liz Stride in Berner Street) and 1.45 a.m. (Catharine Eddowes in Mitre Square). Berner Street was under the jurisdiction of the Metropolitan Police Commissioner, Sir Charles Warren. Mitre Square, however, was just within the City of London boundaries; this meant that Major Henry Smith, who was Acting Commissioner of The City of London Police, was in charge of the Eddowes murder. Out of the five Ripper victims only the killing of Catharine took place within the City.

Newspapers in 1888 record that it was immediately after the discovery of Eddowes's body in Mitre Square that a summons was sent to Major Henry Smith, who, in his memoirs *From Constable to Commissioner*, published in 1910, writes about the event:

The night of Saturday, 29 September, found me tossing about in my bed at Cloak Lane Station, close to the river and adjoining

Southwark Bridge . . . suddenly the bell at my head rang violently. 'What is it?' I asked, putting my ear to the tube. 'Another murder sir, this time in the City.' Jumping up, I was dressed and in the street in a couple of minutes. A hansom cab – to me a detestable vehicle – was at the door . . .

Other less important City of London policemen, such as Superintendent Alfred Foster, were also summoned in the middle of the night to the murder site in the square. Clearly, judging by this documented activity, the homicide of Liz Stride at Berner Street, which had happened around forty-five minutes before Eddowes's attack, would have been immediately relayed to Sir Charles Warren, Berner Street being within the Metropolitan Police boundaries.

Major Henry Smith also relates in his memoirs how, having been informed of the murders, he visited Mitre Square, then proceeded to spend a busy night calling at the morgue and rushing around the area in general. Let me repeat that, although Warren must have been summoned after the discovery of Stride's body, he did not put in an immediate appearance, which is not surprising. My late friend Stephen Knight confirms that although the two earlier murders (of Mary Nichols and Annie Chapman) had occurred in areas under the control of the Metropolitan Police, Sir Charles did not bother to visit either murder site at any time. He didn't seem to be in any hurry to visit the East End after Stride's killing, until he was told about the graffiti that had been found in Goulston Street; on being informed about the writing he rushed to the site. Let us examine the matter of the graffiti once more.

On the night of the double murder, PC Alfred Long walked his Goulston Street beat. Goulston Street was another dreary, overcrowded East End thoroughfare, although efforts at improving the street's housing stock had been made; brick tenements, euphemistically named Wentworth Model Dwellings had been erected. Sets of flats in the Model Dwellings were served by a series of open entrances that led to communal stairs. Nothing out of the ordinary caught the constable's attention as he plodded his beat back and forth past the Model Dwellings. On his 2.20 a.m. round all was quiet. However, on his return beat, just before 3.00 a.m. the constable noticed a piece of torn rag 'lying in the passageway leading to the staircase' of apartments 108–119. Chalked on the wall above the torn cloth were the words:

> The Juwes are
> The men that
> Will not
> be Blamed
> for nothing

This strangely worded, strangely arranged message is written in iambic pentameter – the chosen rhythm of William Shakespeare for most of his blank verse.

At the time of the murders a considerable amount of graffiti was chalked around the East End. As the above message does not make obvious sense, and as it does not mention murder, there was nothing to directly link the piece of blood-stained cloth on the ground to the words above it. Slaughter houses around the East End could easily have been the source of the remnant, however, presumably common sense indicated to Constable Long that this could be an important find. Detectives were called. In the mean time, Catharine Eddowes's body had been taken to the mortuary, and it was noticed that part of her apron was missing. Once reports of the Goulston Street blood-smeared rag had filtered through to the authorities they compared it to the apron on the body and found a perfect match, so this proved that Jack had indeed paused in the entrance to the block of dwellings, where he had thrown away his memento. Such a discovery now made the chalked message supremely important. Possibly it was the only direct clue ever left by the infamous murderer.

Obviously, with Victorian transport, it must have taken at least a few hours to link the torn rag to Eddowes's apron. Warren, on hearing the news, rushed to Goulston Street at around 5.00 a.m., before dawn had broken. To repeat – the sensational murder of two women around three to four hours earlier (one of these homicides being in territory under Warren's jurisdiction) had not proved sufficient bait to lure Sir Charles into the East End – the few chalked words were. Why? Possibly the fact that at last the Ripper's handwriting could be recorded. If that is so, Sir Charles reacted strangely. (His behaviour made me study the graffiti closely.) After examining the graffiti Warren caused astonishment – an astonishment that has lasted up to the present day – by ordering the message be washed away. Several of his senior officers, presumably stunned by the stupidity of such an order, displayed more common sense. They realised that the writing, probably the only clue left to date by the man the whole of the London police force was hunting, could be valuable. Warren was advised against destroying the graffiti, but he was adamant – he insisted that the word 'Juwes' might spark riots. His officers, clearly anxious to save so important a clue, suggested that the message be covered up for an hour or so until it was light enough to take photographs. Warren would not wait even an hour; he insisted that any covering would be torn down. This surely would *not* have been the case. Although the police were generally hated throughout the East End they were also feared. Warren only had to put a few men on guard to prevent any covering being torn down, and this for only approximately an hour.

I assume that at 6 a.m. although the street was used for trading, it would not have been too busy. Once dawn had broken the area could easily have been cleared for a short time, the covering removed and photographs taken; and as the police were the only people who knew that the writing could be directly linked to Jack the Ripper, how could a few meaningless words be dangerous?

The next suggestion made to Warren was one any reasonable person would be expected to follow. Erase the offending word, or even erase the entire top line, leaving an entirely innocuous and totally meaningless phrase:

. . . the men that will not be blamed for nothing.

It was put to Warren that these remaining lines of graffiti could then be photographed at leisure and the handwriting might yield valuable clues. Warren rejected even this most sensible of solutions. He wanted the entire graffiti destroyed. Henry Smith's memoirs suggest that the police chief personally washed out the words. If that is an exaggeration, Warren certainly ordered the destruction. Warren's stupid action was condemned from several quarters, and much criticism in the press. And Warren's supposed intent, to suppress the word 'Juwes', failed miserably. The graffiti became common knowledge although there was widespread confusion about the exact wording. In fact Warren's actions did more harm than good. The message had been seen and rumour spread quickly. The word 'Juwes', which makes no real sense, became commonly translated as the much more damaging 'Jews', but this would not have worried Warren. It is my belief that he was not concerned with protecting an innocent race. As we shall see, he had darker motives and these prompted his actions.

At Catharine Eddowes's inquest, PC Long gave evidence and spoke about his dramatic discovery. Some newspapers reported that the graffiti had read: 'The Jews are the men who will not be blamed for nothing'. Even Long, who had discovered the graffiti, claimed that the words chalked on the wall were, 'The Jews are not the men that will be blamed for nothing.' The City solicitor, Henry Crawford, clearly knew that Long's statement was incorrect. Crawford cross-examined the policeman, paying special attention to the spelling of the word 'Juwes'. Crawford thought that this central word had been spelt 'Juees'. As we now know, they were all wrong. Warren's actions had already started to cause total confusion.

The flustered PC Long stumbled through his cross-examination in court. It was then discovered that he had been testifying from memory, which is strange, as Long had written down all the relevant facts in his notebook; once this was discovered Long was ordered to produce the notebook in court, yet even this did not produce results. The

Constable's notes were incorrect, which is astounding, as, to repeat, it was he who had discovered the graffiti and had initially stood guard over it. One would have expected that he, of all people, would have written down such a startling discovery verbatim, but apparently not: in his notebook, the constable still had the word 'Juwes' written as 'Jews'.

We now know that there was absolutely no need for any of this confusion. Stephen Knight found, among the Metropolitan Police files of confidential letters, a covering note from Sir Charles Warren attached to an exact copy of the Goulston Street graffiti. Mention of this is made by Warren himself in a report to the Home Office. After stating that 'The writing was on the jamb of the open archway or doorway visible to anybody in the street' (a lie), the Police Chief continued: '. . . I considered it desirable to obliterate the writing at once, having taken a copy, of which I enclose a duplicate.' The last phrase seems to infer that Warren made the copy personally, which seems unlikely. Surely the Metropolitan Commissioner would delegate such a tiresome task? And, as I have said, I suspect that the copy had already been made by the time that Warren arrived at Goulston Street, several hours after the original discovery. With one copy sent to the Home Office and the duplicate in closed Police Files, the material remained unseen for almost a century. Surely this was illegal? The vital, double-murder inquests had not yet taken place. Why was at least one copy of the important graffiti not produced at the official inquiry? That would have solved once and for all the farcical contradictions that were taking place in the court-room. And furthermore, such vital evidence should have been automatically presented to the inquest.

Was Superintendent Thomas Arnold trying to help his superior officer, when he wrote, 'I was apprehensive that if the writing were left it would be the means of causing a riot and therefore considered it desirable that it should be removed . . . had only a portion been removed, the context would have remained.' More claptrap. To repeat – what context could '. . . the men that will not be blamed for nothing' possibly convey? We can now view the copy of the graffiti at the Public Records Office in Kew, where it is open to inspection.

As various damaging interpretations of the graffiti were now in general circulation the above message could have been published, as other texts had been, to see if anyone recognised the distinctive handwriting. The Metropolitan Police copied and widely fly-posted a letter and card, asking for help in identifying the handwriting, although there was no certainty that the correspondence came from the killer. Yet handwriting that almost certainly was Jack's was locked away for a century, when, by law it should have been produced in court.

I am amazed that few researchers highlight this fact or find it odd. I find it most odd. Warren's actions appear to be mystifying until they are unravelled. Then his behaviour makes perfect sense. The Police Chief's actions were meant to create confusion, and that is exactly what they did do – until now.

ళ

Several writers have repeated Warren's assertion to the Home Office that the message was written 'on the jamb of the open archway or doorway, visible to anyone in the street.' Let me repeat my research:

P.C. Long (Who found the apron fragment): The rag was 'lying in the passageway leading to the staircase'.

Chief Inspector Donald Swanson noted: '. . . he [P.C. Long] found in the bottom of a common stairs leading to No. 118 to 119 Goulston Street Buildings a piece of a bloodstained apron, *and above it* [my italics] written in chalk, the words, "The Juwes are the men who will not be blamed for nothing,". . .' (Even Swanson uses incorrect wording.)

Detective Constable Daniel Halse stated the graffiti was: 'written on the fascia . . . . the fascia was about the height of a man'.

Superintendent Thomas Arnold wrote that the writing was: 'on the *wall* of the entrance.' (My italics.)

The City surveyor's map stated that the writing was: '. . . on the right hand side of the doorway . . . *found inside entrance* to Model Dwellings.' (My italics.)

This can leave little doubt about the positioning of the graffiti; it was directly above the blood-stained cloth, and that was lying in the entrance hallway. I forcibly contend that this proves my belief that Warren was lying and not just mistaken (he had visited the site) when he wrote that the graffiti was written '. . . on the jamb of the open archway. . .' Warren was trying to emphasise that the writing, and especially the sensitive word 'Juwes' was more visible to the general public than it actually had been – and that necessitated its instant removal. Any graffiti on the jamb of a doorway *would* be more difficult to cover up – but not impossible. So Warren was prepared to lie, even to the Home Secretary, in order to mask his true reason (which will shortly be revealed) for destroying the graffiti. My understanding of the positioning of the message is illustrated here.

1 Actual positioning of the graffiti.

⊗ Positioning of the graffiti according to Sir Charles Warren.

But why did Warren produce the facsimile in the first place? The most likely explanation is that an officer had already made the drawing. Victorian police seem to have had a mania for making on-site sketches recording accurately details of the murders. There are police drawings of the corner in Mitre Square where the body was discovered. There are detailed police sketches of the mutilations to Eddowes's body, et cetera. All of these details were later photographed. It is, therefore, highly likely that a skilled officer had been called to the scene of the discovery in Goulston Street, where he routinely made an exact copy of the graffiti – or maybe even traced it. It would have appeared highly suspicious if Warren had destroyed both the original and the copy and a duplicate.

To summarise, the vital questions that need answering are:

1) Why did Warren fail to visit personally any murder site until he was told of the graffiti? Why did that message make him rush to the East End? (He visited Mitre Square later on.)

2) Why, when there was no reason, did Warren insist on totally destroying the chalked message against the advice of his senior officers?

3) Why did he allow endless arguments – even in a court of law – about the exact wording and form of the graffiti, when there was a facsimile at the Home Office and a copy readily to hand at Scotland Yard?

4) Why was an obviously careful copy of the graffiti not reproduced as other (less suspect) writings from 'the Ripper' had been, to see if anyone recognised the distinctive handwriting?

5) Why did Warren write a report to the Home Office which contained a clear lie about the positioning of the graffiti? Warren had stood on site discussing the fate of the message. He knew full well that the graffiti had been written on the wall at the base of the stairs, and not on his carefully described, 'jamb . . .' There had to be good reason for such a senior officer – the Metropolitan Police Commissioner – to lie; to suppress evidence; to bend the law. What was the reason?

Once these questions are answered the identity of Jack the Ripper will be finally revealed.

∽

Is there any proof that J.K. Stephen wrote the graffiti? If we look at Stephen's poems in *Lapsus Calami*, we see the distinctive layout frequently used in this type of work. Here are a few lines, taken at random, from an 1880 poem printed in *Lapsus Calami*:

Then comes the melancholy, vain,	*The leaves are*
And hopeless struggle to regain	*The men that*
His old unsullied reputation:	*Will not*
Abortive efforts to attain	*be Blamed*
Impossible regeneration.	*for nothing*

The graffiti has identical indentations – certainly an unusual layout for a piece of East End graffiti. And, like the graffiti, the above stanza is also written in iambic pentameter.

After my book was published I wondered if I could take the question of the handwriting further. To this end, I obtained from a highly reliable researcher a copy of a letter written by J.K. Stephen. I laid out the copy of the graffiti, which is on file at the Public Records Office and cannot be disputed, and then scoured J.K. Stephen's letter. If I could find a group of characters – three or four together – that corresponded with the graffiti, I pasted them underneath the chalked message. If I could find only two characters together I used them, and I filled in the blanks with single lower case letters. I could not find any capital Ts. The result is reproduced here. The top line is the graffiti, still on police file: the line underneath is composed from J.K.'s handwriting. On the following pages, some of the characters I have chosen from the letter are underlined for the purposes of demonstration.

I am aware that it will be pointed out that the graffiti is a copy and that the characters may be of a different size. I know all that – and no doubt the dubious midnight anoraks who stalk the Internet thinking that their minor opinions are important, will pounce. That is up to them. I am as surprised as anyone at the above results. All I can do is give an absolute assurance that the facsimile and the letter are totally genuine, and I have used no trickery whatsoever.

the leaves are

the leaves are

---

the men hat

he men hat

Will not

Will not

---

be Blamed

be Blamed

---

for nothing

for nothing

King's College,
Cambridge.
27 Mar.

Dear Lord Houghton,

I am very grateful for your letter, & I will gladly send you a copy of Bothwell if it is printed: only I am afraid it will not be. I think I must have infused into it too much of the apostolic spirit, for the exam

did not add to their award a
recommendation to permit.

We are very much horrified
at what you say about dear Sir
Welton. I hope he will not
adhere to his intention. I will
write to Alfred my brother & ask
him to use his brotherly fraternal
influence. If the President does
find I suppose you — to touch
him President, will appoint another

I suppose the dinner will be on an early Wednesday in June.

We held our last meeting this week term yesterday, & shall begin again about the end of April. I have succeeded Rowe as secretary, and shall be very happy to communicate to you the future subject of discussion, whenever you are able to come to a meeting.

I am your sincerely

James K. Stephen

My handwriting comparison must speak for itself.

I find it interesting that in the graffiti – a very short message – the three lower case 't' characters are formed in three different ways. Those three identical ways can be found in J.K's letter. And the tilt of the writing in both cases is similar. Given the astounding comparison, the only conclusion must be:

1) the graffiti was copied with accuracy and great skill.
2) The writing was carefully traced. I believe this to be the case. There can be no other explanation for such similarities.

To recap, I had now discovered that the layout of the graffiti matches the layout in many of James's poems, as does the iambic pentameter, and there is a startling similarity between the graffiti and J.K's handwriting. Surely this string of inter-linked discoveries could not be random coincidence? And I strongly contend that, given the layout and the rhythm, the graffiti is definitely the work of an educated man. The iambic pentameter even uses the Shakespearean double beat on the word 'blam-ed'. How many working-class East End men would produce such literate graffiti?

A professional graphologist agreed that there are striking similarities in the two scripts, but insisted that she needed to see the handwriting of the policeman who made the copy! Given the obvious similarities in the writing, I have proved to my own satisfaction that the two hands are identical. Professional people who have been shown the above material have agreed with me. As far as I am concerned, J.K. Stephen is the author of the graffiti – therefore, the bloodstained cloth found below the writing proves that he was Jack the Ripper. This would explain why Sir Charles Warren was so alarmed by the message – so alarmed that in his panic he was willing to lie, to suppress evidence and break the law to prevent any identification of the handwriting.

But why would J.K. bother to scrawl a message on a wall? He was insane at the time, but still clever enough to commit daring murders and evade capture. It is well-documented that serial killers have been known to write to the police or newspapers and boast about their crimes. This is a common aberration, which could, I have been told by a leading psychologist, represent a subconscious desire on the part of the killer to be apprehended, so preventing any further deaths: serial killers are capable of extreme self-deception. Or the action might display a total disdain for the men hunting the killer – a challenge. It is my belief that James Stephen belonged to the latter class. In his mania he may well have been proud of what he was doing. To his warped way of thinking the murders would have been entirely justified, as he was preventing a possible insurrection, saving the Establishment, saving the Monarchy in general and saving his close friend Prince Eddy in particular. He was also furthering his own fierce ambition.

There is nothing particularly alarming in the graffiti, apart perhaps from the word 'Juwes', which, as we have seen, could easily have been erased; but why was such convoluted wording used – with unnecessary double negatives and so on? It is almost as though the writer needed certain letters for a hidden agenda. Then I remembered Stephen's fondness for word games. J.K. uses an anagram in his acrostic, and Dr David Abrahamsen, who studied Stephen's life carefully, noted: 'J.K. coined words of duel intent. It was like a personal game of inventing new words, places and names in a code known only to him . . .'

What, I wondered, if the graffiti had been written in code? That might account for the strange wording. I puzzled for a considerable time, trying various ciphers from various specialised books without success. I then began to wonder if a simple anagram had been used? The graffiti contains only forty-six characters, and over one-third of these are vowels. Out of the remaining thirty consonants several letters which are low down on the frequency table of normal usage (even in large texts) were used several times – in only eleven words. For instance, both B and W, which are in the last one-third of normal frequency-usage, are each used twice, despite the low number of consonants available. Eight letters, including the normally high-usage C, are not used at all.

Out of any forty-six letters, it is, of course, possible to find a long list of assorted words or short garbled phrases, but I wondered if any message containing specific names or dates could be discovered? I set to work, and found that from the graffiti's restricted selection of letters, two highly unusual names, along with their initials, could be extracted – F.G. Abberline, and M.J. Druitt. Both of these men are, of course, inextricably linked to the Ripper case. Frederick George Abberline, the police go-between, and Montague John Druitt, the leading suspect. Both of these names used up almost half of the available letters. The odds are high (I checked with a university expert who specializes in ciphers) against two such unusual, pertinent and inter-linked names occurring randomly in so small a selection of characters, in a text that is traditionally linked to Jack the Ripper; especially when, as we shall see, the remaining few letters can be used to form a perfectly coherent and relevant sentence.

Endless numbers of Ripper researchers have tried to explain the graffiti's meaning without success. This is not surprising, as the original message has no sense. It is the hidden words that are so revealing. The full anagram, which uses every letter of the graffiti, is as follows:

The Juwes are the men that	F.G. Abberline. Now hate M.J.
will not be blamed for nothing	Druitt. He sent the woman to hell.

Each message contains:

E 7, T 6, H/N 4, A/L/O 3, W/R/M/I/B 2, J/U/S/D/F/G 1.

J.K. Stephen, in the familiar way of serial killers, was taunting the police. He had left them a mysterious message in anagram form, chalked on a wall for all to see, and, highly improbably, to work out. Most dramatic of all – the message actually named one of the killers. It was Warren's duty to ensure that the writing was totally destroyed, something that he did with singular competence.

To repeat – there is no doubt that the odds are high for two unusual surnames and two sets of initials to occur randomly in only forty-six letters, in writing closely associated with the Ripper, and an anagram ties in perfectly with J.K's love of word games. It is not difficult to imagine James, having been prickled by criticism from Abberline (and, by the malice of displaying Druitt's name, probably having quarrelled with his partner-in-crime) deciding to get revenge on both men in the most extreme way. J.K. Stephen, the man who liked to set word puzzles without answers for his readers, and who so gleefully mutilated the bodies of his victims, must have delighted in his own cleverness as he worked out an anagram that was a confession. The daring shown in this public display aligns with the exhibitionism shown in other aspects of the Ripper crimes. (Interestingly, almost one century later, the serial killer nicknamed Zodiac, who terrorised America during the late 1970s, and who, like Jack, was never arrested, also wrote ciphered letters to the newspapers.)

With his unlikely name appearing in so few letters, I believe that Frederick George Abberline, that shadowy Ripper investigator, who, unlike most of his colleagues, wrote no book of memoirs, knew the reason behind the crimes. As we have seen, despite several denials by the noted detective about knowledge of the killer's identity, he told Nigel Morland, the founding editor of *The Criminologist*, 'not to look for Jack the Ripper at the bottom of London society but a long way up'. A prime clue. Abberline clearly knew more than he would reveal, and he would certainly have disapproved of the insane, exhibitionistic nature of the murders and must have remonstrated with J.K., although the policeman would have been powerless to stop the killings: a policeman, even today, could not interfere with the actions of the Secret Service. State security is all-powerful and Stephen's work must have placed him in that category. However, my evidence points towards the fact that Abberline, although he was powerless to act, was unable to suppress his hatred and contempt for Stephen's insane actions – and the policeman must have said so.

So J.K. Stephen reacted to that criticism in a typically unbalanced, childish manner; a manner that also led him to take revenge on his partner-in-crime Montague Druitt. 'Now hate M.J. Druitt. He sent the woman to hell'. To which woman was J.K. referring? Probably Liz Stride, as she had been murdered by Druitt, although on days following several of the murders he had played cricket. Could Montague have murdered one day and been so carefree the next? I believe that is possible. There is no doubt that the human mind is capable of operating on different levels simultaneously. As an example of self-deception, in 1913 in New York, a much-loved, conscientious parish priest, Father Hans Schmidt, secretly married a young servant girl. Shortly afterwards, overcome with remorse at breaking his sacred vows of chastity, the priest murdered his young bride. Over the next three days, in between conducting masses and other duties, all carried out with devotion and sincerity, Father Schmidt carved up his young bride's dead body and threw the limbs and torso into the river.

I have no doubt that the Goulston Street graffiti was written by J.K. Stephen, but let us examine this curious episode in greater depth, carefully considering the killer's movements and motives on the night of the double murders. Firstly, there was absolutely no need to cut off part of Eddowe's apron and carry it away – indeed, there was every reason not to do so. To wander around an area teeming with policemen after the first murder, carrying indisputable proof that you were the killer, clearly demonstrates some kind of mania. And why would Jack take the nerve-tingling risk of discovery just to eventually throw away his memento in an entrance? What would be the purpose of such a crazy act?

Despite his mania, the Ripper was sly, cunning and intelligent. Quite clearly the killer needed the fragment of apron to highlight the graffiti. Jack was saying, 'this is not just any old scrawl – this message comes from me.' The apron was the marker that spelt out the authenticity of the graffiti. To what purpose? If the killer had merely been compelled to demonstrate anti-Semitism all he had to do was chalk, 'The Jews committed the murders,' or such like. Why use convoluted language that doesn't make sense, along with a made up word, 'Juwes'? And why would the killer risk his life for a few, apparently meaningless, semi-literate words? Clearly the graffiti was important to Jack – so important he was willing to risk his life to make sure that people knew it was from him – therefore the writing must be important to any Ripper investigation.

After the double murders, Jack, even given his steely character, must have been under considerable mental pressure. Any man bold enough to linger around an area teeming with policemen trying to catch him, who pauses to write on a wall in a dark area – an area with possible comings and going from the surrounding dwellings, would hardly be likely to concern himself with presentation. Under immense pressure, the message that Jack clearly felt compelled to write should have been quickly sprawled in a few words. It wasn't. The strange spelling and the double negatives point to a man who is semi-literate, yet – to repeat for further emphasis – the format of the words, set in the layout of a poem, written in iambic pentameter, point to considerable education. My thesis fits the known facts perfectly.

After working on the graffiti, I remembered the distinguished professional cryptographer, Professor Fred Piper, from Royal Holloway College, University of London, telling me that if more than one anagram cross-links with a second document then the odds in favour of the anagrams become astronomical. Even given the forty-six character anagram that I had uncovered, the strange wording of the chalked message continued to intrigue me. The double negatives and so on were unnecessary for a simple word game. I suddenly thought that it would be amazing if Stephen had also worked out a coded message, inserted not in a crossover-document, but in the one layout. It would take an extremely clever fellow to pull off this difficult feat, but J.K. *was* extremely clever.

I once again began to try and find a possible code that might fit the graffiti, and by chance I came across a fascinating book, *Secret Language*, by Julian A. Bielewicz. This outlined a cipher devised by the Elizabethan genius Francis Bacon, thought by many to be the writer of Shakespeare's works. I already knew the Bacon Code – it is fairly common; the distinguished Professor Piper also knew the code, but under a different name. I will continue to use the 'Bacon Code' title.

I knew, as *Secret Language* pointed out, that in Victorian days letters were expensive to post but newspapers could be sent much more cheaply. (That might still be the case. It was certainly so in the not-too-distant past.) What I did not know, and what the book *Secret Language* explained, was the fact that poor folk would often use the Bacon Code to mark passages from a newspaper: this could then be posted and decoded by the recipient – a cheap way of sending expensive letters. This meant that the Bacon Code must have been widely known and used during the time of J.K. Stephen; he would certainly have been familiar with it. Given this fact, could J.K., I wondered, have made use of Bacon's cipher? The code works on the simple premise of the letters 'a' and 'b'. Sentences are grouped into a series of five characters and the code is read according to the position of the 'b'. The difficulty with this cipher is the need to know the placing of the 'b'; it is essential that this letter has some form of identification, such as underlining, marking, spacing and so on.

This is the code:

aaaaa = a	aaaab = b	aaaba = c
aaabb = d	aabaa = e	aabab = f
aabba = g	aabbb = h	abaaa = i or j
abaab = k	ababa = l	ababb = m
abbaa = n	abbab = o	abbba = p
abbbb = q	baaaa = r	baaab = s
baaba = t	baabb = u or v	babaa = w
babab = x	babba = y	babbb = z

The graffiti contains forty-six letters, and Bacon's cipher needs the text to be grouped into a series of five characters, but an extra letter or so at the end of the coded message is unimportant, as the following example will show.

Suppose I wished to send you, the reader, a coded message, 'danger'. I would write an innocuous few words indicating the position of the letter b – in this instance by bold underlining – in a secret message the marker letters would not be so boldly displayed – they can be slightly lower or higher, slightly tilted or whatever, but underlining is the clearest way for this demonstration. So I write:

'The d__og is fi__ne, b__ut I th__ink he m__isses you.'

On receipt of my few cheery words, you, the reader would compress the characters into groups of five, carefully noting the underlining.

THED__O GISFI NEB__UT ITH__IN KHEMI S__SESY (OU)

We know that every unmarked character represents the letter 'a' and the underlined letters denote the letter 'b'. So we get:

THED__O	aaabb. Check the code.	This is letter D
GISFI	a series of 5 characters unmarked is aaaaa.	This is letter A
NEBUT	abbaa	This is letter N
ITH__IN	aabba	This is letter G
KHE__MI	aabaa	This is letter E
S__SESY	baaaa	This is letter R.

My demonstration makes things very easy as the underlining is bold, but no characters in the graffiti appeared to be marked. If they were, I could not pick up the markings. If the Bacon Code had been used by J.K. I had to find some kind of recurring pattern for the letter b. I tried using every capital letter in the graffiti as the marker, then I compressed the graffiti into 5 character groups. That did not work. Only an excess of similar vowels and consonants appeared and no word – never mind a relevant word – could be formed. I underlined all the initial lower case letters of each word. That did not work – I had the same result. I tried underlining the capital and the initial lower case letters, to see if they were the combined marker. That did not work. I tried reversing this process. That did not work. Endless other variations did not work. After a long period of experimentation I was about to admit defeat, yet I remained convinced that there was a hidden code. Otherwise why would such a clever and literate fellow as James risk his life to write semi-literate graffiti, clearly using specific letters in a specific layout, if it was not to hide some word game? He could have written a straightforward, devastating message had he wished to do so.

Examining the Goulston Street message once more, I wondered if the ludicrously long tail on the letter 'O' in the graffiti might indicate a marker? Although in J.K's letter to Lord Houghton one of the 'o' characters trails upwards, the graffiti's letter 'o' soars in a most peculiar manner. Codes often contain subtle clues.

Was this an indication that the letter 'b' was represented by the second character in each word? Importantly, this gap is five characters away from the end of the message, and five is the required grouping for the Bacon Code. Interestingly, *Secret Language* mentions the film *Colditz* in which Robert Wagner's character uses every ninth character in a secret code. ('. . . a staggering task.') Could J.K. Stephen have got there first? I tried underlining every second letter of each word in the graffiti. A totally regular pattern.

The J̲uwes a̲re t̲he m̲en t̲hat w̲ill n̲ot b̲e blamed f̲or n̲othin(g).

The marked message was then grouped into a series of 5 letters.

THEJU̲ WESA̲R ETHEM E̲NTHA TWILL N̲OTBE̲ BLAME
DFOR̲N O̲THIN (G̲).
abaab aaaab aabaa baaba aabaa abaab abaaa aabaa baaaa.
K B E T E K I E R

To my amazement, nine relevant characters appeared. The anagrammed word *'Bertie'* leaps out – almost in sequence. *BERTIE KK E.*

KK (*Kaiserlich-königlich* from Chambers Dictionary) means *Imperial-Royal.*

E. Edward. So, the nine letters represent: *Bertie, Imperial Royal Edward.*

Interestingly, *Kaiserlich-königlich* is German. Bertie spoke German – his English had a thick, guttural accent. In deference to her beloved Albert, Victoria spoke only German at home.

To find two letter k's by chance in nine characters is unlikely – the letter K (along with five others) is in the very last category of usage frequency in the English language.

I discussed this work with the excellent Professor Piper, and the distinguished cryptographer opined that if J.K. Stephen had indeed used the Bacon Code – and if he had taken the second letter as a marker – then the resultant letters were indisputable. I think that if J.K. did not use the above code in the graffiti, then it is astounding that an exact sequence – the second letter in every word of the infamous message, seemingly outlined by a large upward stroke – would yield the exact letters for Bertie – the very basis of my thesis – along with symbols for Imperial Royal Edward.

Had J.K. quarrelled with Bertie, who might have objected to the killings? Or had J.K.'s close relationship with Eddy, Bertie's son, perhaps caused the rift? Bertie was violently anti-homosexual. When one of his aristocratic friends got into trouble over his sexuality Bertie refused to believe the charges. 'No more than I'd rather believe the same of the Archbishop of Canterbury,' he thundered. (Little did Bertie know . . .)

So, from graffiti that is linked to Jack the Ripper, written in iambic pentameter, in the layout of J.K.'s poems, in a hand that is identical to that of J.K., we get:

F. G Abberline. Now hate M.J. Druitt. He sent the woman to hell.

(A simple anagram.)

Bertie, KK E: (A coded anagram.)

All from forty-six characters. To repeat: Professor Piper had told me that if a first anagram cross-links with a second document then the odds become astronomical. A third link-up and the matter would stand in a court of law. In the graffiti I have found two cross-linked anagrams in a single document. For me, that is conclusive. So, to summarise:

> above a piece of apron indisputably discarded by Jack the Ripper, is a chalked, apparently semi-literate message of forty-six letters, written in a hand identical to that of J.K. Stephen, and set in the layout of a poem frequently seen in J.K.'s work, using the iambic pentameter. This hints at a highly educated man. The message contains unnecessary letters in the form of double negatives and so on, which could hint at a code. After analysis, the forty-six characters yield a cogent anagrammed message that contains the names and initials of two men central to the Ripper affair, M.J. Druitt, and F. G. Abberline. Then a popular Victorian cipher, when applied to the graffiti, with a highly restrictive second-character key, produces nine letters that form an easily solved anagram – Bertie, KK E. (Imperial Royal Edward) – two cross-linked messages in the one document. And 'Bertie' forms the very heart of my thesis, especially in regard to J.K. Stephen, who, I suspect, was pouring scorn on the prince in a *Reflector* editorial.

Did Sir Charles Warren know about the coding in the graffiti? It is hard to see how, unless J.K. boasted to friends, or Druitt found him working out the codes. We will never know if it was the handwriting alone that made Sir Charles panic, or knowledge of the hidden messages, or both.

There is one further puzzle. After the insane exhibitionism, why was J.K. Stephen not eliminated? It must have become obvious to the Establishment that his mind was now unbalanced, to say the least. His knowledge was deadly and his insane actions were clearly a threat. Again, we can only speculate, but there could have been several reasons which would explain the Ripper's survival for four years after the murders ended.

1) Recruiting an assassin to eliminate Stephen might have involved further, unnecessary risk for those in the highest echelons of society. The danger of Kelly had been eliminated. Leave well alone.

2) It is possible, and even likely, that after the final killing, J.K.'s murderous fury had abated. After all, his objective had been achieved, and there is nothing to indicate that he killed for fun – he killed for a purpose. The terrible savagery that accompanied the killing merely underlined his disgust at the (to him) worthless women who had threatened his world. That purpose achieved, J.K. may have seemed to have regained his mental stability.

3) J.K. might have ensured that there was a hidden record outlining the secret of his coded material.

∽

J. Hall Richardson, in his previously mentioned book, *From the City to Fleet Street*, has published a document known as 'the Liverpool letters'. Puzzlingly, these two letters are lumped together: 'I quote one...', Richardson says, then he quite clearly quotes two, the second letter undated. Both messages are signed 'Jack the Ripper'. A further puzzle in regard to these letters concerns the time lapse before their publication. Richardson's book was published in 1927, almost forty-years after the murders had ended, and after the letters had been sent. Yet surprisingly, 1927 appears to be the first time that the Liverpool letters were published. Let us look at various dates:

> 'Dear Boss' letter. First use of the name Jack the Ripper, posted to the Central News Agency. Dated 25 September. Postmarked 27 September. Received 30 September. Published in the newspapers 1 October.

> The Liverpool letters, dated 29 inst, and signed 'Jack the Ripper'.

Given the fact that Jack threatens more murders in the 29 inst letter, and more murders occurred, I have taken the date to mean 29 September 1888. The puzzle inherent here is the fact that, if the letters were sent on that date, the writer knew the nickname before it had been published. Only the Central News Agency, who received the 'Dear Boss' letter, and the police (who were sent it) knew the pseudonym before publication. Either the writer of all the above communications was the same man or else he had access to official knowledge. I strongly suspect that J.K. wrote only the Liverpool letters and the graffiti. I will shortly outline why I believe the 1888 date is possible. Further, it seems an odd coincidence that J.K. Stephen should publish a fiendishly difficult acrostic without any answers (finally solved as 'Liverpool') in the same year as the mysterious Liverpool letters were sent, although there was a time lapse.

At one time it was thought that the letters had been posted to the police and had been lost, but it now appears they were probably sent to the *Daily Telegraph*, which would account for their being used in Richardson's 1927 work. Why the letters were not published at the time they were received remains unexplained. Admittedly thousands of crank messages were sent, but as the letters are so carefully set out in Richardson's book, he must have thought them important enough to keep for decades. This singles the material out as being special; J. Hall was a canny newspaper reporter, not easily fooled. And, to repeat, the first Liverpool letters, if sent in 1888, would be only the second time the infamous nickname had been used, which, in itself would have given considerable interest to the documents. I tried hard to trace the letters without success.

I had an argument with a belligerent Ripper writer, the late Melvyn Harris, who insisted that the letters were sent in 1889 (without a shred of proof to back up this assertion). I cannot prove that 1888 is the correct date for the documents, but equally, no one can disprove that year.

If J.K. was indeed at the heart of the killings, as I believe, and if he was in collusion with the police authorities, as I also believe, he may well have been made aware of the dramatic new nickname before publication – and revelled in the title. Was it the prompt use of the infamous pseudonym that alerted J. Hall to the source of the Liverpool letters? Did he then consult with important friends? Richardson was friendly with many top policeman and politicians. He might well have known Sir Charles Warren personally. In his memoirs, J. Hall reveals that he knew many important people, including the highest in the land, such as William Ewart Gladstone, whom he visited at home. Awareness of the limited number of people with access to the new, bizarre nickname might have alerted Richardson, who may well have had inside knowledge himself. If so, it would have been easy to have the *Daily Telegraph* letters intercepted. That would explain the non-appearance of such dramatic material in the newspaper.

From time to time Ripper researchers have paid considerable attention to the contents of the Liverpool correspondence. The second letter gives an address, then says the police are fools because they cannot find the sender; this has aroused the particular interest of many researchers. I remained intrigued by the fact that J.K. Stephen was within easy reach of Liverpool during the time the letters were sent, by Lynda's brilliant acrostic solution, by the long suppression of the document(s), and by the general air of mystery surrounding the correspondence. Had J.K. been playing word games again? I stand firmly by my graffiti theory, but admit to being on much shakier ground with the Liverpool letters, given their length. However, for the above reasons, I decided to work on the first letter, which was sent around three weeks after Annie Chapman's death. Could the insane J.K., overcome by his serial killer's urge to advertise his crimes, have devised a further unusual thrill for himself by carefully anagramming his plans and posting them to the *Daily Telegraph?* What could happen? He is protected by the highest powers in the land. After considerable work I found that the first letter anagrammed into a long list of pertinent names and messages. The second letter boasts an address, and an anagram of this letter does indeed contain a very surprising revelation.

⟡

Sir Richard Holmes was the librarian at Windsor Castle from 1870–1906. The Castle was frequently used by Queen Victoria as it is by our present monarch. Clearly Sir Richard, after such a long period of royal employment, was ideally placed to write a book about the family; his biography of Bertie, *Edward VII – His Life and Times,* was published in 1910 in two large, extensively illustrated volumes. The subject's life is covered in considerable detail, enlivened by many anecdotes. Amongst these anecdotes is a record of the Prince of Wales's well-known love of fires: indeed, so great was Bertie's love of a good conflagration that he, and a number of his close friends, actually rented a flat in Watling Street, near the local fire station. In this flat, 'above a butcher's shop' Sir Richard informs us, the Prince and his friends kept their uniforms at the ready for any alert. This extraordinary revelation illustrates the unconventional lifestyle that Bertie maintained – and certainly relished. The print of Bertie helping out at a blaze is published in this book. Sir Richard relates that the friends who shared the Watling Street premises with the prince included the incorrigible gambler the Duke of Sutherland, Sir George Chetwynd, Lord Richard Grosvenor, and several other unnamed rakes.

Watling Street was (and is) not too far from the streets solicited by

Mary Kelly and many other prostitutes. (Somewhere around a mile, I believe.) It is not difficult to imagine the sordid games that might have gone on in Watling Street, once the cabal of rich, powerful, rampant rakes had escaped from the restrictions of high society. The fire-fighting activities would have provided a perfect cover for a relentless pursuit of sexual adventure. No dates are given for the tenancy of the Watling Street flat, but there is no reason why this should not have been a long-term arrangement, the flat being passed on to others as the need arose. One of the men may well have owned the property. Accommodation in an area where the Prince would be neither expected nor recognised, and away from the prying eyes of Palace officials, would have provided an ideal playground for Bertie, who would have been in his forties during the Ripper affair. The prince was renowned for his low boredom threshold; he required constant stimulation and amusement, and the Watling Street establishment would have provided this in the form that Bertie liked best of all – sexual pleasure.

The Goulston Street graffiti contains only forty-six letters – the first Liverpool letter 170 characters – giving a wide scope for names and phrases to be found. Yet, with careful study, I discovered the astonishing fact that a long list of names inextricably linked to the Ripper affair can be anagramed from close to half of the characters contained in the first Liverpool letter, and even the projected date of Mary Kelly's death can be found. Here is the list, with the names set out as they are used:

> Charles Warren. Annie Chapman. Bertie. Montague Druitt. 'Naive' Kelly. 9 November (the date of her death). J. K. Stephen.

Are such a long list of names in only 170 characters there by coincidence? Let me set out the first Liverpool letter in its entirety:

> Liverpool. 29th Inst. Beware, I shall be at work on the 1st and 2nd inst, in Minories at 12 midnight, and I give the authorities a good chance, but there is never a policeman near when I am at work, Yours, Jack the Ripper.

The extraordinary (revised) anagram of this letter reads:

> Charles Warren 1) Bertie: his 2 articles were not on Annie Chapman. 2) Montague Druitt and I again wish to voice a plan.
>   It is – naive Kelly dies 9 November. Her death might work in a bid to stop 12th hour riot. J. K. Stephen.

The letter and the above anagram both contain:

> E 19, I 17, T/A 15, N 14, R 12, O 11, H 10, S 8, L/D 5,
> W/M/C/P 4, B/V/K/G/U 3, Y/J 1. Numbers; 1, 1, 2, 2, 2, 9.

Each statement in the decoded message fits the facts contained in the main narrative of my book. The anagram of this first Liverpool letter, sent after Annie's murder, boldly states that Bertie's goods were being sought, and that several items had been stolen. 'Naive' Kelly indicates that the Establishment were planning to deceive her, and even the date of Kelly's planned death is accurately given, showing careful advance preparations. Was this date significant? 9 November was *Bertie's birthday*.

Unstated facts are also of interest. There is a clear intent to murder Kelly herself and not a substitute. So can we now assume that, up to that date, Queen Victoria had not interfered? And the murder of Eddowes and Stride are not mentioned – the link is from Chapman to Kelly. This fits in with my thesis that Eddowes's death came only after she had alarmed the Establishment by openly advertising her supposed knowledge of the Ripper's identity, and that the unfortunate Liz Stride was indeed in the wrong place at the wrong time.

The second Liverpool letter, after decoding, is even more startling. This letter has proved a particular puzzle for Ripper researchers. It reads:

> 'Prince William St., L'pool. What fools the police are. I even give them the name of the street where I am living. Yours Jack the Ripper.'

It has been suggested that the Ripper, in his reference to an address, was referring to his earlier letter, which mentions the Minories, an East End thoroughfare. There was great excitement when it was discovered that Druitt's cousin, Lionel Druitt, had possibly once maintained a surgery in the Minories. Another more obvious solution to the puzzle was that the Ripper was indicating that he actually lived at an address in Prince William Street, Liverpool. All of the previous theories are incorrect. When an anagram of the second Liverpool letter is unravelled there is a staggering revelation. As we have seen, the Ripper says, 'I even give the name of the street where I am living . . .' and this is true, but it does not say that the address is given only in code. And, amazingly, that street is Watling Street – Bertie's secret address.

The second letter contains one-hundred and four characters – considerably less than the first communication; even so, there are a great many possible words contained in so wide a selection of vowels and consonants. However, the anagramed message is so potent and factual that it is possible to visualise J.K. Stephen in his most sardonic mood. The decoded message reads:

> I kill. Can the police trap me? I live in a Watling Street harem with people who love to fight fire. Come here. Yours, James Stephen. V.R.

Both messages contain:

E 17, I 10, T 9, L/R/O/H 7, A 6, P 5, S/M/N 4, W/V/C 3, F/G2, K/U/Y/J1.

This is the clearest of messages, and, once again, one that further endorses my thesis. We know from Sir Richard Holmes that Bertie did indeed stay in Watling Street; it is a certainty that the place would indeed have been 'a harem'; and the occupants of the flat certainly loved to fight fire. A further link to royalty is the sardonic V.R. (Victoria Reigns.) With the words 'I kill' was J.K. blaming the murders directly onto Bertie? Or had J.K. been allowed to use the Watling Street flat? It has often been suggested that the Ripper had a safe-house in or near the East End.

∽

Did J. Hall Richardson agree to suppress the dramatic Liverpool documents, holding on to them until their importance had vanished? It is certainly strange that documents of such interest were not published at the time they were received. Perhaps thirty-nine years later, with many of the main players in the drama dead, Richardson felt that it was safe to forget any promises and use the letters as piquant material for his book?

Interestingly, Sir Charles Warren died in the year that Richardson's memoirs were published. Whatever the reason, we know that J.K. Stephen survived for another four years after the murders, whereas Montague Druitt survived for only a few weeks. He died in mysterious circumstances. Did J.K. once more demonstrate his loyalty and usefulness to the Establishment by murdering his former colleague and friend – perhaps on orders? The fewer people who knew the true Ripper story the better. Or might Druitt have initiated a blackmail scheme of his own? Was the £50 cheque found on Druitt's body payment for silence or a final payment for services rendered? Maybe J.K., in the drama of yet another murder – forgot to retrieve that payment?

Michael Harrison quotes a stanza of J.K. Stephen's writing, in his book *The Life Of H.R.H. The Duke of Clarence and Avondale:*

> I've no time to tell you how,
> I came to be a killer,
> But you should know, as time will show,
> That I'm society's pillar.

(Written in iambic pentameter.)

That sums up the whole solution. J.K. killed, but only to save society. Precisely.

The noted crime expert, Colin Wilson, in his introduction to

Donald Rumbelow's book *The Complete Jack the Ripper*, writes: 'J.K. Stephen, the Duke of Clarence's ex-tutor, is a more likely suspect: at least the evidence against him is stronger...'

There are many mysteries regarding the Ripper murders that can never be answered, especially when we consider the destruction of so much valuable material. Bertie's private papers were burned after his death, as were, amazingly, the private papers of his wife. What could Alexandra possibly have had to hide? The papers of Sir William Gull, whose private diaries are said to have named the Ripper, were burned. The private papers of Dr Thomas Stowell, the man who said that he had read Gull's diaries, were burned. Sir Melville Macnaghten, who wrote the Memoranda, declared that he had documentary evidence of the Ripper's identity but he had burned it. Eddy's papers cannot be examined, and there are no known surviving letters between him and his long-time friend and tutor J.K. Stephen, which is odd, because many letters from Eddy to some of his other friends are still in existence. What could all these people have had to hide? Why were valuable papers, that would normally be held for future generations, destroyed? Medical records involving Eddy are also missing from various medical files. What secret was being hidden?

I feel certain that we now know.

Afterthoughts

Since the publication of my book I have received a great deal of correspondence, questioning, and comment about anagrams. I have to confess that some of the comment has been disingenuous; any number of anagrams can be formed from even a short sentence, and the subject must be approached with common sense and an understanding of the rules, which a surprising number of people lack.

Today an anagram is thought to be merely a game, but in the distant past the puzzle was treated with the utmost seriousness – an art tainted by mysticism. A large number of academic books were printed on the subject. (I found over forty titles published during the fifteenth century.) The French believed that a man's destiny was anagrammed in his own name, able to reveal the power of good or evil, and this was taken so seriously, when one unfortunate man found his name contained an evil message, he committed suicide.

Virtually every word in the English language can be anagrammed, so we can only know if a hidden message exists when:

a) we are told (or suspect) that it is there.

b) when there is evidence that something is being hidden or coded – in which case:

c) every character in the puzzle must be used to form a complete, coherent message. (I thought that every schoolboy knew that last rule. Apparently not.)

Further, if you know that an anagram is present, the puzzle can refer to anything, but the original message must point towards a relevant topic. This format is often used in time of war, when a spy might write a few innocent sounding words that are actually an important coded message. There are other rules. The solution should, in general, be better – or at least as good – as the puzzle: the former comes first, written down to be anagrammed, although there is no reason why there shouldn't be some give and take while the puzzle is being worked out, changing the original message to fit a few stray characters that may be needed. However, there should be some indication that the original message had flowed.

Given the wealth of writing on the subject I have been constantly surprised that so many people do not know the rules of an anagram, as instanced by an extraordinary review in the *Sunday Times*, written by Maurice Chittenham who was advised by Melvin Harris (author of three Ripper books). I have recently learnt that Melvyn Harris has died, but I wrote and spoke to the man by telephone outlining the following facts, and as he had not the slightest hesitation about attacking other writers in print, I do not feel that my reply shows a lack of respect to someone who is not here to defend himself. The following text should speak for itself.

Maurice Chittenham reviewed three Ripper books together. First came Harris's tome. Chittenham gave this a favourable review. Along with other critics, I did not agree. (A clever and lacerating review by the distinguished Jonathan Goodman is highly recommended.) Chittenham, having reviewed Harris's effort, sought Harris's collaboration to review my book – a peculiar decision, as we were clearly rivals. Harris immediately pounced on my anagrams, and produced an 'anagram' of his own. This is my work using all forty-six characters of the Goulston Street graffiti.

F.G. Abberline. Now hate MJ. Druitt. He sent the woman to hell.

from this:

The Juwes are the men that will not be blamed for nothing.

Harris produced this 'anagram' from the *nine-hundred-character* 'Dear Boss' letter:

M Druitt and J K Stephen cheat F G Abberline. Go to Whitechapel, exterminate rancid harlots. End with Kelly as tripe

Anyone who thinks that they can anagram a document of around nine-hundred characters is deluded. I wrote to Harris asking if he thought that taking a small selection of letters from a very long document ignoring almost ninety per cent of the characters, and ignoring the numerals completely, constituted an anagram? Harris wrote back (I still have the letter) and explained that the actual wording of his published anagram was not quite right (he clearly still thought he had produced an anagram) as the final word did not fit (as if that would have made the slightest difference to such garbage). Apparently he mentioned this to Chittenham 'while chatting on the phone', before he gave the reporter the final choice. Harris also explained that he had a few extra letters to play with! That statement caused tears of laughter to roll down my cheeks. Harris actually had about around eight-hundred characters to play with; he could have finished his anagram with the cast list of *Gone With The Wind*.

᪣

Select Bibliography

Abrahamsen, Dr David, *Murder and Madness – The Secret Life of Jack the Ripper* (Donald I. Fine Inc., 1992).

Anonymous, *The Prince of Wales* (Grant Richards, 1898).

Ball, T. Frederick, *Queen Victoria* (S.W. Partridge and Co., 1886).

Begg, Paul, *Jack the Ripper: The Uncensored Facts* (Robson Books, 1988).

Begg, Paul, Martin Fido, and Keith Skinner, *The Jack the Ripper A to Z* (Headline, 1991).

Bielewicz, A., Secret Language

Benson, Arthur Christopher, *The Leaves Of The Tree* (Smith, Elder and Co., 1911).

Benson, E.F., *King Edward VII* (Longmans Green and Co., 1933).

Browning, Oscar, *Memories of Later Years* (T. Unwin Fisher Ltd.).

Cowles, Virginia, *Edward VII and His Circle* (Hamish Hamilton, 1956).

Cullen, Tom, *Autumn Of Terror* (Bodley Head, 1965).

Fido, Martin (Also see above), *The Crimes and Detection of Jack the Ripper* (Weidenfeld and Nicolson, 1987).

Harris, Frank, *His Life And Adventures* (Various editions from a privately published book, 1920).

Harrison, Michael, *The Life of H.R.H. The Duke Of Clarence and Avondale* (W.H. Allen, 1972).

Holmes, Sir Richard, *Edward VII: His Life And Times* (The Amalgamated Press Ltd., 1910).

How, F.D., *Six Great Schoolmasters* (Methuen and Co., 1904).

Howells, Martin and Keith Skinner (Also see above), *The Ripper Legacy* (Sidgwick and Jackson, 1987).

Knight, Stephen, *Jack the Ripper, The Final Solution* (George G. Harrap) and Co. Ltd., 1976).

Lang, Theo, *My Darling Daisy* (Michael Joseph, 1966).

Lee, Sir Sydney, *King Edward VII* (Macmillan and Co. Ltd., 1925).

London, Jack, *The People of the Abyss* (Nelson and Sons Ltd., 1902).

Martin, Sir Theodore, *Life Of The Prince Consort* (Smith, Elder and Co., 1882).

Matters, Leonard, *The Mystery of Jack the Ripper* (W.H. Allen, 1948).

Mayhew, Henry, *London Labour and The London Poor* (Various editions, first published in 1851).

Odell, Robin and Colin Wilson, *Jack the Ripper* (Bantam Press, 1986).

Pearson, John, *Edward The Rake* (Weidenfeld and Nicolson, 1975).

Richardson, J. Hall, *From The City To Fleet Street* (Stanley Paul and Co. Ltd., 1927).

Rumbelow, Donald, *The Complete Jack the Ripper* (Penguin Books, 1988).

Smith, Sir Henry, *From Constable to Commissioner* (Chatto and Windus, 1910).

Stephen, J.K., *Lapsus Calami* (Macmillan and Bowes, 1896).

Stow, John, *The Survey of London* (1598).

Trowbridge, W.R.H., *Queen Alexandra* (T. Fisher Unwin Ltd., 1921).

Victoria, Queen, *Letters, 1837–1861* in three volumes, edited by A.C. Benson (John Murray, 1908).

Vincent, James, *His Royal Highness the Duke of Clarence and Avondale. A memoir* (John Murray, 1893).

Young, G.M., *Victorian England* (Oxford University Press, 1936).